# LISTEN LEARN & LOVE

## Improving Latter-day Saint Culture

# Listen Learn & Love

## Improving Latter-day Saint Culture

## RICHARD H. OSTLER

CFI
An imprint of Cedar Fort, Inc.
Springville, Utah

This is not an official publication of The Church of Jesus Christ of Latter-day Saints. The opinions and views expressed herein belong solely to the author and do not necessarily represent the opinions or views of Cedar Fort, Inc. Permission for the use of sources, graphics, and photos is also solely the responsibility of the author.

ISBN 13: 978-1-4621-3956-9

Published by CFI, an imprint of Cedar Fort, Inc.
2373 W. 700 S., Springville, UT, 84663
Distributed by Cedar Fort, Inc., www.cedarfort.com

Library of Congress Control Number: 2020942523

Cover design by Shawnda T. Craig
Cover design © 2022 Cedar Fort, Inc.
Edited by Trina Caudle and Marci McPhee

Printed in the United States of America

10 9 8 7 6 5 4 3 2 1

Printed on acid-free paper

This book is dedicated to all those who have shared with me your stories with honesty and vulnerability. You are some of my heroes. Your perspectives and insights help us better understand how we can improve Latter-day Saint culture to create Zion—a Zion where we all feel loved, needed, and that we belong.

# CONTENTS

# CONTENTS

# INTRODUCTION

I am a committed member of The Church of Jesus Christ of Latter-day Saints and love our restored doctrine revealed through the Prophet Joseph Smith. This restored doctrine includes Heavenly Parents who love us, with whom we can have a personal relationship; the infinite Atonement of Jesus Christ to forgive sin and heal our hearts; the plan of salvation that gives us understanding of and perspective for our mortal life; the power of covenants; and personal revelation.

My hope is that more Latter-day Saints are able to stay in the Church and more can join, so they too can experience the healing, hope, and peace of our restored doctrine. **However, I have come to understand that it is often the culture that causes some of our dear friends to step away from the Church.**

Indeed, this is what Sister Carol F. McConkie of the Young Women General Presidency taught in the video message, "Lifting Others": "The gospel of Jesus Christ does not marginalize people. People marginalize people. And we have to fix that."[1]

President M. Russell Ballard talked about improving our culture for single Latter-day Saints, which I think applies more broadly. He invited us to "disregard old notions and ideas that have sometimes

---

1. Carol F. McConkie, "Lifting Others," Gospel Media, The Church of Jesus Christ of Latter-day Saints, March 2016, churchofjesuschrist.org/media/video/2016-03-0018-lifting-others.

unintentionally contributed to their feelings of loneliness and that they do not belong or cannot serve."[2]

This book is a practical application of Sister McConkie's statement and President Ballard's challenge to *listen, learn and love* to improve our culture. I feel we can improve in a number of areas such as reducing our tendency to judge others; not seeing Church callings as achievements; addressing less-than-equal treatment of women; using better tools to end pornography use; viewing repentance in a more positive light; removing stigma around mental illness and suicide; understanding scrupulosity; fully accepting, loving, and supporting missionaries who return home "early," are called to a service mission, or feel their path is not to serve a mission; reducing suspicion around political differences; and compassionately encouraging those who have questions about the Church's history and practices.

Improving our culture by disregarding old notions and ideas doesn't require us to change doctrine—but rather look inward to see how each of us can do better—so more people feel welcomed, loved and a sense of belonging.

I wish I had read a book like this decades ago. It would have given me tools to be more thoughtful, helpful, and inclusive. "When [we] know better, [we] do better."[3] Even though I am the author of this book, I am not at the finish line—it is a work in progress for me to improve so I can better see and support others.

As we are open to learn, we are following the counsel of Elder Dieter F. Uchtdorf:

> Brothers and sisters, as good as our previous experience may be, if we stop asking questions, stop thinking, stop pondering, we can thwart the revelations of the Spirit. Remember, it was the questions young Joseph asked that opened the door for the restoration

---

2.  M. Russell Ballard, "Hope in Christ," April 2021 general conference, churchofjesuschrist.org/study/general-conference/2021/04/28ballard.

3.  @DrMayaAngelou (Maya Angelou), "Then when you know better, do better." Twitter, August 12, 2018, 1:29 p.m., twitter.com/DrMayaAngelou/status/1028694898239791104.

of all things. We can block the growth and knowledge our Heavenly Father intends for us. **How often has the Holy Spirit tried to tell us something we needed to know but couldn't get past the massive iron gate of what we thought we already knew?**[4]

In writing this book, I sought input from many voices who you will hear in these pages, including those who have had negative experiences with our culture. I'm grateful for their courage to share their stories, which give us better perspective and insights. Many shared their personal experiences; others wrote about their understanding of various gospel principles. Their names are listed in the Contributor Index. Some participants' names have been changed so they would feel more comfortable being honest and telling their full story. Still more do not have their thoughts shared within this book, but their contributions are nonetheless valuable and appreciated.

It is my hope that their insights will help us open our "iron gates" so we can set aside past assumptions and develop new perspectives to help others.

I would like to introduce to you a few people in particular, who wrote entire chapters.

I asked my friends Cynthia Winward and Susan Hinckley to write chapter 3 about improving our Church culture for women. These two wonderful, committed Latter-day Saints produce a podcast called *At Last She Said It*.[5] I have learned so much from Cynthia and Susan. I recognize that I need to listen to the experiences of a wide range of women to better understand their concerns, learn what I need to change, and learn how I can improve things in my circle of influence. This benefits not only women but all Latter-day Saints, as women's contributions are more fully used to build Zion.

---

4.  Dieter F. Uchtdorf, "Acting on the Truths of the Gospel of Jesus Christ," (worldwide leadership training address, Salt Lake City, February 11, 2012), thechurchnews. com/archives/2012-02-11/president-dieter-f-uchtdorf-acting-on-the-truths-of-the-gospel-of-jesus-christ-53389?fbclid=IwAR0WPoya3KMMvVHQSeDmEFU 2ETT4Awlx7UKP6f4ebN-4kjGTT0z55B5dSOQ, emphasis added.

5.  See atlastshesaidit.org.

I asked my friend David Cook to write chapter 9 about changing our Church culture in the area of politics. His professional work as a lawyer in Rochester, New York, combined with his lifelong Church service, result in some unique insights. I respect his thinking. He presents what I feel is a balanced point of view that can help us listen to all kinds of voices in the political arena so that we can work together, instead of against each other, to improve our world. I hope we can find common ground and make space for all kinds of political opinions in our Church family so that all will feel welcomed. No one should be labeled as "less faithful" because of their political views.

A few topics about improving Latter-day Saint culture are *not* addressed in this book. For example, toxic perfectionism is not addressed here. Neither is improving the experience and valuing the contributions of LGBTQ[6] Latter-day Saints. That topic was addressed comprehensively in my first book, *Listen, Learn and Love: Embracing LGBTQ Latter-day Saints,*[7] and in other books by other authors. Nor is the issue of race and racism in our church culture addressed in this book. That topic deserves many books as well, written by Black Latter-day Saints and other minority races. In the meantime, we have several excellent podcast interviews at the Black Latter-day Saints tab at listenlearnandlove.org.[8] We will continue to amplify their voices on our podcast. I have learned so much from our Black brothers and sisters. My heart aches at some of the things they have endured, even from fellow Church members. I hope much more work will be done to address racism in the Church, as we "lead out in abandoning attitudes and actions of prejudice,"[9] as President Russell M. Nelson has charged us to do.

---

6.  LGBTQ stands for lesbian, gay, bisexual, transgender, and queer/questioning.

7.  Richard Ostler, *Listen, Learn & Love: Embracing LGBTQ Latter-day Saints* (Springville, UT: Cedar Fort Publishing, 2020).

8.  See listenlearnandlove.org/black-latter-day-saints for episodes with Black Latter-day Saints.

9.  Russell M. Nelson, "Let God Prevail," October 2020 general conference, churchofjesuschrist.org/study/general-conference/2020/10/46nelson.

Throughout the book, some of these insights and experiences may cause us to feel uncomfortable, perhaps with an initial reaction to defend the Church or dismiss others' experiences. I have learned to sit with that discomfort, as it often leads to changes I need to make to get past my iron gate. As each of us improve, our church is one step closer to our vision of a unified Zion. Further, as we validate others' experiences, it can help them feel heard, provide a measure of healing, and increase the chance they can put the experience behind them and move forward.

I have always loved the symbolism of lower lights in this hymn:

> Brightly beams our Father's mercy
> From his lighthouse evermore,
> But to us he gives the keeping
> Of the lights along the shore.
>
> Eager eyes are watching, longing,
> For the lights along the shore.
>
> Trim your feeble lamp, my brother;
> Some poor sailor, tempest-tossed,
> Trying now to make the harbor,
> In the darkness may be lost.[10]

Sometimes we see the brighter lights: people who speak more naturally or have more privilege, but the lower lights can also provide us with insights that often go unseen and unheard. Those insights can help us become better and more unified. I love the lower lights. While we may only have a "feeble lamp," ours may just be the light that is needed by "some poor sailor, tempest-tossed, trying now to make the harbor." Perhaps you are exactly the light

---

10. *Hymns* (Salt Lake City: The Church of Jesus Christ of Latter-day Saints, 1985), 335.

needed by some "eager eyes" who are "watching, longing, for [your] lights along the shore."

If you feel marginalized, try to stay burning brightly. Even though you may feel pain and are not sure about your future in the Church, we need you. If you are in a position of privilege, we need you too. Perhaps you can help the lower lights shine more brightly by magnifying their voices.

I am grateful to so many who contributed their stories, thoughts, and comments to this book. You are some of my heroes. I hope and pray that we can see each other as beloved children of Heavenly Parents and eliminate cultural checklists that can divide and prevent us from becoming the unified body of Christ. As we truly build Zion, everyone can develop a sense of belonging and know that their contributions are needed and valued.

I invite you to join with me as we read these stories and act on impressions to improve our culture—blessing the lives of those around us—and helping to create Zion.

# CHAPTER 1

# IMPROVING OUR CULTURE TO BE NONJUDGMENTAL AND MORE LOVING

How can we collectively reduce judging so everyone can feel welcome in Latter-day Saint congregations and enjoy the fruits of our restored doctrine? How can we root out judgmental attitudes or comments and become more like Christ? When we look inward, what work do we each still need to do, as we try to be a loving people?

Sister McConkie urges us to see others as Jesus Christ does:

> I know people who come to church every Sunday so that they can be inspired and uplifted and who just simply walk away feeling judged and unloved, unneeded, like there is no place for them at church. We need to do this differently. We need to be deeply aware of what the purpose of coming to church on Sunday is, and make sure that everyone who comes feels loved, needed, accepted, and lifted. . . .
>
> We cannot allow judgment to dictate the way we interact with people. It's simply not right. . . . We just cannot be, or even call ourselves, a disciple of Christ if we are not helping others along that path.
>
> The gospel of Jesus Christ does not marginalize people. People marginalize people. And we have to fix that. . . . [All]

have talents and abilities and personality that is needed in the kingdom of God. And if we're going to build the kingdom of God on the earth, we need everyone to come and do their part.[1]

These are powerful words: "The gospel of Jesus Christ does not marginalize people. People marginalize people. And we need to fix that." I think about her words frequently and ask myself if my words or actions are making it difficult for people to consider joining or continuing as a member of our restored Church. As you read this book, I hope ideas will come into your mind and heart about what you can do within your circle of influence to implement Sister McConkie's vision.

I became more aware of this topic during my Young Single Adult (YSA)[2] assignment. For the first time, I met with many individuals who were not regularly attending church. Before this experience, I had assumed that those not attending church did not believe in our restored doctrine. However, I soon learned that many did hold core Latter-day Saint beliefs but were not participating because they felt judged or not good enough, or they lacked a sense of belonging.

I had also supposed that those who had been hurt were simply too easily offended and they should "learn not be to be offended," putting all the responsibility on their shoulders to resolve a painful experience. However, I have come to honor how people feel. Asking them not to be offended can invalidate their experience, potentially deepening the wedge between them and the Church and decreasing the likelihood they will return. Validating their feelings is often vital in helping them put difficult experiences behind them.

I have also tried to ask more often, "Lord, is it I?" as taught by Elder Uchtdorf:

---

1. McConkie, "Lifting Others."
2. YSA is a Latter-day Saint congregation specifically for single adults ages 18–30.

It was our beloved Savior's final night in mortality, the evening before He would offer Himself a ransom for all mankind. As He broke bread with His disciples, He said something that must have filled their hearts with great alarm and deep sadness. "One of you shall betray me," He told them.

The disciples didn't question the truth of what He said. Nor did they look around, point to someone else, and ask, "Is it him?"

Instead, "they were exceeding sorrowful, and began every one of them to say unto him, Lord, is it I?" (Matthew 26:22)

I wonder what each of us would do if we were asked that question by the Savior. Would we look at those around us and say in our hearts, "He's probably talking about Brother Johnson. I've always wondered about him," or "I'm glad Brother Brown is here. He really needs to hear this message"? Or would we, like those disciples of old, look inward and ask that penetrating question: "Is it I?"

In these simple words, "Lord, is it I?" lies the beginning of wisdom and the pathway to personal conversion and lasting change.[3]

Elder Uchtdorf's words motivate me to reflect with an open mind and heart so that the Spirit can guide me to the changes I need to make in my attitude and behaviors. Making those changes allows me to be part of the solution.

## "Is She Wearing Her Temple Garment in that Wedding Photo?"

Sister McConkie's vision and Elder Uchtdorf's counsel apply to an experience I had after performing a ring ceremony for a beautiful, newly married couple. I posted a photo of the event on social media, and a few days later, someone commented to me that something was missing from the photo. They gestured to the bride's shoulder, inferring a "missing" temple garment sleeve.

---

3. Dieter F. Uchtdorf, "Lord, Is It I?" October 2014 general conference, churchofjesuschrist.org/study/general-conference/2014/10/lord-is-it-i.

That led me to write a Facebook post titled, "Is she wearing her temple garment in that wedding photo?"[4] I talked at length about the need to not judge others. The response far surpassed anything I have ever posted by a hundredfold. It went viral with more than 5,100 comments, 22,000 likes, and 19,000 shares. The post was also shared by *LDS Living*. I say this not to bring attention to myself but to show that clearly this subject struck a nerve, with Latter-day Saints discussing how to apply the principle of non-judgment in a practical way.

In that post, I explained that as a YSA bishop, I officiated at many ring ceremonies that took place after temple sealings. The purpose of a ring ceremony is to bring families and friends together in celebration of a couple making commitments and covenants with each other. After posting a photo of a ring ceremony, I received questions like, "Did you notice what was missing in that photo?" and "What was missing below her shoulder straps?" It was disappointing that this was the focus that some chose to discuss, rather than the goodness and beauty of that wonderful couple. It gave me a better understanding of why some in our church feel marginalized and withdraw.

I reflected on that ring ceremony. I never noticed that her garment may have been missing—it never entered my mind. All I saw was the beauty of that young couple coming together to be married, her tender-hearted father walking her down the aisle to join her new husband. Was she possibly wearing her own mother's wedding dress? Could they be new converts and their families were not members? Could this wonderful woman be a recent convert without a lifetime of instruction on and preparation for this issue?

---

4. Richard Ostler, "Is she wearing her garment in that wedding dress photo?" Facebook, May 13, 2017, facebook.com/richard.ostler.5/posts/10211600652005026 and in *LDS Living*, May 15, 2017, ldsliving.com/YSA-Bishop-s-Viral-Message-About-Being-too-Quick-to-Judge-Others/s/85373.

The garment represents a covenant between the individual and Heavenly Father.[5] But that personal covenant is not to be used as a measuring stick to judge others' commitment to *their* personal covenants. Some people may need time to figure out wearing the garment, and each will come to their own conclusions with their Heavenly Parents about what is right for them. Deciding what is right for me does not give me permission to project my choice onto other people.

In saying this, I am not endorsing a casual approach to temple commitments or wearing the garment. My garment reminds me of the Savior, His sacrifice for me, and my temple covenants. There is power in those covenants that gives me great spiritual strength.

But this is not about the temple garment! Rather, it illustrates a broader challenge in the Church: the culture of judging based on appearance and sometimes shaming others. As I meet with so many on the fringes of the Church, I learn that it is often this culture—not the doctrine or the commandments—that causes them to withdraw. They feel judged. Instead of coming to church to enjoy the Savior's healing touch where everyone is loved and accepted, with friends walking with them as they move forward in life, they feel critical eyes and judgmental attitudes.

Do we have thoughts like these?

- That skirt is too short.
- Is that a double pierced ear?
- Why are they home from their mission early?
- Why are they in that political party?
- Are they acting on their same-sex attraction?
- Why didn't they take the sacrament?
- Why aren't they dating anyone?
- Why didn't their marriage work?

---

5. For more information about the covenants represented by temple garments, please visit "Garments," Gospel Topics, The Church of Jesus Christ of Latter-day Saints; accessed June 15, 2021, churchofjesuschrist.org/study/manual/gospel-topics/garments.

- I'm not sure about her working outside the home.
- Why is he not wearing a white shirt?
- Why do they have tattoos? Don't they know their body is a temple?
- I heard they messed up at school.
- Why haven't they submitted their mission papers yet?
- Why didn't they serve a mission?
- Why did they march for that cause?
- I wonder why they go skiing (play sports, eat in restaurants) on Sunday.
- Why haven't they had kids yet?
- What's going on with that bishopric member with a goatee?

Do we ask newly engaged couples which temple they will be sealed in, partly as a way to assess their worthiness? Do we do the same when reading a wedding invitation?

We sometimes extend this type of seeing to social media posts. Do we see that outdoor activity photo collage and notice that it was posted on a Sunday? Do we look at that glass in a restaurant photo and wonder what is in it? Do we notice that swimsuit and rate its modesty based on our own family rules?

Does this focus on appearance and behaviors actually add to our own mental load and increase the burden to fit in and be the "perfect" Latter-day Saint ourselves? By enumerating the ways that others fall short, is our inner voice turning to criticism of ourselves as well?

I don't want to be too negative, as many individuals and congregations are doing a great job with welcoming all, but there is room for improvement.

I invite everyone to keep the commandments and enjoy the blessings that follow. One of the most important commandments was named by the Savior: to love one another (see John 13:34). We need to retrain our brains and eyes to stop focusing on others' possible shortcomings. After meeting with so many on the margins and hearing their stories, I now "see" how our church culture looks through their eyes, and it has changed my heart and feelings toward these good people. I now try to understand everyone as my equal—a daughter or son of loving Heavenly Parents, trying to do their best as they move forward in life, measured by their own yardstick and not my yardstick for them. I look for their Christlike attributes, talents, the way they are contributing to society, and what I can learn from them. I seek to see them the way I believe our Heavenly Parents see them. I accept them where they are and extend my love, understanding and encouragement.

I love what Elder Uchtdorf said about judging others:

> Stop it! It's that simple. We simply have to stop judging others and replace judgmental thoughts and feelings with a heart full of love for God and His children. God is our Father. We are His children. We are all brothers and sisters. I don't know exactly how to articulate this point of *not judging others* with sufficient eloquence, passion, and persuasion to make it stick. I can quote scripture, I can try to expound doctrine, and I will even quote a bumper sticker I recently saw. It was attached to the back of a car whose driver appeared to be a little rough around the edges, but the words on the sticker taught an insightful lesson. It read, "Don't judge me because I sin differently than you."[6]

Do I need Elder Uchtdorf's counsel? Yes, absolutely! Do you need this counsel? I will leave that up to you. The only person in a Latter-day Saint congregation who has any right to judge is the bishop, and that is *only* in a private and thoughtful visit to discuss temple worthiness, help someone return to full church participation, or explore a specific calling.

At the same time, don't we each have a duty as a member of the Church to "warn our neighbor"? Yes, but I believe the principle behind this concept is love. In my mind, I replace "warn" with "love our neighbor." When our neighbor feels our genuine love for them—meaning we will walk with them and our friendship is not

---

6.  Dieter F. Uchtdorf, "The Merciful Obtain Mercy," April 2012 general conference, churchofjesuschrist.org/study/general-conference/2012/04/the-merciful-obtain-mercy, emphasis in the original.

conditional on any specific outcome (like commandment keeping or joining the Church)—then our ability to lift, build, and help them increases. They trust us. They know we did not befriend them as a Church assignment or to fulfill a quota, but because we truly care and see them as an equal daughter or son of Heavenly Parents.

After that loving and trusting relationship has been built, I might feel impressed to visit with them in a quiet moment about an item or two on the previous list. I may ask, "Do you want to talk about your feelings about coming home from your mission early?" or "How do you feel about the temple?" Or you might say, "I am here if you want to talk about (fill in the blank)." You might gently ask them the story behind that tattoo and discover that sharing the story brings you closer together. These questions should be asked only from a position of love and friendship, and not judging their actions. People need trusted friends to process the experiences behind those questions, and those conversations are often both helpful and healing. I am not suggesting that we avoid sensitive subjects entirely, but wait to open that door until love and trust are established. In addition, our friends who are not members of our Church—on the receiving end of love without an agenda—might feel safe opening up to us about their faith-related questions and open to invitations on how our church might be their path. I am honored to have walked several into our church over the past few years.

If we truly listen to those on the margins, we might be surprised to learn their true feelings and feel their pure hearts. They are some of the finest people I know. They are *not* on the margins because they are weak or because Satan has got hold of them, or they are not reading their scriptures. They are often there because others put them there. One good young man articulated it this way: "I don't feel Mormon enough to belong." Yikes! Everyone should feel "Mormon enough" to be welcomed, valued, and loved in our congregations.

Elder Uchtdorf taught, "The Church is a home for all to come together, regardless of the depth or the height of our testimony. I know of no sign on the doors of our meetinghouses that says, 'Your testimony must be this tall to enter'."[7] Bishop Gérald Caussé of the Presiding Bishopric added, "In this Church there are no strangers and no outcasts. There are only brothers and sisters. . . . Our wards and our quorums do not belong to us. They belong to Jesus Christ. Whoever enters our meetinghouses should feel at home. . . . Unity is not achieved by ignoring and isolating members who seem different or weaker and only associating with people who are like us."[8]

It is true: "Our wards and quorums do not belong to us. They belong to Jesus Christ." And when He was on earth, how wide did He open the doors to those wards and quorums? Here are His instructions to the Nephites:

> [Do] that which ye have seen me do. And ye see that I have commanded that none of you should go away, but rather have commanded that ye should come unto me, that ye might feel and see; even so shall ye do. If ye know that a man is unworthy to eat and drink of my flesh and blood ye shall forbid him. Nevertheless, ye shall not cast him out from among you, but ye shall minister unto him and shall pray for him unto the Father, in my name; and if it so be that he repenteth and is baptized in my name, then shall ye receive him, and shall minister unto him of my flesh and blood. But if he repent not he shall not be numbered among my people. Nevertheless, ye shall not cast him out of your synagogues, or your places of worship, for unto such shall ye continue to minister; for ye know not but what they will return and repent, and come unto me with full purpose of heart, and I shall heal them; and ye shall be the means of bringing salvation unto them (excerpts from 3 Nephi 18:24–5, 29–32).

The Lord could not be any clearer: He wants us to welcome ALL through our chapel doors and into our hearts.

---

7. Dieter F. Uchtdorf, "Receiving a Testimony of Light and Truth," October 2014 general conference, churchofjesuschrist.org/study/general-conference/2014/10/receiving-a-testimony-of-light-and-truth.

8. Gérald Caussé, "Ye Are No More Strangers," October 2013 general conference, churchofjesuschrist.org/study/general-conference/2013/10/ye-are-no-more-strangers.

Some have used the terms "big tent" or "the gate is wide" to describe their vision for Latter-day Saint congregations. The big tent view is that our congregations are safe, welcoming, loving, and healing for everyone who considers our Church their spiritual home—all those who still want to "give it a go" and try to make it work. They may not fit the cultural mold, they may have work-in-progress testimonies, they may be working hard to keep the commandments. But they may want to attend to feel the Spirit, worship their Savior, take the sacrament, and hear uplifting talks and music. They need to feel the support of other members, figuratively putting their arms around them and saying, "You are welcome. I am your friend: no ifs, ands, or buts." They also may want to provide that support for others in a mutually uplifting environment. Christ practiced big tent Christianity during His ministry as He reached out to those on the margins of society, spent time with them, served them, talked about their goodness, and invited them to join Him. Likewise, Christ wants our congregations to be welcoming for all God's children.

While the gate is wide at the congregational level, the temple is different as the gate narrows with belief and behavior requirements discussed in a temple recommend interview. Our congregations should be a safe place to help more people toward the temple. Let's be careful not to use the temple recommend questions to decide if others (or ourselves) should feel welcome in our congregations (or homes). As Elder Uchtdorf taught, there is no measuring stick to attend our wards and branches.[9] Let's follow what Christ taught, making our congregations and our families judgment-free zones, where the path is wide and everyone feels welcome.

Unfortunately, some Latter-day Saints do not feel that home or church are safe places for them. Some have shared with me this painful scripture that prophesies of the Savior but also resonates with them: "And one shall say unto him, What are these wounds in thine hands? Then he shall answer, Those with which I was wounded in the house of my friends" (Zechariah 13:6).

---

9.  Uchtdorf, "Receiving a Testimony of Light and Truth."

This scripture is profoundly heartbreaking, both for the Savior and for anyone who has been wounded. The safest place of all should be at our parents' house—both our earthly and Heavenly Parents' houses. Our congregations should also be a deeply safe place for everyone, where the cares of life are left behind as we seek the Savior's healing. No matter who we are, where we are, or what road we are walking, when we come to church, I hope we do not feel judgment, only love.

I believe deeply in our church! My purpose in discussing this issue is to make the Church work for more of our dear sisters and brothers, leading to more partaking of the fruits of our restored doctrine. Becoming less judgmental and more accepting is essential to people feeling welcome and like they belong within the Church. This encourages them to contribute to our wards and stakes, bringing us more fully together to create Zion.

## "All God's Critters Got a Place in the Choir"[10]

Without everyone's voices, we are all impoverished, both in our own lives and as a church. As we become more Christlike in our attitudes and abandon judgment to make others feel more welcome, we are all enriched. Elder Jeffrey R. Holland's memorable talk "Songs Sung and Unsung" illustrates how this works:

> I would ask us, especially the youth of the Church, to remember it is by divine design that not all the voices in God's choir are the same. It takes variety—sopranos and altos, baritones and basses—to make rich music. To borrow a line quoted in the cheery correspondence of two remarkable Latter-day Saint women, "All God's critters got a place in the choir." When we disparage our uniqueness or try to conform to fictitious stereotypes—stereotypes driven by an insatiable consumer culture and idealized beyond any possible realization by social media—we lose the richness of tone and timbre that God intended when He created a world of diversity.

---

10. Bill Staines, "All God's Critters Got a Place in the Choir," in Laurel Thatcher Ulrich and Emma Lou Thayne, *All God's Critters Got a Place in the Choir* (Murray, UT: Aspen Books, 1995), 4.

Now, this is not to say that everyone in this divine chorus can simply start shouting his or her own personal oratorio! Diversity is not cacophony, and choirs do require discipline [or] discipleship—but once we have accepted divinely revealed lyrics and harmonious orchestration composed before the world was, then our Heavenly Father delights to have us sing in our own voice, not someone else's. Believe in yourself, and believe in Him. Don't demean your worth or denigrate your contribution. Above all, don't abandon your role in the chorus. Why? Because you are unique; you are irreplaceable. The loss of even one voice diminishes every other singer in this great mortal choir of ours, including the loss of those who feel they are on the margins of society or the margins of the Church.[11]

I have heard lovely solos in my life. I also appreciate beautiful harmonies with every voice singing out. We need to follow Elder Holland's words to bring individuals from the margins into the center of our fellowship so *they* can help *us* become better followers of Christ. Their participation and inclusion in our congregations strengthens everyone, and the Church itself. Creating an environment of inclusion allows everyone to stay comfortably in the choir and gives them courage to sing out. We all are needed.

## Insights from Al Carraway

One of my favorite Latter-day Saint authors is Al Carraway. This remarkable convert to our church shares her journey as a new member in her best-selling book, *More than the Tattooed Mormon*.[12] Sister Carraway has several tattoos and shares some painful situations when she was judged because of them. I am guilty of this same kind of judging. Fortunately, she was able to navigate those difficult

---

11. Jeffrey R. Holland, "Songs Sung and Unsung," April 2017 general conference, churchofjesuschrist.org/study/general-conference/2017/04/songs-sung-and-unsung.

12. Al Carraway, *More than the Tattooed Mormon* (Springville, UT: Cedar Fort Publishing, 2018). She has published multiple books, all of which can be found at alcarraway.com and cedarfort.com.

comments and remains a committed Latter-day Saint. This book and her other excellent books are eye-opening.

Sister Carraway's honest blog post, titled "Nothing about this woman is Mormon anymore," was written in March 2020, ten years after her baptism. It is deeply moving and causes me to look inward and examine how I may be adding to others' burdens. She said:

> PERMISSION?
>
> STOP— just stop scrolling for a sec to read this.
>
> Ten years. It's been 10 years and still this morning I woke up & the first thing that happened was I ended up in tears. Multiple comments from multiple members of our church, and those who chose to hit the follow button on my Instagram, creating a long strand of how disgusting I am.
>
> NO, no, this had nothing to do with my tattoos– they mentioned specifically my weight & the color of my hair????
>
> They all quite literally said "nothing about this woman is Mormon anymore." (Apparently spirituality is based on that??????)
>
> 10 years I've been a member. TEN YEARS straight I have been told by ONLY members of my church that for every reason you can THINK of, (probably ones you wouldn't believe), that no matter what I'm doing or how I dress or look, or what I write:
>
> That I'm doing it wrong.
>
> Y'all have been extremely creative through these 10 years to find the most bizarre reasons to tell me that I do not belong.
>
> Only members of my church have told me, still, for 10 years straight, word for word, that God does not love me.
>
> As a convert from the east coast, "Brothers & sisters" is a literal term. Church family is quite literally family. In every way. Oooooh how ignorantly excited I was to follow the spirit away from my small east coast branch knowing where I was going completely by myself, abandoning literally everything to follow my new-found God, I would still have "family" there for me.
>
> TEN YEARS and it's my "family" that are the only ones that continuously cause unexpected tears in the morning right when I wake up. How ironic this all has been to me, because I thought we were all supposed to be in this together? Why is it people are so set on driving people away?

Nothing I hate more than when my integrity and intentions are assumed and exploited by people I'll never meet. Nothing worse than your entire character and SOUL destroyed by people who I thought were in this together with me, because there will always be someone waiting to get offended by something because they hold the world to their own personal expectations.

But here I am, 10 years later & through it all—the hurt, the tears, the confusion, the loneliness, the judgment—

I really like me. I reaaally truly like me.

And when you have found contentment and love in yourself THERE IS POWER that comes to you & protects you.

The power to keep going. The power to move past it. The power to show up still. The power to laugh minutes after tears during breakfast with your husband.

I'm not letting anyone turn me away from a REAL God and I hope everyone invests to get to that point, too.

LISTEN—PLEASE, LET GO of any hurt or weight caused by others. Who is anyone to say you don't belong here or part of this church? Who is anyone to tell you that God is not your Father & you are not His????

LISTEN—PLEASE, please please please, with ALL THAT I HAVE LEFT IN ME—

INVEST in taking the time to learn how to like yourself.

PLEASE, pllleaaaassseeee invest in being able to see yourself the way that God sees you.

THERE IS A PROTECTING POWER that comes— there is a contentment & happiness that comes—

And wow does life blossom when you invest in building and knowing in what really matters.

It's God that matters. it's your SOUL that can never die that matters. It's taking advantage of every second we have to LIVE on this planet, in this phase of life we will never have again, that matters. It's you that matters. It's how God sees us is what matters. And He sees us as someone capable of becoming like Him.[13]

---

13. Al Carraway, "Nothing About This Woman is Mormon Anymore," *Al Carraway* (blog), March 20, 2020, alcarraway.com/2020/03/20/nothing-about-this-woman-is-mormon-anymore/.

## Personal Stories

Below are stories about painful experiences within our faith community. I am not sharing these to be critical of the Church or anyone in it, but stories give us real life experiences to help us understand how we can implement Sister McConkie's vision to "make sure that everyone who comes feels loved, needed, accepted, and lifted."[14] I wish I had heard stories like these earlier in my life, to increase my opportunities to lift rather than add to someone's burden.

### SUSAN DOHRMAN

Many years ago, I was working a Level 1 Trauma Center in the SICU (surgical intensive care unit), caring for those who had been in auto accidents, shot, stabbed, you name it. It was extremely stressful because many patients were young, with their whole lives ahead of them. Many were gang members, some were under arrest, handcuffed to their beds and a sheriff at the door.

One Saturday night, I'd had a particularly difficult shift. I left the hospital at 7:30 Sunday morning, pretty upset over the night's events. I just needed to take the sacrament. I needed to ground with my Father in Heaven, who I knew loves each of us equally, despite the roads we've taken in life. My ward met midday and I had to return to work Sunday night so, like it or not, I had to go home and get some sleep.

But I knew there was a ward building along the freeway, and I supposed there would be a sacrament meeting at 9 a.m. So I stopped at the building and waited. Sure enough, people began arriving prior to 9:00. I determined to go in, sit in the back so I could take the sacrament, and leave immediately to go home. I had no makeup on, my hair was not done, and I was wearing hospital scrubs, not even a skirt. Plus, I'd been up all night.

As the ward members arrived, everyone was greeting their friends. I noticed there was a swath of about six feet around me where no one sat. No one spoke to me. It was odd, but I didn't really look like I belonged there. I thought about the sign in the front of the building that says, "Visitors Welcome." What if I was a visitor? What if I was someone who just needed to feel the Spirit? What if I was an inactive member trying to return?

---

14. McConkie, "Lifting Others."

Eventually the missionaries spoke to me. I explained why I was there, and they welcomed me.

This was a life-changing event for me. Now, when I attend church, I look for the unfamiliar face, the one who isn't dressed properly. Quite truthfully, if I met someone in church who smelled of cigarettes or alcohol, I'd still welcome them.

## ABBY HARRISON

I remember my Young Women leaders teaching us about appropriate Sunday dress. They told us that as girls, our Sunday best meant that we had to wear pantyhose. I dutifully wore them most weeks. But one week, I ripped my last pair, so I went to church without. One of the leaders was at the door of the Young Women room, pinching the leg of each girl checking for pantyhose. I was promptly shamed and told that if a young man doesn't wear a white shirt, he doesn't participate in passing the sacrament and I needed to take dressing for church as seriously as they do.

The other time I felt very judged was just before my mission, when my younger sister got engaged. I already had my mission call, and I was grateful she was getting married before I left so I could attend the ceremony. A few days before the wedding, a Church member said to me, "Oh, your younger sister is getting married this week? How exciting! How does that feel, you know, her getting married before you? Are you going on a mission because you could not get married?" I was twenty years old.

I felt that in the eyes of my fellow Church members, I was a failure simply because I was about to turn twenty-one and was unmarried. It made me reconsider serving a mission. I had actually received a proposal and felt that I was only valuable to God as a man's wife. The pressure to get married was overwhelming. Even though I was going to serve a mission and had been at BYU earning a degree, nothing seemed to matter except getting married and presumably popping out babies as fast as I could.

Thankfully I did serve, and my life has been blessed for it.

## RUBY WALCH

My husband is a convert to the Church. He was born in China and raised predominantly atheist, but always felt that there was a higher power in the universe. His conversion story is amazing. To sum it up, he met with the missionaries after he graduated from our local university, we got engaged, and he was baptized shortly after. At first, we thought to wait the year to be married and sealed,[15] but ultimately decided that was not a good plan for us. We moved our wedding up to December that same year.

My neighbor, a very faithful Saint who watched me grow up, was supportive and kind at first. But the tide changed quickly as she began telling me I was "wasting my time because he wasn't a returned missionary" and if I wasn't going to get married in the temple, I "might as well not get married at all, because God won't recognize your marriage and you will be living in sin." (In her defense, she had a stroke about ten years prior to this and has never been the same since.)

That was bad enough, but then the majority of my own relatives couldn't be bothered to attend the ceremony because we were not getting married in the temple and it was an "inconvenient" day of the week.

My husband has never felt truly welcome in our ward. His closest friends are still literally on the other side of the world; I don't think he really has any friends in this hemisphere. He doesn't look or act like the standard cookie cutter priesthood holder. I think our bishop is the only person who has truly tried to get to know him in the five years we've been in this ward as a married couple.

At family events, my husband tries very hard to be friendly and outgoing toward my cousins, aunts, and uncles, but interactions are only now seeming to be authentic with them.

We all wish to be seen as people with hearts and feelings and interests. Above all else, I just wish someone would befriend him. My story, while similar to many others, is something that has drastically changed the course of my life, particularly pertaining to my membership in the Church.

## EMMA RYDBERG

I grew up in Illinois and didn't know what a "Mormon" was. I have always been fascinated by cults and religious groups that do not follow the ways of the world, so my interest was piqued from the beginning.

I was baptized at eighteen years old in 2014. My baptism was the result of a multi-year journey to get closer to God. I went through some extremely hard trials as a teenager and lived at a mental health rehabilitation facility for twelve months when I

---

15. At the time, the Church policy was that those who married outside the temple were not eligible to be sealed for a year. This policy has since been changed.

was fifteen. It was located in Montana close to the Idaho border, and the vast majority of the staff and a few of the other residents were active LDS members.

My heart was softened, and my interest bloomed into desire to know more, to feel closer to Heavenly Father, to know more about this life. When I left the rehab program and went back to Illinois, I never forgot about the Church and the feeling I got from studying about it.

I went to college about an hour away from Nauvoo. I had learned about its history and kept telling myself that I would make time to visit and see what it was all about. However, my desire to see Nauvoo was eclipsed by an increasingly intense drug and alcohol problem. I was expelled from college and felt defeated, embarrassed, and irritated. Just before I moved out of the dorm, I had an overwhelming feeling that if I didn't go to Nauvoo, when would I ever have the opportunity again? Every mile closer, more excitement and light filled my soul. How could I be so excited for something I'd never seen or been to? Around 2:30 in the morning, the light of the Nauvoo temple pierced the night sky. Seeing the temple filled my whole being with what felt like electricity.

I drove back to my dorm, slept for a few hours, packed up, and drove home as though the extremely profound experience had never even happened. I continued to struggle with alcohol abuse and mental health problems until I developed a liver infection and sepsis, had emergency surgery, and was hospitalized. This experience shook me to my core. Being eighteen and so close to death was the wake-up call I desperately needed. Three weeks later, after I was released from the hospital, I contacted the sister missionaries, took the discussions, and was baptized a member of The Church of Jesus Christ of Latter-day Saints on September 20, 2014.

The first year of my membership in the Church was, for the most part, unremarkable. I was very active in the gospel; it seemed my testimony was doubling every day. I was going out to work with the missionaries almost every day. I received my temple endowment thirteen months after my baptism. I felt very comfortable in my ward and stake. The Church in Northern Illinois is the most beautiful mosaic of every walk of life. Rich. Poor. Black. White. Asian. Hispanic. Young. Old. Straight. LGBTQ+. I felt welcome despite my tattoos, my prior substance abuse, and my prior trials. Everyone was on a level playing field.

I moved to Rexburg, Idaho, in January 2016 to finish college at BYU–Idaho. This was the first time since being part of the Church that I felt that I was not wanted, I was not worthy of being wanted, and I did not deserve to take up space in the gospel. I was kicked out of class for my tattoos showing. I almost lost my ecclesiastical endorsement for publicly supporting my LGBTQ+ friends on social media. I lost my calling as a temple ordinance worker once they knew I had tattoos. The list could go on and on and on. I had a mindset that my unique, worldly experiences brought me closer to the Savior, but that decayed into a belief that those experiences obstructed me from being a "real" member of the Church, from having a "real" relationship with Heavenly Father. My testimony was never weaker than at BYU–I. I was told that I was a worthless sinner who would never have a genuine place in the gospel, so I started acting that way. I once again started abusing alcohol, got more tattoos, broke the commandments.

After graduation, I moved to Idaho Falls, where I now work as a registered nurse. I have attended my current ward only a handful of times and for the foreseeable future, I will not be going back. Once mothers see my outward physical appearance, they pull their children away from me and look at me in terror. I have shared my thoughts in Sunday School, only to be told that I don't understand what the passage actually means and maybe the Gospel Principles class[16] would be better suited for me. I have been denied access to the temple because of my tattoos, and my stake president had to be contacted in order to verify my recommend.

I don't want anyone to feel sorry for me, but I do want my experience to be a teachable one. We are all sinners. We all fall short of the glory of God. The only difference is that some of my sins are visible. They have been washed away spiritually by the Atonement of Jesus Christ, but they will forever keep a physical residence on my body. How would we treat one another if we could not only see all of their shortcomings written across their body, but if our shortcomings were written across our bodies too? Would we be more empathetic? Would we be more patient? What behaviors would we start or stop? Would we be

---

16. The Gospel Principles class was usually attended by new members, investigators, or others learning basic gospel principles. This class was discontinued when the Sunday meeting schedule was shortened from three to two hours. See First Presidency letter, The Church of Jesus Christ of Latter-day Saints, October 6, 2018, media.deseret.com/media/misc/pdf/2018-fall-general-conference/first-presidency-letter.pdf.

better about keeping our covenants? Would we be better about helping our brothers and sisters keep their covenants?

This is something I often think about. How grateful I am that only a few of my sins are written on my flesh. Heavenly Father and His Son, Jesus Christ, know everything that I have done. They have been beside me through every heartache, every tear, every time I have been rejected, every time I have been made to feel less-than. I have a testimony that They choose to look beyond my physical countenance every single time. They see my soul and through Their infinite grace and mercy, I am wiped clean of all imperfections and am made whole again.

I know that my days of being judged are not over, not even close. But I choose to remember that there is only one judgment that matters, only one judgment that is bound on earth as it is in heaven. By focusing on my relationship with Christ and His gospel, I am able to "keep my eye on the prize."

## E. DOYLEN

I love black. Growing up, my style icon was more Morticia Addams than anything you'd find in fashion magazines. While remaining modest, I found myself gravitating toward a look somewhere between gothic and punk, all while remaining an active participant in the Church.

I wish I could say people who claim to love the Lord extend that love to all, but that's not always been my experience. Because I didn't look the way some people wanted me to, I've deliberately been left out of activities, Church-sponsored and otherwise. I've been ignored or closed out of groups when I tried to make connections. I've been called vicious hurtful names. I've had active attempts to drive me out of wards. I've had people tell me to my face that they hated me, though they didn't take the time to get to know me. I was bullied to the point that I considered ending my life.

Many may shrug this off, thinking, "She brought it on herself. She had a choice to change how she identified. She could have just kept that part of herself from the public." For years, I did just that. I changed my entire look to bright colorful clothing that was "in style." I never felt comfortable with myself in this look, but I feared that returning to who I had been would lead to more bullying.

I kept my new look until college, until one night I realized I honestly didn't like anything about myself anymore. My mental and physical health had changed in unexpected ways, and I felt lost and unlovable. I spent many nights in tearful prayer, wondering who I was supposed to be. The Lord answered me through a series of experiences (one of which was with the loving man writing this book) that I needed to quit hiding who He made me to be. Our loving Father designed me purposefully to not fit the mold because He needed me to reach certain people with my appearance who perhaps couldn't be reached otherwise. I wish I could say that returning to an Addams Family-approved look as an adult was smooth sailing and prejudice-free, but it hasn't been. I've perhaps received even more hurtful responses than in my youth, but now, I'm armed with the love of my God, who I know is proud of who I've become.

I firmly believe God gave us innate traits as part of a divine creation (beyond the obvious things such as race and sexual orientation). There are things you were made to love, to care about, to excel at, in order to reach every corner of this earth with God's light and glory. When someone is judged for any single characteristic of their design, we miss the opportunity to see the beautiful masterpiece that God created us each to be.

## MARY BEXTONEN

My first wakeup to "Church culture" was as a BYU student in the 1980s. My first year was ideal with great roommates and a wonderful ward. My second year was the exact opposite—I lived off campus in a dump of an apartment. My home teachers refused to visit me because of where I lived. My roommates stole things from me frequently. One roommate made a show of praying and reading the scriptures, and liked to let me know I was not up to her standards. She got pregnant and had to quickly get married. I was rarely asked on dates. The guys who did ask me out wanted to know my life goals on the first date, which I did not share because they were very personal to me, so I was scoffed at and given a lecture about goal setting.

After that year, I decided to transfer to a public university in another state to save my sanity and church membership. Everyone in my home ward, including my parents, was concerned I would never find a member to marry, and wondered how I could leave the "Lord's University" to go to a public university with all the drinking and partying. Well, it was easy because no one judged me, there was no weird culture to deal with, and most people were very friendly and accepting.

I was married for twenty-two years to a Black African man who was a returned missionary and a member in good standing. My parents, bishop, and stake president were supportive of our marriage. My ward was generally loving and didn't say much other than congratulations. However, one grandmother wrote me a letter that I needed to talk with my priesthood leaders because this couldn't happen. I disregarded her, as she was known for being crusty and I had already talked to my priesthood leaders. A couple in my ward from Utah talked to my parents but got nowhere, so they pulled me aside to inform me (as if I did not already know) of the "curse of Cain,"[17] which would become my curse and my children's and on and on. I politely listened, then told them the story of how my husband and I became acquainted. There had been many miracles for us to meet and get engaged. The couple said they could see the hand of God and were then supportive, but the assumption had been made that I could not possibly know what I was doing.

We lived for a time in a Midwestern city, in a ward which was very educated and used to diversity in thought. We were widely accepted, and when our first child was born, it was a joyous time with our ward family. We later moved to a different city—a very segregated city. Our new ward members did not say much directly, but there were looks and whispers. My second child was born with complications requiring medical help the first two years, and the ward did rally to our aid.

We also had our third child in that ward, and at one point, I needed childcare assistance when she was an infant. Black and bi-racial children are often born with a Mongolian spot on their bottoms. It is common in dark-skinned infants and often disappears over time. All three of my children had it. Well, the sister who watched my baby asked me how I handled my children. I told her my parenting perspective, which is a normal parenting view, and she did not say anything else. But I overheard whispering that I possibly abused my children. I still went to church and carried on without saying anything, but I was mortified that this is what was being said about me. I was never allowed into the "inner circle" of that ward.

About twenty years ago, we moved to Utah. After my experiences at BYU, I never, ever wanted to move back to Utah. Our first ward was wonderful, accepting, and supportive. I went through my divorce in that ward, and they were amazing! The kids and I still talk about some of the members there.

---

17. This damaging former teaching is untrue and has been denounced. See "Race and the Priesthood," Gospel Topics, The Church of Jesus Christ of Latter-day Saints, accessed March 20, 2021, churchofjesuschrist.org/study/manual/gospel-topics-essays/race-and-the-priesthood.

After the divorce, my husband left the United States. I had no money, no child support or alimony, so I had to sell my house and move. Our second ward in Utah was the complete opposite of the first. We were openly stared at when entering. The bishop let me know I would need to reach out to the sisters in the ward as they were not likely to befriend me (including his wife!). He said they were not an "open bunch." He was right on the money. But I was too busy working three jobs to feed, clothe, and house my kids. I had been through an abusive marriage, so I knew I could go it alone.

Alone I went. My home teacher let me know that he could not visit me because I was single—which felt like a slap in the face. Was I now some pariah? I couldn't have the missionaries over because I was single—another slap in the face! We got to sacrament meeting a few minutes late and saw an open pew at the back. When we sat down, I was instantly told I could not sit there and had to move. They did not say why, and I did not want to disrupt the meeting, so we moved. By the time I sat down again, I was bawling. I was hanging onto life by my fingernails, and there was no comfort anywhere at church. I did find out later that a man in a wheelchair and his family usually sat in that pew, but it remained empty that day.

In seminary, my daughter was taught about temple marriage and that if you are divorced, you can't go to the celestial kingdom. She told me that she can't believe in a church that would teach I could not go to the celestial kingdom because I was divorced. I tried to explain that I still believed the Lord would work things out on my behalf, but she stopped attending church.

The last Sunday my son attended church was the day he was ordained a priest. He won't tell me what happened, but something did, and he has never gone to church since.

My younger daughter hung in there until she was fifteen. She came home from school and said she would never go to seminary again. She was tired of hearing about her teacher's practically perfect family and how "our family" did not fit in culturally or racially. I tried to talk with her and emailed the seminary teacher to no avail. The bishop was disappointed in me for not "making" her attend. Then the Young Women leader lit into me about my bad example since I did not attend every Sunday (I worked every other Sunday) and that is why my daughter was starting to miss meetings. I was so taken aback that I just said I needed to go home, and left crying. I later called her and said in no uncertain terms that she was in the wrong. I did not know the bishop had called her to check my attendance and it was none of her business anyway.

After being in the ward at least four years, I was called to teach Relief Society but was treated as though I did not know the gospel and had been inactive. It was my fourth time being an RS teacher, and I had been in RS presidencies, but that showed how little my ward knew me. A couple of years later, I was called into the Relief Society presidency in that ward. I served until my cancer diagnosis. The ward was great during my cancer and took good care of me, but as soon as my treatments were over, I was dropped like a hot potato.

I finally felt like I had found my true gospel home when I was called to work in the temple. I knew the temple president and matron personally, and it was a joy to serve under them and to have them warmly greet me when they were there. I loved the inclusive instruction received in prayer meetings: that love should prevail in all we do in the temple. I was called to be an assistant coordinator and loved to see how the Lord made things work out in the temple. It was a true honor to serve.

I was preparing to move in 2018, and everything came to a head when I overheard two men talking in the hall at church about helping me with my move—they did not want to do it and felt I should handle it all on my own. One was my neighbor across the street, and the other was the elders quorum president. After serving in that ward for twelve years, apparently I did not deserve their help. On moving day, those two men never showed up. Ten others did, with a couple of my brothers and friends not in the ward. We had an 1800-square-foot house loaded in less than two hours, and I was gone from that ward. FAREWELL!!!!

As of January 2019, I have not attended church. When I met with the new bishop, I asked for some time, as I was dealing with my younger daughter's suicide attempt and my own depression. I was in counseling, so I was emotionally getting help, but I didn't have the stamina to put on the Happy Mormon Sunday face. He did not listen and told me I just needed to attend my meetings, pray, and read the scriptures. He is now the stake president. That was the final straw that helped me decide to stop attending.

I'm tired of not being listened to. I'm tired of being told I need to be the strong one, I have to be the one to reach out. . . . I'm tired. I've usually held multiple callings since the age of twelve, even in wards in Utah, and I've given all I can right now. I can't go to church and hear politically or racially charged talk with people oblivious to how it affects others. I'm tired of dear friends who don't or won't hear me when I express my racial experiences or concerns. I just can't do it anymore. Only two brothers and their wives in my family know that I'm not attending church. My parents and the rest of the family have no idea, and I won't be telling them because I can't handle the self-righteous lectures. I have grown up in the Church and been active my entire life until now. Church is not a safe place for me, and I need to feel safe.

## KIMBERLY J. JOHNSON

I have an amazing career that I love, in which I help people have experiences to change their lives for the better. I love the people I work with, and my job helps me feel fulfilled. It has also given me the opportunity to see the world, which broadens my view.

I am married with four beautiful children who are the lights of my life. My career helps provide for them, and it helped pay for my husband's PhD. After the birth of our third child, I tried the stay-at-home-mom thing. So many of my fellow ward members were stay-at-home-moms. They had things in common and brunches and play dates that I felt my kids and I were missing out on. I heard in Relief Society about the importance of being home with your kids while they are little, that *not* being there was doing them a great disservice. It was everywhere I turned. The guilt was immense and swallowed me whole. So I left the job I loved and became a stay-at-home-mom. I fell into a deep depression and lacked balance in my life.

After a year and a half, I returned to my career, and luckily my employer welcomed me back with open arms. Later, a man who is a member of the Church stopped me in the kitchen at work. He said, "I was at your wedding reception several years ago. It was lovely." I agreed. He said, "It has been over ten years now. Right?" I agreed. He said, "Don't you have any children yet?" I was shocked at the audacity of the question but told him we have four. He exclaimed, "Four children? What are you doing here? Who watches your kids?" My face turned red as I told him my sister-in-law does. "Well, at least *SOMEONE* is loving your babies!"

That was the turning point for me. My Savior and Heavenly Parents know I am a good mother. They know I love my babies and do my best. What this man implied was absolutely false but is not an uncommon attitude within the Church. From that moment, I was DONE berating myself and letting other members of the Church do the same to me. We DO NOT have the right as members of The Church of Jesus Christ to judge each other this way. Luckily for me, instead of devastating me, this experience turned me around, and I try to be a support to ALL mothers. There is no perfect way to mother, whether working outside the home or staying home.

## MAGGIE SLIGHTE

From the week I first joined the Church, I've dealt with judgment from members who were quick to notice that I wasn't like most of them. Sideways glances from people who noticed I wasn't dressed as well or spoke differently didn't affect my life, and I did my best to ignore them.

I was baptized when I was homeless, but no one understood that I was homeless, since I hid it well.

After my divorce in 2017, I embarked on a journey across the Southern states in the car I lived in to search for a warm place to wait out the winter. My branch president was careful to make sure I knew to ask for help from any bishop in my path. I agreed but wanted to be as self-sufficient as my disability pension would allow.

When I stopped at a ward in Florida one Sunday, the lesson was on "the Stranger." I felt an impression to request help from the bishop. A food order would help the hunger pain in my gut, and I was worried about some mechanical issues with my car. But when I met with the bishop, he was certain and stern: there would be NO help from him or anyone in his ward. I should have thought about food before becoming homeless.

Dejected, I went to the Relief Society class. I felt an impression to open up about my circumstances again, this time to everyone. God rewarded my humility with one invitation for lunch and another for dinner. The angel who invited me to dinner commiserated with me about my situation. She and her family allowed me to stay a night, filled my gas tank, and gave me groceries and a little cash. They still keep me in their prayers.

Sometimes, even when people judge, God sees us and rewards us for our humility and strength in the face of judgment. I've included many of these examples in a memoir about my journey across the country and my final year of being homeless, *The Car That Ran on Prayers.*

## JOSIE L.

Many years ago, I was in an abusive relationship and didn't have the courage to get away. I was married at age twenty and lived in a pretty bad situation for a year and a half. I tried to leave a few times, but he always convinced me to stay. When I finally left, I was determined to stay active in the Church. My bishop made it very hard for me. He knew my ex-husband and thought highly of him despite the circumstances. He made hurtful remarks like, "How does it feel to be twenty-two and divorced?" and "I don't think the Church should help you pay for counseling since you chose to leave. You chose to get divorced." It was a struggle.

Being a young divorcée has an unfortunate stigma. I knew the decision to get divorced shouldn't be taken lightly. Despite the abuse, it was a very difficult decision. The lessons in Relief Society, sacrament meeting, and general conference can make you feel guilty even if it was 100% the right decision.

When I chose to get remarried, I had an amazing singles ward bishop who treated me so well. He never once was judgmental. He went to great lengths to keep my location private from my ex-husband when handling the sealing cancellation paperwork. He understood why I needed my information confidential and respected me.

## SHANNON STAHLE

Due to a lot of family turmoil and feeling not seen or heard, I openly rebelled against the Church when I was a teen. I had sex, partied, and mocked the Church and my family to my friends.

Despite years of going further and further down this path, I hit a point that I knew I needed to make a choice about where my life was headed. I started praying and knew I needed to attend church and start repenting. It was so hard. Friends from earlier in life when I was active didn't seem to know how to treat me when I returned to church. One friend treated me like garbage when he found out I had been sexually active and gotten a tattoo. He commented on my clothes, that I needed to dress more "modestly." He regularly told me what a disappointment I had been and that he could never date me seriously because I wasn't a virgin. In hindsight, I can see how it was an emotionally abusive friendship, but at the time I thought I deserved it. I eventually cut contact with him, simply because it was too painful for me to deal with regularly.

I started dating another man when I was nearing the end of my repentance process. I felt like this relationship could move to a more serious level, but I was terrified about revealing my past to him. He felt the same way about our relationship moving forward, and we agreed to talk about the important things about ourselves. I sobbed as I poured out my soul to him, telling him about my sins and mistakes. I was fully prepared for rejection as I had experienced before.

His response was nothing that I had imagined. He said, "Okay." I was confused, I asked what he was thinking. He said, "You aren't your past. I don't really care about who you were, but you seem to be working really hard on your future, and that's what matters to me." He said it so genuinely, without even a hint of disapproval.

It was the first moment in my life that I felt accepted and truly seen for what my efforts were. I have since tried to model how I treat others after I was treated then. Christ would never judge. He would never scoff or wrinkle His nose at someone's sins. He would love and encourage. And that's what my husband did for me.

## KELCI WOOD

I am a convert and was baptized when I was twenty-one, after meeting with the missionaries for just three weeks. I was over the "college scene" and needed something concrete in my life, like a strong church family. Growing up, I was very active in my parents' church until I went to college. Like many people away from home for the first time, I was trying to discover myself. I spent a lot of time with the wrong kinds of people who didn't uplift me and enabled my drinking problem. I am also hard-headed about a lot of things. When someone tells me I can't do something, that is my quickest motivator. I want to prove them wrong. That helped me join the Church, actually. A lot of people told me how awful it was, and I wanted to prove them wrong. It ended up being the greatest blessing for me to join the Church. It saved my life.

How does this relate to being judged? Absolutely every-thing. In 2018, I had major issues with migraines. This wasn't a new thing for me—I've had migraines off and on since I was nine years old. I talked with my doctor about medication and some alternative options. The recommended medication was a heavy narcotic, which I did not want. I ended up getting extra piercings in my ears, which has eliminated my migraines.[18] As a result of these piercings, I was judged by several members of my ward.

Many of them knew how strong a member I appeared to be. They frequently told me about President Gordon B. Hinckley's talk from October 2000 general conference, "Great Shall Be the Peace of Thy Children."[19] President Hinckley

---

18. This is called daith piercing, based on the same principles as acupuncture.

19. Gordon B. Hinckley, "Great Shall Be the Peace of Their Children," October 2000 general conference, churchofjesuschrist.org/study/ensign/2000/11/great-shall-be-the-peace-of-thy-children.

passed away before I joined the Church, but I was quite used to people referencing him and his talks often. After I received the additional piercings in my ears, the members kept telling me, "Ya know, Sister Wood, President Hinckley has stated that having multiple piercings is against the rules. You could lose your temple recommend for that." The bishop actually told me that he was going to take away my recommend. That statement alone, from this bishop, pretty much crushed me. I had lost my temple recommend once for not obeying the law of chastity, but losing it over having additional piercings seemed unfair.

So I looked up this talk because I was done with being judged about having multiple piercings for medical purposes. In the talk, President Hinckley clearly states, "We discourage tattoos and also the piercing of the body *for other than medical purposes*." The extra piercings in my ears relieved pain from migraines AND I didn't have to take highly addictive medication, so I was like, "Sign me up!" Now I quote this very talk back at people who say I need to take out my earrings.

There are a lot of people in this world who are going through much more than you realize. These people may never share exactly what they are going through. Judging them before knowing and understanding their situation is NEVER okay. This causes unnecessary thoughts about not feeling wanted. It is our job on this earth to love one another and not judge them. That is the job of God alone.

## The Inn

As we have read this chapter, we can reflect on Elder Gerrit W. Gong's April 2021 general conference talk, "Room at the Inn," as he compares the inn from the parable of the good Samaritan to our Church with these insights for all of us to consider:

> Yet we all have something needed to contribute. Our journey to God is often found together. We belong as united community—whether confronting pandemics, storms, wildfires, droughts, or quietly meeting daily needs. We receive inspiration as we counsel together, listening to each person, including each sister, and the Spirit. . . .
>
> He entreats us to make His Inn a place of grace and space, where each can gather, with room for all. As disciples of Jesus Christ, all are equal, with no second-class groups.

All are welcome to attend sacrament meetings, other Sunday meetings, and social events. We reverently worship our Savior, thoughtful and considerate of each other. We see and acknowledge each person. We smile, sit with those sitting alone, learn names, including of new converts, returning brothers and sisters, young women and young men, each dear Primary child.[20]

---

20. Gerrit W. Gong, "Room in the Inn," April 2021 general conference, churchofjesuschrist.org/study/general-conference/2021/04/16gong.

# CHAPTER 2

# MEASURING PROGRESS BY COMING TO CHRIST, NOT CALLINGS

This is a vulnerable chapter for me to write as I share some of my most honest feelings and painful church experiences—not to be critical of our church but to help us improve our culture so more can partake of the blessings of our restored doctrine, feel they belong, and come unto Christ more wholeheartedly. I pray this chapter will help us better come together as Latter-day Saints to love, see, and support each other.

Starting as a young man, I have been hardwired as a committed Latter-day Saint to occasionally measure my progress in life and see my worth based on my church callings. I do not believe this is how my Heavenly Parents want me to measure my life. I share this personal aspect of my life to help us improve our church culture so that others do not feel the pain I have experienced by tying my worth to something outside of my control. Rather, my hope is our culture hardwires us to measure our progress in life by coming unto Christ, developing Christlike attributes, and honoring temple covenants—all things within our control.

## "So Were You an AP on Your Mission?"[1]

When I meet a newly returned elder, I find myself silently wondering if he was an assistant to the president (AP). I decided to not ask this question of anyone, but it bothers me that I still think it. Within Latter-day Saint culture, we have created a way of "seeing" that often measures a missionary's success by leadership assignments and causes Latter-day Saints to measure their feelings of self-worth, value, and worthiness by their callings.

I have spent a lifetime of hearing good folks in our church defined by their callings. How many conversations like these have we participated in?

- "He's dating the daughter of the stake president."
- "They just moved into the ward; he was in the bishopric of his prior ward."
- "She is marrying the elders quorum president in her singles ward."
- "My new walking partner is the stake Primary president."
- "He is having a great mission; he was just made a zone leader."

I have been in meetings where people introduce themselves by a list of their church callings. I have been in quorum lessons where a good brother answers a question beginning with, "When I served as a [former calling] . . ." I have been in settings where we tell the youth that they are the future leaders of the Church: "Maybe one of you is a future bishop, Young Women president, stake president, or even Relief Society General President or General Authority." Further, sometimes women are defined and mentioned only in the context of their husband's calling, such as wife of the bishop, wife of the patriarch, or wife of the mission president.

---

1. Richard Ostler, "So were you an AP on your mission?" Facebook, July 1, 2017, facebook.com/richard.ostler.5/posts/10212030741076984 and in *LDS Living*, July 8, 2017, ldsliving.com/We-Need-to-Stop-Judging-Each-Other-and-Our-Righteousness-Based-on-Church-Callings/s/85828.

I heard about the funeral of a prominent Church member, at which the presiding authority asked all former and current General Authorities in attendance to stand to show love for this good person. I have heard that some parents size up their potential future son-in-law by his callings. I have heard talks describing someone returning from inactivity and then stating his calling ("He is now serving as a bishop") to illustrate a return to full activity. I have heard of meetings in which all returned missionaries are called to the stand to participate in a missionary song. I have read biographical sketches of newly sustained leaders that list prior Church callings. And I have mentioned being a YSA bishop in my social media posts, books, and articles.

These are all innocent comments. No one intends to make others feel slighted or overlooked. Past or current callings do not need to be treated as confidential information. However, in that funeral when General Authorities were asked to stand, what message was presented to children and youth about what is valued in our culture, or to the other adults who were never called to comparable positions? Do we need to list prior leadership callings in a published profile?[2] What is the impact over a lifetime of having worth and value for some defined by leadership assignments?

This focus has inadvertently created in a way of seeing—starting in our youth—that can cause one to measure their progress in life by the callings they receive. It can be damaging. It can make some of our best and most capable members feel marginalized. It can lead some to step away from the Church as they don't feel they measure up or are needed. I have felt it in my own life and have spoken with many who have felt the same pain—wondering if they are somehow less worthy in the sight of their Heavenly Parents.

Similarly, some wonder if they had some early leadership opportunities, they would have the same senior callings some of their peers are experiencing. I know many wonderful members who

---

2. This list of church callings is necessary sometimes, as seen in my own profile in this book.

would make incredible ward/stake leaders but are not called, which may be partly because they have never had some of the experience that comes through earlier callings that helps prepare them for a more senior calling. I think of them in our meetings and wonder how they feel, as I rarely hear some of them offer a comment. Isn't their voice just as important?

To be completely honest, I have felt the pull of desiring church callings. Why? I have internalized and "hardwired" the message of "worth" it sends about those who are called. I have yearned for that same feeling of validation—the signal of worth it sends me—and to our congregation, family, and community about me.

Realizing this is unhealthy, over the past decade I have spent a great deal of effort trying to deprogram myself from measuring my progress in life by my church callings. I am seeking to reprogram myself to measure progress by developing Christlike attributes, being a good husband/father, having a strong relationship with my Heavenly Parents, honoring my covenants, and being a worthy priesthood holder—all things in my control. I have a long way to go. Yes, I will accept any calling that comes my way—I will do all I can to honor my covenants—but I am focusing on things I can control. Still, I often get triggered, and it is a work-in-progress.

I have deep respect for and sustain those who are called. They need all the support, prayers, understanding, and "hands at their back" they can get. Their road is difficult, time intensive, and lonely at times. And I don't want anyone in leadership (or those who were an AP or Sister Training Leader) to be diminished by my thoughts or feel guarded in sharing your experiences. We need to hear your faith-promoting stories and are grateful for your service to bring others to Christ.

I have recently heard incredible homecoming talks as some wonderful returned missionaries shared their love of the Savior and how they helped to walk people into the gospel of Jesus Christ. They didn't mention anything about "serving in the office" or "spending a lot of time with the President." Well done.

During his mission, one our own sons never once mentioned anything about his leadership assignments. Further, his mission did not update us on his leadership assignments. I remember getting up in fast and testimony meeting on the last Sunday of his mission and mentioned that as far as I knew he was a junior companion for all twenty-four months of his mission and how proud I was of him that he made his mission about bringing people to Christ and not his leadership assignments. Yes, upon returning home we did have a private conversation about his various leadership assignments and the wonderful lessons learned and those he served—but we both knew that didn't define his mission—and our approval of his mission (like his Heavenly Parents) was not tied to any leadership assignments. (Now, in sharing this example, I do not want any parent to feel guilty for sharing the excitement of their missionary's leadership assignment with others—I'm just providing some additional perspective.)

Our son reminded us that when missionaries are assigned to areas and leadership positions, they are not set apart again, because they are already set apart in their calling as a missionary. We should be focusing on less on internal mission assignments and more on the calling of being a missionary. Interestingly, this is one of the few callings you can choose, because anyone can be a missionary.

## Hardwired in Youth to Measure Worth by Callings

As I mentioned, I am trying to deprogram myself from measuring my worth around church callings and instead focus on coming unto Christ and developing Christlike attributes. For me, multiple factors occurred in my youth to cause this way of seeing leadership. As a child, I developed an interest in reading obituaries in the local Salt Lake newspaper. Each day, I noted the name of the person with the most years married, to track how many days in a row I could find someone with fifty years of marriage. This quirky interest resulted in reading amazing life stories that gave me vision and perspective for the kind of life I wanted to live and the way I wanted to serve. The obituaries for Latter-day Saints often included a list of church callings—something very appropriate in recapping their life-long dedicated service. However, that contributed to my way of seeing leadership, as I noticed how successful Latter-day Saints are measured in a final summary of their lives.

I also grew up in a wonderful family where many served in significant Church leadership assignments. My great-grandfather was an Apostle, and my grandmother was in the Relief Society General Presidency. These two relatives were part of my life well into my adult years, and their example of selfless service had a great influence on me. Many other family members served as stake presidents and mission presidents. I am honored to be part of a family contributing to building the kingdom of God, and I hope to respect their legacy with my own service. My distinguished ancestors were humble about their assignments, never flaunting their positions, simply wanting to serve wherever they could be useful. But the seeds of how to measure my worth were innocently planted in my soul through this implied cultural link between church assignments and goodness.

During my Aaronic Priesthood years, I listened to parents speak about their missionary sons and daughters, often mentioning leadership assignments. During my era, in a missionary homecoming sacrament meeting, the bishop often read a letter from a mission president about the missionary in front of the entire ward. Such letters gave great insight into the goodness of their service, but frequently mentioned leadership callings, reinforcing the definition of success in this way. Further, missionaries in their homecoming reports sometimes mentioned leadership assignments or made vague references to "when I served in the office."

## England Manchester Mission

As I boarded the plane in May 1980 for the England Manchester Mission, I was filled with a deep testimony of our restored gospel and a genuine desire to help others find the blessings of membership in our restored church. But I'm sure part of my motivation to be a good missionary was so I could climb the ranks and serve as an assistant to the president, which I had internalized as the cultural badge of a successful missionary. Maybe I was even thinking that my future wife or father-in-law might measure me up by mission leadership, and I wanted to be seen as a capable future husband and son-in-law.

After about six months, I realized that my mission president, Ellis Ivory, was working to change that perspective. Instead of progressing as if up a ladder—junior companion, senior companion, trainer, district leader, zone leader, assistant—a good missionary could be a zone leader one transfer and a junior companion the next. Or he be a zone leader without ever being a district leader. I experienced these type of assignment changes, as I went from zone leader to junior companion. In most missions, an assignment lower on the "mission ladder" only happened if a missionary was disciplined for a behavior issue. But for us, having no ladder became part of the culture.

I believe this resulted in a culture focused less on leadership ranks and more concentrated on bringing people to Christ through our restored church. I also believe it gave more individuals the opportunity to grow during leadership assignments and elevated the mission to a higher spiritual level that might not otherwise have been possible. It perhaps removed shame from those whose assignment was changed because of a behavior issue. It helped all of us to be humble. We lived a higher and holier way, allowing us to bring many to our restored gospel. In fact, during some months, we were the highest baptizing English-speaking mission in the Church— perhaps partly because our mission culture was focused on bringing people to Christ rather than climbing the mission leadership ladder.

I was asked to serve as an assistant to the president in my mission and did my best in that assignment. I learned a lot serving with President and Sister Ivory, two of my heroes, and enjoyed the chance to interact with more missionaries and help people come unto Christ. I wish every missionary could serve as an assistant to the president and experience the personal growth.

As I flew home from England in 1982, I had the sweet peace of knowing I helped many find our Savior through our restored Church. I am also sure that some of the satisfaction I felt was related to being an assistant to the president. I had reached cultural expectations and met my own goals. This assignment also maintained my hopes for future church callings. Could I be one of those mentioned in youth gatherings: "one of you may be a bishop, stake president or even a General Authority"? The dream was alive.

## Falling Behind

In my twenties and thirties, I served as an elders quorum president twice, stake Young Men president, stake mission president, high councilor, and bishopric member. I was honored to serve and did my best to bring people to Christ through the restored Church.

During my mid-to-late forties, I noticed that men my age were being called to more senior leadership assignments than I was (bishops, stake presidencies, mission presidents).

Feelings gradually crept into me of falling behind men my age. I started to wonder if I measured up to the men receiving those callings and if my Heavenly Parents saw me differently than others being called.

## Twenty-six Good Men

In my early fifties, a particularly difficult experience occurred with the reorganization of our stake presidency. Leading up to this reorganization, there was a lot of chatter about who would be called, and some started to refer (in a good-natured way) to others as "President." Some of those comments were directed to me, which, I admit, met my desire for this type of validation, and I wondered if I would be called. However, I did not feel any impressions I would be called and pragmatically realized I likely would not be since I had not served as a bishop. That seemed to be necessary experience to be a stake president.

The morning of the stake conference, I had a strong impression about who would be called, which was confirmed when David Sturt was sustained as our new stake president. My wife, Sheila, and I are good friends with Dave and Stacie Sturt and their family, and we were pleased that this good man would be guiding our stake. Several of our children would likely serve missions and/or be married while he served, and we looked forward to his participation with us in those milestones.[3] I felt at peace and looked forward to stake conference.

However, something happened to make it one of the most painful church meetings I have ever attended. It was not because I was not called—it was the explanation of one of the presiding authorities about "interviewing twenty-six good men" and "we got this right." Perhaps other stake members needed to hear this message, but I did not need comments laying out the case that the right person was called to lead our stake. I believed in and trusted the process. Hearing "twenty-six men"—knowing I was not one of them—made me feel othered, something I had never felt before in a Church setting. I felt the walls of the chapel closing in on me. I felt a line in the sand drawn, not between me and our new stake president, but between me and those twenty-six men—and perhaps on a deeper level between my perception of myself and my true worth. I felt judged. There was no mention of the good men who were not called or who were not among the twenty-six interviewed.

I knew to separate this painful experience from our beautiful restored doctrine, and I continued to participate and serve in the Church. But in another meeting a few years later, a different visiting Area Seventy described the process of calling a stake president, mentioning that they "go in and interview the top men in the stake." I felt sort of traumatized all over again.

Perhaps I overreacted to these experiences as I realize there was no malice behind these comments. In writing about it now, it does not seem like a big deal. Someone my age and hopefully my spiritual maturity should be able to handle this type of situation. Perhaps I am the only person who was hurt by what was said—but the pain I felt was real.

I hope we can learn to believe another's pain and not require them to prove it. In my experience, dismissal just adds to the pain. The

---

3. President Sturt, who served nearly ten years, was a great stake president and blessed our family immensely. Sheila and I will be forever grateful to him for his dedicated service.

entire experience has given me more empathy, compassion, and better ministering tools for those with difficult church experiences—including many women who feel their voice is not valued or heard, and those often on the margins like our LGBTQ members, BIPOC,[4] and others. Some call this church-generated pain, which is a unique type of pain because it results from a place that is intended to be a place of healing. Feeling this pain firsthand has helped me understand this pain in others when they open up about difficult church experiences and the need for the Atonement of Jesus Christ to heal our hearts and souls. I have tried to lean back into the pain (continuing to enter my local ward building which reminds me of the experience) as a way to move forward. I have also better understood why some need to take a break from attending church (not a break from living the gospel) while they heal from difficult experiences, and trusted them to know what is right for them to move forward.

A couple of years later, with a desire to put the experience behind me, I wrote to the visiting authority from stake conference and shared my feelings. His response was excellent. Here are some of the things he said, which give insights to improving our culture in the way we handle leadership changes.

He validated my pain with, "I am sorry for the pain you experienced as a result of the statements made at the stake reorganization. I understand how the 'twenty-six men' comment could make one feel excluded and undervalued." His next statement was also very helpful: "In most stakes, there are scores of men not interviewed who could successfully serve as a stake president." I feel this is key in how we should look at leadership callings. *Many* are qualified—but only *one* is chosen for a season to lead. Yes, I wish this principle had been communicated during the stake reorganization and ingrained in our culture. It would not have taken anything away from the divine nature of the person called, but rather helped me not feel othered and judged.

---

4.   BIPOC is an abbreviation for Black, Indigenous, and People of Color.

The late Elder Clayton M. Christensen, when he was Area Seventy of the North America Northeast Area, shared some of his feelings in an *Ensign*[5] article:

> "Inasmuch as ye have done it unto the least of these my brethren, ye have done it unto me" (Matthew 25:40). "Out of small things proceedeth that which is great" (D&C 64:33). Despite the Savior's assurances that the small things are the big things, many in the Church feel inferior for never having served in presidencies or bishoprics. Others who have served in leadership positions feel "put out to pasture" when given a less-prominent calling.
>
> I once felt passed over when another man was called to a leadership position I had felt I might receive. In the crisis of self-confidence that ensued, I realized that because our minds are finite, we create hierarchies and statistically aggregate people. We perceive stake presidents to be higher than bishops and Primary presidents higher than Primary teachers because they preside over more people. But God has an infinite mind. He needs no statistics above the level of the individual in order to have a perfect understanding of what is happening. This means, I realized, that the way God will measure my life is not by the numbers of people over whom I have presided but by the individual people whose lives I have touched with His love and with the gospel of Jesus Christ.
>
> With this sense of my most important calling, I began to fast and pray that God would give me opportunities daily to bless and help people. As I acted upon the promptings I received, it was as if God spoke to me more frequently because He knew I was listening. This period in my life proved to be one of extraordinary spiritual growth.[6]

---

5. The magazine for adults published by the Church was called *Ensign*. Now it is called *Liahona*.
6. Clayton M. Christensen, "My Ways Are Not Your Ways," *Ensign*, February 2007, 54–59; media.ldscdn.org/pdf/magazines/ensign-february-2007/2007-02-00-ensign-eng.pdf.

## "Lift Where You Stand"

Even today, I find myself aware of ward and stake leadership changes and wonder if I will be called. Being called as a bishop in a Young Single Adult ward in 2013 didn't resolve this issue, as I felt that other men my age had already checked the bishop box and were on to more senior callings. I realize that this negative perception perhaps held me back from completely focusing on my stewardship and being the most effective in my assignment. Instead, I wasted mental energy wondering how this assignment fit into or could lead to future callings, or if I measured up to other YSA bishops in my circle who generally had more church leadership experience. It is also possible that I over-served in this assignment because of this hole in my soul, which led me to seek therapy for the emotional fatigue I experienced. Did I feel I needed to be the best YSA bishop who ever served to feel equal to my peers, or catch up to their more senior callings?

I also feel this way of measuring self-worth will not be fulfilled with increasingly senior callings. Instead, it needs to be fulfilled by things within my control: building my relationship with my Heavenly Parents, receiving the healing power of the Atonement of Jesus Christ, keeping my covenants, and being a good husband and father. I share my honest and vulnerable feelings with you, my reader, in hopes that they might be helpful for you.

Elder Uchtdorf's general conference talk "Lift Where You Stand" provides helpful guidance to improve our church culture to create a way of seeing that we are all equally needed:

> Some years ago in our meetinghouse in Darmstadt, Germany, a group of brethren was asked to move a grand piano from the chapel to the adjoining cultural hall, where it was needed for a musical event. None were professional movers, and the task of getting that gravity-friendly instrument through the chapel and into the cultural hall seemed nearly impossible. Everybody knew that this task required not only physical strength but also careful coordination. There were plenty of ideas, but not one could keep the piano balanced correctly. They repositioned the brethren by strength, height, and age over and over again—nothing worked.

As they stood around the piano, uncertain of what to do next, a good friend of mine, Brother Hanno Luschin, spoke up. He said, "Brethren, stand close together and lift where you stand."

It seemed too simple. Nevertheless, each lifted where he stood, and the piano rose from the ground and moved into the cultural hall as if on its own power. That was the answer to the challenge. They merely needed to stand close together and lift where they stood.[7]

Elder Uchtdorf was teaching that each calling is needed, and we should not rank callings. He continued:

There is a better way, taught to us by the Savior Himself: "Whosoever will be chief among you, let him be your servant." (Matthew 20:27)

When we seek to serve others, we are motivated not by selfishness but by charity. This is the way Jesus Christ lived His life and the way a holder of the priesthood must live his. The Savior did not care for the honors of men; Satan offered Him all the kingdoms and glory of the world, and Jesus rejected the offer immediately and completely. Throughout His life, the Savior must have often felt tired and pressed upon, with scarcely a moment to Himself; yet He always made time for the sick, the sorrowful, and the overlooked.

In spite of this shining example, we too easily and too often get caught up in seeking the honors of men rather than serving the Lord with all our might, mind, and strength.

Brethren, when we stand before the Lord to be judged, will He look upon the positions we have held in the world or even in the Church? Do you suppose that titles we have had other than "husband," "father," or "priesthood holder" will mean much to Him? Do you think He will care how packed our schedule was or how many important meetings we attended? Do you suppose that our success in filling our days with appointments will serve as an excuse for failure to spend time with our wife and family?

The Lord judges so very differently from the way we do. He is pleased with the noble servant, not with the self-serving noble.

---

7.  Uchtdorf, "Lift Where You Stand."

Those who are humble in this life will wear crowns of glory in the next. Jesus taught this doctrine Himself when He told the story of the rich man who was clothed in purple and fine linen and ate sumptuously every day, while the beggar Lazarus yearned merely to taste of the crumbs from the rich man's table. In the next life, Lazarus appeared in glory next to Abraham, while the rich man was cast into hell, where he lifted up his eyes in torment.

In the same talk, Elder Uchtdorf also addressed spiritual impressions some may receive about being called and how each is called where we are needed:

> When traveling to the stakes of Zion for the purpose of reorganizing a stake presidency, I have sometimes been surprised when, during an interview, a brother would tell me that he had received an impression that he would be in the next presidency.
>
> When I first heard this, I wasn't sure how to react.
>
> It took some time before the Holy Spirit gave me understanding. I believe that the Lord has a certain calling for every man. Sometimes He grants spiritual promptings telling us that we are worthy to receive certain callings. This is a spiritual blessing, a tender mercy from God.
>
> But sometimes we do not hear the rest of what the Lord is telling us. "Although you are worthy to serve in this position," He may say, "this is not my calling for you. It is my desire instead that you lift where you stand." God knows what is best for us.

When I feel "passed over" for a leadership calling, it is a good time to remind myself that it is not where I serve, but how. It is a time for me to discern what my Heavenly Parents want me to learn and whom They have asked me to bless, right where I am.

## More Can Grow into Becoming Leaders

Elder Christensen, quoted earlier, was also a prolific writer about disruptive innovation. He had a similar approach to that of my mission president, Ellis Ivory, about mixing up junior and senior companions. Elder Christensen suggested in that same *Ensign* article that our strongest leaders be called to mentor others from "underneath," sort of like experienced junior companions! He said,

Some wards and branches suffer from inadequate leadership. The reason is often that we rely on the same qualified people to fill key callings, denying others experiences in which personal growth can occur. When a branch is just emerging and there are no alternatives, leaders extend callings to people who don't fit the traditional mold of talented, capable leaders and invite them to assume important responsibility. During such periods, the branch and its members often grow in exciting ways.

Many times, however, there comes a point when a group of talented, experienced leaders and teachers has coalesced. When there are capable people available to ensure that Church programs run efficiently, we often stop drafting people from the periphery of capability into the positions of responsibility in which they can grow. Because they seem less qualified than those in the experienced core, we leave them on the periphery. The experienced leaders and teachers play musical chairs, exchanging positions of responsibility.

This is not the Lord's way. Building His Church on the backs of the simple and weak (see D&C 1:19) was not a temporary, stop-gap staffing plan to tide the Church over during its early years until enough experienced, committed, qualified leaders had arrived on the scene. The Lord deliberately weakened Gideon's army so that Israel wouldn't get confused about whose power had led them to victory (see Judges 6–7). None of Jesus's original Twelve Apostles had evidenced adequate experience or commitment when He called them. Enoch, Moses, Samuel, David, Jeremiah, Amos, and Joseph Smith were unqualified by the world's standards when the Lord put them to work. But God transformed them.

We will build greater strength and our wards and branches will grow when we stop relying solely on the strongest members—when the experienced and most talented of our leaders are called to supporting roles, to train and help those who can become strong as they serve in positions into which they can grow."[8]

8.  Christensen, "My Ways Are Not Your Ways."

I love Elder Christensen's idea of helping others grow into leadership positions, instead of relying on the same leaders. Potential new leaders may come from many walks of life. Personally, I have benefited tremendously from different points of view. People who are different from me have contributed insights from their life experiences and professional training that would never have occurred to me. If I just surround myself with people who are like me because that is where I am most comfortable, I may not be as effective in my church assignments as I seek to reach and bless the lives of others. Similarly, expanding the diversity of our leadership benefits everyone, by drawing on the richness of a variety of experiences.

We know from various studies that all kinds of organizations (religious and otherwise) function better with diversity in leadership.[9] So when we are seeking inspiration on who to call, we should be open to considering people from all socioeconomic backgrounds and experience levels, and *then* praying for God to reveal who should be called.

Many have reached out to me about this topic. They notice a group of relatively young people receiving callings with significant responsibilities, allowing them to grow and develop spiritual and administrative skills, which qualify them for consideration for more senior callings. We have come to see them as leaders. However, there are also good men and women who never received early leadership positions which would have opened the door to later callings. Now that they are older, they are generally locked out of those more senior callings. Some of these members and their spouses have expressed to me how difficult this cultural aspect is for them. They feel that their voices are less valued because of their lack of church leadership experience. Over time, they might be viewed as not having the ability to serve in those assignments—in

---

9. See, for example, Juliet Bourke and Andrea Titus, "Why Inclusive Leaders Are Good for Organizations, and How to Become One," *Harvard Business Review*, March 29, 2019, hbr.org/2019/03/why-inclusive-leaders-are-good-for-organizations-and-how-to-become-one.

reality, the ability is there—but the person has never been given the chance to use their talents to build the kingdom in this way. Feelings like these remind me of Sister McConkie's words shared earlier: "The gospel of Jesus Christ does not marginalize people. People marginalize people. And we have to fix that."[10]

A few years ago, I realized I lacked the tools to unwire myself from measuring my self-worth from church leadership positions. I realized it was becoming a stumbling block to my emotional health and relationship with the Church. I turned to a trusted therapist to help me. I wanted my self-worth to be tied to things in my control (my relationship with Heavenly Parents, a strong relationship with my wife and family, commandment keeping, serving others) and not things outside of my control (church callings). But a lifetime of cultural programming made this difficult, and I needed tools acquired through therapy to move forward. This is still a work in progress. I am grateful to my dear wife, Sheila, and her positive role in this whole process and her lifelong unconditional love regardless of my church assignment.

I think the pain of this situation has given me greater empathy. Even though I am in the bullseye of Latter-day Saint privilege, I have felt pain that usually someone in my position would not face. That pain has built within me a greater ability to validate and sit with people in their own pain. While still far from perfect, I have become more sensitive to members who feel marginalized than I would have been without these painful experiences.

Sometimes I get the impression that this is all part of the plan as I try to "lift where I stand." Recently, a transgender Latter-day Saint asked me for a blessing. It was a sweet, Spirit-filled experience. Afterwards, the thought came to my mind, "Richard, you are just where I need you to be to speak the words that I needed one of my transgender children to hear." In reality, being what God wants us to be and doing what He asks us to do is the essence of building the kingdom and gathering Israel.

---

10. McConkie, "Lifting Others."

## All Are Needed in the Body of Christ

The church family is often referred to in the scriptures as the body of Christ. I love this metaphor because it accurately describes that ALL are needed in the kingdom, not just heads (leaders). Brother David Dickson wrote these insights in the *Ensign*:

> Have you ever tried picking up a pencil with your toes? Or walking on your hands? Neither activity is especially easy for the obvious reason that walking is for feet and pencil lifting is for fingers. But that's the wonder and beauty of our bodies. Each part serves a unique and critical function in our everyday life.
>
> The Apostle Paul understood this principle when he compared the early Church to the body of Christ. He taught, "For by one Spirit are we all baptized into one body" (1 Corinthians 12:13), meaning that when we join the Church we are added to and function like a critical part of a body. Each of us has unique talents, gifts, and abilities that make us crucial to the work. That's true whether we're from Boston or Buenos Aires; whether we're old, young, single, married, widowed, divorced, from a part-member family, childless, or have a house full of kids. Whoever you are, wherever you are, you're a valuable member of the body of Christ.
>
> And just as a person can't function as well without hands or eyes or feet, neither can the Church function as easily without you. Or as Paul put it, "The eye cannot say unto the hand, I have no need of thee: nor again the head to the feet, I have no need of you" (verse 21). Remember that you are an absolutely essential part of that body. Just as a body needs fingers and feet, the Church needs you. [11]

The kingdom would be pretty lopsided if everyone were a leader. Imagine a ward with nothing but bishops. Who will play the piano? Who will work the broadcast system? Who will teach people how to research their family history? Who will teach the children the

---

11. David Dickson, "Strengthening 'The Body of Christ,'" *Ensign*, September 2019, churchofjesuschrist.org/study/ensign/2019/09/strengthening-the-body-of-christ.

beloved Primary songs? Every bishop is good at something, but no bishop is good at everything.

All are needed—leaders, servers, gifted teachers, skilled family history researchers, accomplished technicians to handle our ever-increasing technology needs, loving nursery leaders who have the gift of making a little child feel welcome, shadow leaders with encouraging personalities that support youth to lead but are not direct leaders themselves, etc.

Gifts of the Spirit work like this too. Leadership is not the only valuable skill in the Church. Doctrine and Covenants 46 lists gifts of "administration" (verse 15) and "operations" (verse 16) that are needed in leadership callings. But the rest of that section lists other gifts that are equally valuable in advancing the Lord's work: wisdom, knowledge, faith to be healed and faith to heal, work miracles, prophesy, discern spirits, speak with and interpret tongues, etc. (verses 17–22). God reminds us, "For all have not every gift given unto them; for there are many gifts, and to every man is given a gift by the Spirit of God. To some is given one, and to some is given another, that all may be profited thereby" (verses 11–12).

Everyone has gifts and skills that are needed in the Church, and God gave them to us to magnify our own calling, not to covet another's calling. Each of us is important, wherever we are called to serve. And when we sing "I'll go where you want me to go, dear Lord,"[12] that includes doing whatever is needed at the moment, with our own particular combination of God-given gifts and talents. Just as a body needs more than a collection of heads, the body of Christ needs more than leaders. God needs *you*, right where you are, just as you are.

## Obtaining Personal Advice from Senior Church Leaders

I am uncomfortable with the cultural notion that personal advice or counsel is better if it comes from an increasingly more

12. *Hymns*, 270.

senior Church leader. This suggests that if only we could meet with a General Authority (or better yet, a member of the Twelve), we would get the right answer to our question. I have sometimes heard members one-up each other based on the calling of the person giving the advice, almost in a competitive way. This creates a culture in which people wonder if they could have gotten better advice for a critical life decision, if only they too had the chance to meet with a senior Church leader.

I believe the General Authorities do not want to contribute to the idea that the best advice comes from only them. I believe they want to cultivate the principle of personal revelation through prayer with our Heavenly Father, using foundational concepts outlined in scriptures, general conference talks, and other study materials. In short, I think they want to teach us correct principles and let us govern ourselves, inviting us to seek further specific guidance for our lives directly from our Heavenly Parents.

When I served as a local leader, I rarely told someone what to do. Instead, I pointed them to core doctrines and principles so they could get personal revelation for their situation. I realized that my advice, based on my limited understanding, might be different than what they would receive through personal revelation from their Heavenly Parents.

A senior leader of the Church would have great advice for each of us. They have a lifetime of experiences in their sacred mission. I am grateful for general conference where we can hear (and later, study and ponder) their words. But it is not the way our Heavenly Parents work, to give personal revelation through individual meetings with senior leaders. It's not realistic or scalable across the vast worldwide membership of the Church. When we hear about someone acting on personal advice from a senior leader of the Church, let's not perpetuate the idea that to receive the very best advice, we too need to follow that path. Instead, those stories should help us better realize the importance of personal revelation in our lives.

Further, I don't believe our leaders want us to feel they are the experts on every topic. President Ballard taught this principle at a November 2017 BYU devotional:

My calling and life experiences allow me to respond to certain types of questions. There are other types of questions that require an expert in a specific subject matter. This is exactly what I do when I need an answer to such questions: I seek help from others, including those with degrees and expertise in such fields.

I worry sometimes that members expect too much from Church leaders and teachers—expecting them to be experts in subjects well beyond their duties and responsibilities. The Lord called the apostles and prophets to invite others to come unto Christ—not to obtain advanced degrees in ancient history, biblical studies, and other fields that may be useful in answering all the questions we may have about scriptures, history, and the Church. Our primary duty is to build up the Church, teach the doctrine of Christ, and help those in need of help.

Fortunately the Lord provided this counsel for those asking questions: "Seek ye diligently and teach one another words of wisdom; yea, seek ye out of the best books words of wisdom; seek learning, even by study and also by faith" (D&C 88:118).

If you have a question that requires an expert, please take the time to find a thoughtful and qualified expert to help you. There are many . . . who have the degrees and expertise to respond and give some insight to most of these types of questions.[13]

If I had the opportunity to visit with one of our senior leaders for personal advice, I would jump at that chance! I would bring a few questions and write down every word or impression. However, I do not believe my mortal plan or eternal destiny is dependent on such a visit with a senior leader. Our Heavenly Parents have given us tools—personal revelation, scriptures, public words of our leaders—to make righteous decisions for our mortal journey and return to Them.

---

13. M. Russell Ballard, "Questions and Answers" (devotional address, Brigham Young University, Provo, Utah, November 14, 2017), speeches.byu.edu/talks/m-russell-ballard/questions-and-answers/.

## The Focus Is Our Heavenly Parents and the Savior

Our Church leaders are sometimes elevated to a level that I do not believe that even they feel is entirely appropriate. For example, I have been at church meetings when the presiding authority is introduced like this: "We are here for one reason: to sit at the feet of [presiding authority] and learn from him." Maybe I am hypersensitive, but these kinds of statements don't feel right to me—not because I do not support the presiding authority or want to hear his inspired counsel but rather because it elevates the leader above the real reason we are at church: to worship and partake of the sacrament. Instead of creating a way of "seeing" that places worth on being a future leader, our culture should point us to our Heavenly Parents and the Savior—with the words of our inspired leaders as a means to get there.

Further, I have felt the discomfort of comparison as some seek to elevate themselves based on how many senior leaders they know. They may share insights from a senior leader, not from a sincere desire to teach the gospel, but with a sense of competition, seeking to elevate their own status because of their access to and interactions with senior Church leaders. This feels like the pride of comparison that President Ezra Taft Benson asked us to avoid[14] when he shared the words of C. S. Lewis: "It is the comparison that makes you proud: the pleasure of being above the rest."[15] Our self-worth should not be tied to how many General Authorities we know, but rather from coming unto Christ and living His gospel.

## We Must Not Inhale

Elder Uchtdorf's efforts to improve the culture in the Church on this topic continued with his October 2010 general conference talk, "Pride and the Priesthood":

---

14. Ezra Taft Benson, "Beware of Pride," April 1989 general conference, churchofjesuschrist.org/study/general-conference/1989/04/beware-of-pride.

15. C. S. Lewis, *Mere Christianity,* (New York: Macmillan, 1952), 109–10.

When I was called as a General Authority, I was blessed to be tutored by many of the senior Brethren in the Church. One day I had the opportunity to drive President James E. Faust to a stake conference. During the hours we spent in the car, President Faust took the time to teach me some important principles about my assignment. He explained also how gracious the members of the Church are, especially to General Authorities. He said, "They will treat you very kindly. They will say nice things about you." He laughed a little and then said, "Dieter, be thankful for this. *But don't you ever inhale it.*"

That is a good lesson for us all, brethren, in any calling or life situation. We can be grateful for our health, wealth, possessions, or positions, but when we begin to inhale it—when we become obsessed with our status; when we focus on our own importance, power, or reputation; when we dwell upon our public image and believe our own press clippings—that's when the trouble begins; that's when pride begins to corrupt.

There are plenty of warnings about pride in the scriptures: "Only by pride cometh contention: but with the well advised is wisdom" (Proverbs 13:10).

The Apostle Peter warned that "God resisteth the proud, and giveth grace to the humble" (1 Peter 5:5). Mormon explained, "None is acceptable before God, save the meek and lowly in heart" (Moroni 7:44). And by design, the Lord chooses "the weak things of the world to confound the things which are mighty" (1 Corinthians 1:27). The Lord does this to show that His hand is in His work, lest we "trust in the arm of flesh" (D&C 1:19).

We are servants of our Lord and Savior, Jesus Christ. *We are not given certain callings so that we can take our bows and bask in praise.* We are here to roll up our sleeves and go to work. We are enlisted in no ordinary task. We are called to prepare the world for the coming of our Lord and Savior, Jesus Christ. We seek not our own honor but give praise and glory to God. We know that the contribution we can make by ourselves is small; nevertheless, as we exercise heavenly power in righteousness, God can cause a great and marvelous work to come forth through our efforts. We must learn, as Moses did, that "man is nothing" (Moses 1:10) by himself but that "with God all things are possible" (Matthew 19:26).[16]

In his April 2017 talk, Elder Uchtdorf reminded us:

> In the eyes of God, there is no calling in the kingdom that is more important than another. Our service—whether great or small—refines our spirits, opens the windows of heaven, and releases God's blessings not only upon those we serve but upon us as well. When we reach out to others, we can know with humble confidence that God acknowledges our service with approval and approbation. He smiles upon us as we offer these heartfelt acts of compassion, especially acts that are unseen and unnoticed by others.[17]

President Ballard taught:

> I tell every General Authority when they are set apart, I try to get to them one way or another, either collectively or individually, and remind them that adulation is a very dangerous thing. You must not let people, or you must not think that, because you are a General Authority, you are above them. Keep yourself humble, and keep yourself teachable and reachable. That's what Jesus would do, and that's what we have to strive to try to do. And I think, to be honest with you, the General Authorities of the Church do a very good job of it. They understand that principle, I believe.[18]

---

16. Dieter F. Uchtdorf, "Pride and The Priesthood," October 2010 general conference, churchofjesuschrist.org/study/general-conference/2010/10/pride-and-the-priesthood; emphasis added.

17. Dieter F. Uchtdorf, "The Greatest Among You," April 2017 general conference, churchofjesuschrist.org/study/general-conference/2017/04/the-greatest-among-you.

18. Sarah Jane Weaver, "Sarah Jane Weaver interviews President Ballard about his 35 years as an Apostle," *Church News*, The Church of Jesus Christ of Latter-day Saints, October 20, 2020, thechurchnews.com/podcast/2020-10-20/episode-1-president-ballard-sarah-jane-weaver-35-years-apostle-testimony-195867?utm_source=twitter&utm_medium=churchnews.

## Shiblon in the Shadow

It is not only our modern leaders who seek to serve without elevating themselves. We find similar people in the scriptures. I was deeply touched by Elder Michael T. Ringwood's general conference talk, "Truly Good and without Guile." I still remember where I was during this talk and discussing it afterward with my wife and brother. I loved how Elder Ringwood gave us more insights into Shiblon, Alma's middle son, and his much-needed work—sometimes in the shadow of his brother Helaman. Elder Ringwood taught:

> It appears that Shiblon was a son who wanted to please his father and went about doing what was right for right's sake rather than for praise, position, power, accolades, or authority. . . . In a world where praise, position, power, accolades, and authority are sought on every side, I honor those wonderful and blessed souls who are truly good and without guile, those who are motivated by a love of God and their neighbors, those great women and men who are "more anxious to serve than to have dominion."
>
> Today there are some who would have us believe our search for relevance can be satisfied only by obtaining position and power. Yet, thankfully, there are many who are uninfluenced by this perspective. They find relevance in seeking to be truly good and without guile. I have found them in all walks of life and in many faith traditions. And I find them in large numbers among the truly converted followers of Christ. . . .
>
> I thank my Heavenly Father for Shiblon-like souls whose examples offer me—and all of us—hope. In their lives, we see a witness of a loving Father in Heaven and a caring and compassionate Savior. I add my testimony to theirs with a pledge to strive to be more like them.[19]

This is the kind of culture of humility we want to create, as we simply and quietly try to "go about doing good" (Acts 10:38).

---

19. Michael T. Ringwood, "Truly Good and Without Guile," April 2015 general conference, churchofjesuschrist.org/study/general-conference/2015/04/truly-good-and-without-guile.

## The Jonathan Principle

One of my institute teachers, S. Michael Wilcox,[20] taught that one of the best scriptural accounts of someone who was "qualified but not called" was Jonathan in the Old Testament. The prophet Samuel had to decide between Jonathan and David to replace Saul as the next king (see 1 Samuel 16). Both men were wonderful candidates.

Jonathan, Saul's son and a great leader, was the logical choice to take his father's place as king. But after David was called instead, Jonathan stood by him when Saul (his own father) wanted David killed. Over and over, Jonathan supported David. There is no record of jealousy, although Jonathan might have felt that he was rightly entitled to the throne. This is one of the best examples in the scriptures of Paul's declaration that "charity seeketh not her own" (1 Corinthians 13:5). Brother Wilcox explained:

> [Jonathan's] humility and selflessness are unprecedented. I know there are many Jonathans among us who, figuratively speaking, will never be king, but who display some of the deepest qualities of a godly character. I do not know why God chose David instead of Jonathan, but I am certain it was not because David was a better man, or because God approved of David above Jonathan, or because David had progressed to a higher level than had Jonathan. God does not measure or equate approval or progress by position. Nor must we! I wish we could get rid of that whole idea in our thinking. We are in danger of creating in people the feeling that callings in the Church, or positions, are equal to approval and progress.[21]

There are so many Jonathans among us in our congregations, fully qualified for any leadership calling and always lifting where

---

20. I am grateful to my dear wife, Sheila, for introducing me to Brother Wilcox.

21. S. Michael Wilcox, *Seeing as God Sees: Discovering the Wonder of Ourselves and Others* (Salt Lake City: Deseret Book, 2009). Section E: "Approval and Progress" (audio book section title). See also "The Jonathan Factor" (e-book section title).

they stand. Many are serving in meaningful ways in our community or quietly behind the scenes in our Church—serving as Jesus served. But that service may not be part of an official Church calling and may not show up on their LDS Tools profile—but it is honoring their covenants to mourn, bear, and comfort (see Mosiah 18:8–9). Let's work harder to hear their voices, see and value their service, pray for them, and help our youth want to become the Jonathans of tomorrow. Let's promote each other's intrinsic value rather than position or status, so our young people measure progress in life by developing Christlike attributes, building a strong relationship with the Savior, and honoring their covenants. Yes, many will be called as leaders—that is needed and wonderful. But we can improve our ward and stake cultures when we focus on our own and each other's Christlike attributes and less on leadership callings.

A Jonathan in my life is my friend Hal McEwan—a personal hero to me. Hal was my father's missionary companion in England (what a great companionship). Hal and I served together as Salt Lake Temple workers for several years. I wrote a shout-out to him on Facebook in March 2019:

> Hal, age 88, is the oldest man on our Friday morning shift at the Salt Lake Temple (he also serves on Thursday mornings). Here are some of the things I love about Hal:
>
> Hal started working at the temple about 35 years ago under President Victor Brown (the 15th temple president). Hal has served under 13 subsequent temple presidents.
>
> Hal has never told me his resume of church callings. As far as I know, his only callings have been ministering brother and temple worker. He never became a temple sealer. When we talk, he tells me about his love of the Savior and how much he loves serving in the temple. He defines himself by his relationship with our Savior and humbly serving others.
>
> With adjustments to the dialog of the temple in January 2019, I wondered how Hal would adapt to memorizing these changes at age 88, after thirty-plus years with the old dialog (it was hard enough for me at age 58). The other day our shift coordinator Malen Earl mentioned that Hal was one of the first to

"pass off" the new dialog. This past Friday, I saw first-hand Hal do the dialog perfectly. Respect.

The other day I saw Hal carrying several tuxedos to the men's dressing room and then working in the laundry. Like Christ, nothing is below Hal's service.

Hal is real. The other day when we got back to the study room in the temple, Hal and I shared a smile regarding me mixing up some of my words.

Hal is a great teacher. Because I know Hal loves me, he took me aside in a private moment and pointed out a few mistakes in my presentation. I was so grateful to Hal for his kind and welcome suggestions.

So this shout-out is to Hal McEwan. A true behind-the-scenes "lift where you stand" disciple of Christ. Thank you for your example of humility and service.[22]

## Balancing Parents and Leaders in Home-centered, Church-supported Gospel Learning

In the October 2018 general conference, President Nelson and Elder Quentin L. Cook outlined principles of a more home-centered church. This is now known as the "home-centered, Church-supported" approach to gospel learning—an emphasis my wife and I fully support and are grateful for. Indeed, with the COVID-19 global pandemic, this proved prophetic as almost the entirety of gospel learning shifted to within the walls of our homes, using the *Come, Follow Me* scripture curriculum.

I am immensely grateful for so many local and general Church leaders who have served and helped our children. When we started our family, my wife and I prayed that we would live in a neighborhood with good leaders and examples to lift and support our family. Those prayers were answered with many incredible men and women

---

22. Richard Ostler, "Meet my friend Hal McEwan," Facebook, March 17, 2019, facebook.com/richard.ostler.5/posts/10216641776909998.

who have blessed the lives of our children. We are eternally indebted to them.

However, as a Latter-day Saint father, sometimes I feel an imbalance that seems inconsistent with our new emphasis on a "home-centered, Church-supported" focus. I have noticed that my children have sometimes been culturally programmed to seek gospel learning, doctrinal insight, and temple and missionary preparation from Church leaders rather than their parents. This struck a nerve when one of our wonderful sons was preparing for his mission. He participated in a temple preparation class taught by a former temple president and a mission preparation class taught by two former mission presidents. He also had excellent stake and ward priesthood leaders. What a wonderful blessing for our son to have their insights in this important preparation time. It was an answer to prayer that he had these good men and their experiences to help him. Those men were acknowledged with appreciation at his mission setting apart.

But my own role as his father seemed diminished, even though I had served a mission and was a current temple worker. I had some uncomfortable feelings that these men had somehow replaced my responsibility to teach and prepare my son for his mission. I felt that our culture had conditioned my son to look to our leaders for this needed preparation, elevating their role over parents. I noticed patterns that can create a "Church leader-focused, parent-diminished" culture. In my darkest moment, I felt that the only unique role I provided was financial support; everything else was covered by Church leaders and teachers. Other men and women may not feel this way, but my feelings were strong and painful.

I recognize there are things that require priesthood keys held by our leaders, such as worthiness interviews and the wonderful setting-apart blessings our stake presidents have given to our departing missionaries. I am not implying that fathers take over these responsibilities. I am suggesting a greater sensitivity in leading our children to look to their parents first for gospel learning and spiritual preparation for missions and the temple.

In the words of Elder Tad R. Callister:

As parents, we are to be the prime gospel teachers and examples for our children—not the bishop, the Sunday School, the Young Women or Young Men, but the parents. As their prime gospel teachers, we can teach them the power and reality of the Atonement—of their identity and divine destiny—and in so doing give them a rock foundation upon which to build. When all is said and done, the home is the ideal forum for teaching the gospel of Jesus Christ.[23]

## Personal Stories about Improving Culture around Leadership

### TAYLOR ROSECRANS

In many areas of the Church, there are more faithful, capable adults than there are leadership/teaching callings. When we do not have a large responsibility at church, we can feel under-utilized and resentful. Many of us are used to insular thinking, where the service we give is primarily in the Church.

But the whole world is full of God's children! There are many community organizations that need capable and compassionate leaders and volunteers, where we can also do God's work. Christ needs hearts and hands in so many places outside a church building. Instead of telling youth they can be future leaders in the Church, tell them they can be future leaders and disciples in their homes and communities! Tell them about the meaningful work done to serve God's children in food pantries, shelters, tutoring, caregiving, and refugee services. A church calling is just one way to lead and serve.

### GERTRUDE LYNDWALK

While attending a youth function, one of the speakers asked for all bishops and their wives to stand. He said to the youth attending that these individuals were the people they wanted to aspire to be like.

In the audience was a dedicated Young Women leader whose husband was inactive and most likely will never become a

---

23. Tad R. Callister, "Parents: The Prime Gospel Teachers of Their Children," October 2014 general conference, churchofjesuschrist.org/study/general-conference/2014/10/parents-the-prime-gospel-teachers-of-their-children.

stake president or bishop, AND she may never become the wife of one. I observed that the youth in the audience, due to the commentary of this well-meaning individual, may never come to see her as a version of themselves: someone aspiring to become more like the Savior, full of testimony and truth, committed to serve as He would have them do. Side by side, this sister and those leaders have the same goals and motivation. They just have different duties.

Statistically speaking, most youth in the meeting will never become bishops or stake presidents or a wife of one. But the Lord always has a place for them, whatever their formal calling or service may be.

## PORTER MCKAY

My patriarchal blessing explicitly states, "You will be called on to be a leader on your mission" and that after my mission, "you will be called to be a leader from a young age and the burden of leadership would not be lifted from you for the balance of your life." This set me up for massive disappointment on my mission. As I approached the halfway point of my mission, I kept wondering when I would be called as a leader. Most of the other missionaries from my MTC[24] group were already leaders. After I was finally placed as the senior companion, I was "demoted" after only one transfer to be a junior companion again to a missionary who was struggling. I was completely devastated. My spirit was crushed. I stayed as a junior companion to various missionaries until the last transfer of my mission, when I was finally brought back up to senior companion and placed as a district leader.

I vented to my dad in an email, feeling like a complete and utter failure having only been a district leader for one transfer. My dad shared that I had been a leader despite not having the title. He told me that he and my mom had been in contact with the parents of one of my companions. This elder had severe anxiety and depression. I remember his stack of medications and our weekly trips to a therapist. Apparently, his emails home were consistently one or two sentences and very negative. Our time together completely changed his mission. I don't say this about how great I am. I tell this story because I know I could have done better if I wasn't so upset about not being senior companion at the time. My time with this elder was the best

---

24. MTC: Missionary Training Center.

part of my mission. I'm sad I was so prideful and obsessed with a title that I couldn't see the Christlike opportunity in front of my face. Even with all of that, after returning home there was still a feeling of failure when some talked about their leadership on their mission.

## GINGER MCKNIGHT PRICE

Sadly, this too carries over into a wife measuring her husband's level of "priesthood righteousness" by his callings. I carried resentment for years toward my husband because he didn't seem to be "bishop material."

## KRISTIN LAMBERT ASHTON

From a slightly different perspective, I think it's wonderful when a ward takes the orientation of "all hands on deck" and doesn't assume you need to have the gospel perfectly down in order to serve. I have a wonderful friend living in NYC who was a Young Women president and asked for a newer member to be one of her counselors. When the bishop extended the call, the new member said she was struggling with the Word of Wisdom. The bishop asked what she would teach the Young Women and then said, "Sister, the Lord needs your service and wants you as you are. Will you accept this calling?" We need every member. When Christ called his Apostles, it doesn't seem to have been based on their ability to look like they were keeping the commandments, but on their willingness to follow Him.

## GEORGIA BETH SMITH THOMPSON

As The Church of Jesus Christ of Latter-day Saints has grown in membership, more rules or regulations become part of the institution to help assure uniformity and orderliness. One of the challenges with structural growth is not to make the framework into the measurement tool of the worth of individuals in the sight of God. This structure can allow us to rely too much on callings or tangible commitments as we interact with individuals.

We are a bit suspect of men who did not serve missions. We wonder about a couple who has not been sealed in the temple. Senior-aged LDS men cannot serve missions without a wife; certain temple callings are not issued to single people. It seems difficult sometimes to separate our real Christlike behavior from the tangibles, such as callings, levels of priesthood ordination, or a temple marriage. Sometimes we casually ask a member, "What are you doing in your ward now?" If they think their calling is not of "great value," they may reply, "Oh, I'm just in the nursery." We hear stories from the pulpit about members who geographically cannot attend a temple regularly, but they have a current recommend.

These levels of behavior are designed to assist us in our worthiness and are important factors. So how do we learn not to rely on them to measure a person's value? How do we learn to make "he/she is a child of God" the most important measure we use and not revert to an institutionalized checklist?

## SHANNON ROBERTSON SPICER

I have reflected on my own tendency to place importance on church callings as if that speaks to a person's righteousness. I believe it's our worldly culture that evokes this from us, not our divine gospel. When applying for jobs or college, it is expected that we include these leadership callings to give us an edge on other applicants. But using these perceived "important" callings to mark our status and compare ourselves to others within the Church needs to stop. And I say that with humility because I am absolutely guilty of this!

But now as a mama dragon of a beautiful gay 20-year-old son, who is faithful and compassionate and Christlike in every way that matters, yet incredibly socially anxious, I know his personal contributions to building the kingdom and bringing others to Christ will NOT be through leadership callings or a full-time mission. It will be through personal connections and the radiance of that inner light that makes him so special. I hate that he might be perceived as or made to feel less important in the work of gathering Israel.

## MATT ROBERTSON

I got used to hearing the question, "What were you on your mission?" Meaning, "What leadership callings did you hold?" I remember the day it dawned on me that the only appropriate response to the question would be if I could honestly say, "I tried really hard to be a disciple of Christ, and I'm still trying now."

## STEVE BLUTH

I once drew a cardboard sign that said, "Buzzards' Nest" for guys like me (Life Scout, three merit badges short of an Eagle) who were about to attend an Eagle Court of Honor and be shamed yet again by those sitting in the Eagles' Nest. I chickened out and left it home. No guts, no glory.

## EVAN SMITH

It's not uncommon for us to say "Congratulations" to someone who is sustained to a new calling. While that may mostly just be an innocuous way of showing support, it is also technically a way of acknowledging an achievement, at least according to the dictionary. But Church teachings discourage us from thinking of callings as accomplishments. Instead, we are taught to avoid aspiring to any calling and to simply serve as best we can in whatever responsibilities we are given. We are also encouraged to not bemoan Church service. Rather, we are encouraged to rejoice in our ability to serve.

When I was called as a counselor in our stake presidency, one brother in my stake said "Congratu-dolences" to me when he shook my hand after stake conference. We joked that such a phrase represents a combination of two sentiments, neither of which we should probably encourage: praise for an achievement on the one hand, and sorrow for an added burden on the other. In lieu of expressing either one of those notions after someone has received a new calling, perhaps more appropriate words might simply focus on gratitude or expressing support. For example, we could say something like, "Thanks in advance for your service" or "Let me know how I can help." While I don't think this issue is a big problem in the Church by any means, I believe that being careful about what we say may help reduce the tendency to view a calling as either an accomplishment or an unwanted responsibility, especially for callings of perceived prominence, like bishop, Relief Society President, or other leadership callings.

## ABE PALMER

I applaud your courage in addressing this issue. It's not just a culture issue within the Church in the Utah/Idaho areas. I have witnessed it in many parts of the US and world, and that is sad. I believe this culture stemmed from long ago. As a kid living in Hyrum, Utah, it was the same back then. I have stories but they are too heartbreaking for me to share.

## TRINA CAUDLE

It's not a Utah/Idaho problem. I've never lived in either. I've lived all over the US and it's a thing everywhere I've been. There's just an undercurrent—even though no one would ever, ever say it—that these callings are important and those callings are not.

## WALT WOOD

My wife and I dated during my senior year of high school and while I was attending college before I left on my mission. Her family became very important to me, including her father, who was in the stake presidency. He was a wonderful and kind man whom I deeply respected.

As I prepared for my mission, he would often say, "Oh, I am positive that you will be an AP when you serve." At first it was very flattering to me, but when I arrived in the mission field, it was just one more added pressure to learning a language, adjusting to a new culture, memorizing the discussions, and dealing with homesickness.

I desperately wanted to please him, because I felt it would positively impact his daughter's opinion of me as well. As I look back on it now, I realize how detrimental to my service this added burden was.

## TED BUCKWALTER

Where did we get the notion that a man with a good job will be a good Church leader? At age thirty-four, I was still building a career and contemplating my next moves, so it was somewhat easy to accept that I would not be in our new bishopric in a small ward on the East Coast, even though at the time I was the elders quorum president. A year later in a different state, I wondered if accepting a holiday welfare food box from the bishop would disqualify me from future leadership.

At age thirty-eight, I had to check my cynicism when it seemed like our new bishop was chosen from a short list of high priests who were former associates of the stake president.

At age forty-five, seeing another new bishopric and thinking about all my prior callings and my failure to break into the upper ranks, I also wondered what had previously been said in ward council about my "wild" children.

I'm almost fifty now and have honored the free agency of my children and supported them through their darkest times. Down the road, at my funeral, I just want them to say that my love for them was unwavering.

I love this quote from Elder Christensen: "There is a calling far higher than that of stake president, bishop, or Relief Society president. It is to be a doer of good, a disciple of Christ, an interme-diary through whom God answers others' prayers."[25]

I just want to be the essential worker helping the fallen wounded. I want to follow the lines from my favorite missionary song: "I'll go where you want me to go, I'll say what you want me to say, I'll be what you want me to be."[26]

---

25. Christensen, "My Ways Are Not Your Ways."
26. *Hymns*, 270.

# CHAPTER 3

# WOMEN IN THE CHURCH

By Cynthia Winward and Susan Hinckley

Women are more than half of Church membership, so it may be hard to understand how it is possible that many women struggle to feel valued or included. The best way to illuminate solutions may be to first highlight some of the problems, because we cannot fix what we don't see. In a culture where accepted roles are well-defined and supported by most members, it is sometimes difficult to see things for which we are not in the habit of looking. Problems become less visible when we are accustomed to them.

In 2020, we started a podcast[1] with the intention of sharing our personal Church experiences as lifelong members. We hoped we might create new space to discuss some of the challenges we and other women have found in the Church. Through this project, we've interacted with hundreds of members and found that many more women share similar experiences and concerns than we imagined. It appears that women are not used to speaking up in the Church. This reluctance may make it difficult for all of us to acknowledge, understand, or resolve persistent challenges. In

---

1. See atlastshesaidit.org. The *At Last She Said It* podcast is available on all major platforms.

this chapter, we'll each contribute some of our personal experiences and insights from other women. First Cynthia will address some of the issues women face generally, then Susan will focus on how we might more successfully retain our young women as they transition to adulthood.

## Despite Being the Majority, Women Frequently Have No Voice at the Church's Decision-making Tables

**Cynthia:** Several years ago, my husband held a stake calling while our stake was being reorganized. The General Authority tasked with calling the new stake president asked the current stake leaders and bishops to submit the names of five men they thought would make a good stake president. My husband submitted his five names, as did approximately twenty-five other male leaders. I asked my husband if the stake Relief Society president was asked to submit names. No. What about the Young Women or Primary leaders? Were any women asked to submit names? He said no.

Despite there being more women than men in the Church, no women were asked. If male priesthood leaders are leaders to women as well as men, why were no women asked to contribute names? It is possible that women may have specific qualities they would like to see in a leader, and bypassing the women was a missed opportunity to include their voices. Would the input of women matter when bishops are chosen? How about when our own leaders, like Relief Society presidents, are chosen? We have heard from our podcast listeners that some women are specifically asked for input on callings for women, but not always. For example, sometimes an outgoing Relief Society president is asked by a bishop who her replacement should be.

As a woman who has been a president of an organization, I was not asked, but I did offer my advice to my bishop as I was being released about a potentially great leader to take my place. This bishop took my advice. The same thing happened in another presidency in which I served as a counselor. In both cases, these men humbly took our advice. How often this happens, we cannot say. Some male leaders go out of their way to solicit the opinions of women, at least when it comes to women leading women. In our experience, these are rare instances and not prescribed officially in the handbook, nor is there any cultural expectation that it should happen.

The same tendency to bypass the voices of women also exists when ward boundaries are realigned. Women may have specific input about neighborhood dynamics and school boundaries, yet women are not part of that process either. The handbook only states that a stake president "may propose creating a new ward or branch in the stake."[2] Women are not prohibited from this process, opening a possible opportunity for stake presidents to involve women. (Side note: when considering the creation of a new ward, the handbook stipulates a ward must have twenty active, full-tithe-paying Melchizedek priesthood holders.[3] However, there is no requirement as to how many women are needed to create a ward.)

The input of women could substantially affect outcomes at the ward level. Several years ago, I served in the Primary presidency of a very large ward, with nearly two hundred children. Our weekly presidency meetings included trying to come up with possible people for the approximately seventy-two Primary callings we needed to staff. Week after week, we submitted names, and a week or two later, we were told why most of those individuals would be denied.

Having studied business management at BYU, I remembered a business operations class where we were tasked to find the bottleneck in a particular process. A bottleneck is basically where production slows down, backing up the process, thus making the entire operation inefficient. This bottleneck was easy to see as a Primary presidency. With a two-week lag in finding out if submitted names were approved or denied, it was clear what could solve the problem: have the Primary president attend bishopric meetings when callings

---

2. Section 36.2, *General Handbook: Serving in The Church of Jesus Christ of Latter-day Saints*, (Salt Lake City: The Church of Jesus Christ of Latter-day Saints, 2020), churchofjesuschrist.org/study/manual/general-handbook/36-creating-changing-and-naming-new-units.

3. Ibid.

were discussed. I made an appointment with a priesthood leader, explained where we saw that the bottleneck could be eliminated, and proposed a possible solution, asking if the Primary president could be allowed to attend bishopric meetings during at least the portion when callings are discussed. I was immediately told she could not attend for confidentiality reasons. I thought the same confidentiality assumed by the ward clerks, secretaries, and bishopric counselors could also apply to the Primary president, but he disagreed.

We finished serving in that presidency, never having a good solution to the problem. We were exhausted trying to staff our large Primary and felt powerless to solve the problem. Several of us voiced concerns that never again would we serve in a Primary presidency unless certain guidelines could be agreed upon with priesthood leaders. Again, there may be exceptions where some bishops invite female presidents to bishopric meetings, but without a policy, a bishop has full discretion.

When women are not even allowed behind closed doors where decisions are made, whether that be assigning callings or realigning ward boundaries, we are effectively eliminating the majority of the Church population in small and large decisions—decisions that affect men and women alike.

## We Don't Hear Women's Voices as Often as Men's

In the center spread of the conference issue of the *Ensign* in November 2020, male leaders outnumbered women leaders at the general church level by 119 to 9. That means that general conference talks throughout history are lopsidedly given by males. Current general conference speakers (overwhelmingly men) frequently quote speakers from previous general conferences (also overwhelmingly men). Men quoting men perpetuates the imbalance.

Women's insights often add a valuable dimension from their unique experience and perspective. Our entire church is enriched when we hear ALL the voices.

The April 2021 general conference consisted of twenty-seven talks by men but only two talks by women. In the previous conference, October 2020, again, only two women spoke to the general membership out of twenty-six talks. During the women's session in October, three women and three men spoke.

It often takes years to get to know the personality of the apostles and to gain a sense of their style through general conference talks, but once that happens, I find I am drawn to certain speakers when I better understand who they are. This is difficult with our female leaders, who do not serve for life but for just a few years. Before we get more than a hint of their personality and speaking style, they're already released.

When the Church held separate general Young Women meetings and Relief Society meetings, there were more opportunities for women to address women. Julie B. Beck, former Relief Society General President and counselor in the Young Women General Presidency, delivered fifteen general conference talks in her nine years of service between 2003–2012 (an average of 1.7 talks per year). Contrast this with Jean B. Bingham, who served as a counselor in the Primary general presidency before becoming Relief Society General President. She has only delivered four general conference talks in her first five years of service between April 2016 and April 2021 (an average of 0.8 talks per year, less than half of Sister Beck's airtime).

We understand the efforts of the First Presidency and Apostles to simplify the meetings surrounding general conference. As of July 2021, the Saturday evening session was no longer to be targeted to a specific audience but would instead become a general session.[4] We are hopeful that this change will bring more female speakers to the Conference Center pulpit, but there is a long way to go to overcome such an extreme disparity.

---

4. "The First Presidency Continues the Saturday Evening Session of General Conference," *Newsroom*, The Church of Jesus Christ of Latter-day Saints, July 27, 2021, newsroom.churchofjesuschrist.org/article/general-conference-saturday-evening-session-update.

## Women's Roles (as Defined at Church) Can Feel Reductive—Motherhood Is Valued Over Any Individual Accomplishment

A common argument often heard in the Church about the different roles of men and women is that men have priesthood responsibilities, and women have motherhood responsibilities. Women are primarily responsible for managing the home, and men are primarily responsible for managing the Church.

There are several problems with the rhetoric surrounding this division of labor. Mainly, we are comparing work in the Church organization to work in the home. Home responsibilities should be our first priority for women *and* men, yet so often our wards and stakes demand more time from men while relegating women to a home where they may not necessarily be needed. A woman's marital status can vary from single, divorced, married, or widowed. A woman's parenting status changes over time. Motherhood adjusts with toddlers, teenagers, and grandmothering. Yet the one-size-fits-all policy surrounding women's church service assumes first and foremost that a woman is a busy mother with a house full of small children. Why else would women not be allowed to serve as membership clerks, financial clerks, executive secretaries, and so on? We often say women can't serve in those callings because those are priesthood responsibilities, but that may be more tradition than anything else. We have seen that things can and sometimes do move from the "priesthood responsibility" category to the "regular callings" category. A recent example of this is that women can now be called as stake auditors.

We have often seen a woman released from a busy calling when her husband later receives a busy calling. Many years ago, my ward bishopric was reorganized. All the men called to the bishopric had wives serving in the Young Women presidency. These women were doing a fine job and had been serving just nine months when they subsequently were all released due to their husbands' new bishopric callings. Have we ever seen the reverse: an entire bishopric released so their wives can serve in a Young Women presidency? These experiences send the message that men's callings are more important, more valued, and more needed in the Church.

A young boy has priesthood responsibilities from the age of eleven until the end of his life. Assuming a long life, a man has priesthood responsibilities in the Church for approximately seventy years. Contrast that with a woman who has full-time mothering responsibility for a shorter portion of her adult life, twenty to thirty years maybe, while many women never have the responsibility of parenthood at all. Most girls and women, whether they become mothers or not, have decades when greater leadership opportunities within the Church could be a reality. Yet there is no equivalent responsibility for an eleven-year-old girl to that of an eleven-year-old boy when he is ordained a deacon. At a very young age, a girl sees the disparity between her lack of official responsibility and that of the boys in her class.

It is difficult as women to explain to girls and young women why this disparity even exists. What does a mother say to her four-year-old daughter when she asks when will she be able to pass the sacrament? It's tough, and tiring, to admit to a daughter that she never will help pass the sacrament, nor is there any comparable duty for her at age eleven, or any of the other priesthood milestones that exist for young men.

When I was a young woman about to graduate from high school in 1992, I attended a career night for a Young Women activity. Several women in the ward were asked to present information about their different professions. Our leaders made sure the final career presented to us was that of being a mother. It was really emphasized to us that this was the best career choice. I was perplexed: could a woman not have a career *and* be a mother? Did I have to make a choice? Did the Young Men activity down the hall have the same presentation, with fatherhood being the final career presented to the boys? I know my leaders were doing their best to present accurate information to us about marketable skills, but these are the confusing messages we send to our young women.

Yes, young women *can* be anything, but whenever possible, Latter-day Saint young women are told that they should choose only motherhood. Perhaps because I grew up in the wake of President Benson's 1987 fireside talk published as a pamphlet, *To The Mothers in Zion*,[5] I was still very much taught in that activity in 1992, and in countless other meetings for years to come, that full-time motherhood was the correct choice, the unselfish choice.

A few months after that activity, I left to attend BYU. The message I received, loud and clear, was that my education was to help my future children and in the tragic event something happened to my husband, *then* I could work outside the home. Thankfully, that explicit message (full-time motherhood is the only righteous option for married women) is waning, partly because times have changed but also because we are now a global church. Telling many mothers around the world to avoid working outside the home may be asking her to put her children in danger of starvation.

As times are changing, so are our messages to the next generation of Latter-day Saint women. Girls still absorb the messaging that full-time motherhood is the best choice, but a wise Young Women leader offered her class this advice: make choices that will increase your options instead of decreasing them. The girls pushed back and said they wanted to be full-time mothers, to which she asked, "But can you guarantee that?" Many women understand that what a young girl professes to want often will change with age and maturity, as will her life circumstances. So teaching a girl to make the best decisions for *her* life, as an individual, is preferable to assuming her main job will be that of wife and full-time mother, roles she cannot fully control.

Recently in a Relief Society meeting, a new ward member, a woman in her fifties, was asked to introduce herself. She mentioned that she is a college student and made sure to say, "Nobody tells you that when you're done raising your children, you'll often have decades of life ahead of you." I was proud of this woman, for

---

5.  Ezra T. Benson, "To the Mothers in Zion" (fireside address, Salt Lake City, February 22, 1987), churchofjesuschrist.org/study/manual/eternal-marriage-student-manual/womens-divine-roles-and-responsibilities/to-the-mothers-in-zion.

not only making her dreams of working toward a fulfilling career happen, but for being honest and vulnerable with her Relief Society class, letting them know it's hard to begin your education and career in your forties and fifties. Women need to be given greater latitude in preparing for complex lives that invariably lay ahead.

In addition, there is a lack of full visibility or acceptance for women living outside the idealized role (single women, LGBTQ women, or women without children). These and other women are leading fulfilling lives without fitting neatly within the "ideal" lines presented in so much of our messaging at church. They may struggle to feel represented, seen, or valued in talks and lessons. Holding up ideals that more fully reflect the diversity of women's lives and circumstances could help us all understand that as individual sisters, we are an important part of the whole.

## In Some Ways, Women Are Complicit in Our Own Marginalization

I attended BYU Education Week many years ago with a friend. As we planned the classes we would attend, she made it clear she preferred to see men speak and avoid female speakers. I was shocked to hear a woman say this. I have also heard men and women joke about the female speakers in general conferences, saying that's when they get up to get a snack, or worse, the women speak in "Primary voice," making it easy to dismiss them all together.

In a church where we do not see women lead nearly as much as men, are we conditioned to prefer men as better teachers and leaders on gospel and doctrinal subjects? As Latter-day Saints, our entire lives are spent seeing men conduct our Sunday sacrament meetings, issue the callings, bless the babies, confirm the children, and bless and pass the sacrament. And this is just a list for one meeting! Are men and women less likely to see women as leaders because in our church women only have stewardship over women and children, whereas men can have stewardship in their callings over all?

Because men, and not women, preside in church meetings, it is not surprising to see women defer to men in any mixed-gender meeting. For example, female leaders often ask a bishopric member to give closing comments for a Young Women Evening in Excellence or a Relief Society birthday party dinner. A stake president is often the keynote speaker on the final night of Young Women camp or seminary graduation. Sometimes a priesthood leader insists that he speak, but very often women prefer to hear from a man to "close" a meeting, rather than another woman in that specific organization. This is a problem in society at large, but surely in a church bearing the name of Jesus Christ we can do better. It may have been the norm in Jesus's time to marginalize women, but the Master Himself shows us time and time again how He elevated women. We can do better.

A few years ago, my stake had the wonderful opportunity to have Sister Sharon Eubank of the Relief Society general presidency attend our stake women's conference. As the meeting was opened, the conducting female stake leader made sure to mention that our stake president, sitting on the stand, presided at the meeting. It was difficult to realize that if Sister Eubank had been male, she would have been the presiding authority.

Is there no meeting in the Church where a woman, even a general officer of the Church, can preside if a male leader is present? Did the stake Relief Society presidency member conducting choose to defer to the male as the presiding leader because we are conditioned to have men preside? Was he invited by the women to sit on the stand and preside? Or was she explicitly told to recognize the man as the one presiding? Regardless, women notice these inequities. It is difficult to understand how women are equal to men in the Church when men always preside, even in a women's meeting.

In March 2021, a layer of female leaders was added to help amplify women's voices outside the US and Canada. These area organization advisers will be mentors and guides to the Relief Society, Young Women, and Primary organizations. When this change was announced, several general leaders expressed their opinions. Former Relief Society general president Linda K. Burton said of this change, "It is the link that has been missing," while Young

Women general president Bonnie H. Cordon said, "It truly feels like the missing piece of the puzzle."[6]

These women recognized that something was lacking, but the everyday women of this church also recognize we have missing puzzle pieces. Expressing what is missing can have real consequences for women. It is difficult for women to notice perceived inequities and be given no means to express problems and challenges. Men and women are told not to write letters to General Authorities, but instead to counsel with their local leaders.

The problem with this is multi-layered. First, a woman expressing concern can often be viewed as less faithful and a complainer who does not "support the brethren." If her bishop or stake president sees her as such, they may also assume she is less committed, which can affect the callings in which she is allowed to serve. Second, her local leaders cannot make policy or handbook changes either. In a hierarchical church, that leaves very little room for a woman to express her concerns and hope for change. Yet President Nelson has repeatedly said that the Church needs "women who can speak out."[7] Third, only men have the ability to make structural or policy changes in the Church. That means a woman's role in any change is dependent upon her ability to convince a man that a concern, problem, or need for change even exists.

## Unfortunately, Many of Today's Young Women Will Not Be Part of the Next Generation of Adult Latter-day Saint Women

**Susan:** Some are separating themselves from the Church intentionally, some are merely slipping away, but the result is the same:

6.  Sydney Walker, "Area organization advisers: Women leaders in international areas to provide instruction, mentoring," *Church News,* The Church of Jesus Christ of Latter-day Saints, March 17, 2021, thechurchnews.com/leaders-and-ministry/2021-03-17/area-organization-advisers-relief-society-young-women-primary-local-instruction-207196.

7.  Russell M. Nelson, "A Plea to My Sisters," October 2015 general conference, churchofjesuschrist.org/study/general-conference/2015/10/a-plea-to-my-sisters.

we are losing many young women in the transition to adulthood,[8] and our congregations are less rich for the loss of their voices, their energy, and their faith.

This failure to retain young members is happening in all churches, not just ours, and so is a reflection of larger societal trends, but it still bears asking why we're not doing better at bridging the gap between adolescence and adulthood for girls who have grown up in our Primary and Young Women programs. Either we're not giving them what they need, or they don't find a place within the walls of our chapels and Relief Society rooms for their adult selves—their desires and priorities as individual women in unique educational, professional, relationship, family, and social contexts. Some younger hearts and minds are not at ease with our doctrines, teachings, and practices. In short, it seems many of our young women simply don't feel their lives are made better as a result of participation in, or association with, the Church.

My own daughters, who spent their childhood and teen years fully immersed in Church programs and teachings, have not chosen to continue to engage as adult women. Their reasons vary, but having watched and listened as they wrestled with that very personal decision and its implications, there are some lessons that seem clear. A wise stake president once advised me that my number-one job was to preserve the relationship. I can't emphasize how much I have come to value that simple advice.

It is difficult when your children reject the church you love and have built your life in. I could not fix any of the problems my daughters experienced at church, nor supply what they found lacking in the organization or its programs. But I could honor their personal choices and continue to love and accept them. I'm ashamed to admit that required some very real—and painful—growth on my part. My natural reaction did not tend toward extending grace or honoring their agency. I had real love lessons to learn. Having

---

8. Jana Riess, "How many Millennials are really leaving the LDS Church?" *Religion News Service*, March 27, 2019, religionnews.com/2019/03/27/how-many-millennials-are-really-leaving-the-lds-church/.

emerged from that painful experience with a better understanding of Heavenly Father's love for me and my children, I can't help but wonder whether we, collectively as a church, are struggling with some of those same lessons.

Apparently I am not alone in needing to grow my ability to love—to offer empathy, grace, and understanding—in all the ways an increasingly complex world requires. In her book *The Next Mormons: How Millennials are Changing the LDS Church*, author Jana Riess references a study in which Millennial-generation women who are no longer in the Church were asked their reasons for leaving. The number-one reason cited was "feeling judged or misunderstood."[9] To me, this suggests a combination of failings on multiple fronts—apparently, neither leaders nor members projected the love and acceptance the respondents needed and wanted to feel. We didn't provide them what they believed Jesus Christ's church should. We can do better.

I believe our young women understand things about their own world that their parents and grandparents undoubtedly do not, but if we are unwilling to be taught or insist on denying the reality in which they are living, it follows that the Church will become increasingly irrelevant in their lives.

## Young Women's Church Experience Is Not on Pace with Their World Experience

The equal opportunities offered to our young women educationally and professionally are not available to women within the organization of the Church. From the time they are children, many girls see a church structure in which they have little voice and make few highly visible contributions. While that is unlikely to change significantly, by expanding our thinking about men's and women's roles, and becoming proactive in providing women every opportunity they can have to contribute at all levels, we could make

---

9.  Jana Riess, *The Next Mormons: How Millennials Are Changing the LDS Church*, (New York: Oxford University Press, 2019), 225.

improvements in many areas without disturbing underlying doctrine. We could significantly narrow that gap.

Many years ago, our family lived in a ward that staffed the Primary organization almost entirely with men. All the teachers were men, the pianist and chorister were men, and even the secretary was a man. My husband still talks about how much he loved teaching the five-year-olds, and they loved him too. I was deeply appreciative that our daughters, who were in Primary at the time, saw men filling unexpected roles in that ward.

How might we level the playing field between young women and young men, so that our young women clearly understand their equal value, beginning with their earliest experiences in our church and its programs? We're organized in a patriarchal system, which makes some inherent disparities easy to see and difficult to counteract. Creative thinking in the administration of our programs with a willingness to try new things will be key. Small changes could have a big impact to increase the visibility of women and amplify their voices.

And I believe we can do more than just allow more women to speak and teach. In April 2014, President Dallin H. Oaks gave a talk titled "The Keys and Authority of the Priesthood." He stated:

> We are not accustomed to speaking of women having the authority of the priesthood in their Church callings, but what other authority can it be? When a woman—young or old—is set apart to preach the gospel as a full-time missionary, she is given priesthood authority to perform a priesthood function. The same is true when a woman is set apart to function as an officer or teacher in a Church organization under the direction of one who holds the keys of the priesthood. Whoever functions in an office or calling received from one who holds priesthood keys exercises priesthood authority in performing her or his assigned duties.[10]

---

10. Dallin H. Oaks, "The Keys and Authority of the Priesthood," April 2014 general conference, churchofjesuschrist.org/study/general-conference/2014/04/the-keys-and-authority-of-the-priesthood.

To me, this assertion suggests that women's roles might yet expand in the Church, even without significant structural changes, under the direction of those with the necessary authority. Under such authority, women might begin to perform some callings where specific priesthood keys are not required, even when those callings have been traditionally extended only to men.

## In Addition to Desiring Equal Opportunities, Our Young Women Expect and Value Authenticity in Themselves and Others

Authenticity may be difficult to find or feel in a culture that tends to celebrate conformity over individuality. If the stereotypical mold is not a natural fit, the discomfort of sitting in lessons and hearing talks week after week that don't reflect the realities of her life may cause a young woman to feel unwilling to make the sacrifice required to stay.

One of my adult daughters was serving as the Primary chorister in her ward, and also as a human rights commissioner in her city. The job required her to consider how the needs of different population groups in the community might best be served, and the rights and well-being of all protected. In preparing for an upcoming sacrament meeting presentation with her Primary children, she was assigned to teach them a song that simply didn't reflect the actual family situations of the majority of the children in her urban ward. She worried about causing them pain or confusion, and felt inspired that her specific Primary might be better served by substituting a different song. She was refused permission to make any substitution, despite explaining her feelings repeatedly as she took her concerns up the ladder. Eventually she resigned from the calling. The inflexibility she experienced sat in deep conflict with her personal insight and inspiration on behalf of the children in her ward. Though some might not understand that choice, it was for her an issue of personal morals that mattered deeply.

## Our Messaging to Young Women Is Not Creating an Environment in Which They Feel Empowered

Remaining relevant in the lives of young women may require that we do all in our power to demonstrate acceptance of women in their full diversity of life choices and circumstances. Young women who find their experiences at odds with more common roles and milestones in Latter-day Saint women's lives might struggle to feel that the Church provides a comfortable space to be themselves and fully embrace their unique path. Creating an inviting and nurturing Relief Society organization will require space for young women to feel they can show up whole, no matter what stage of life they're in, and have their individual voices, ideas, and experiences equally valued. A woman who chooses to delay marriage or childbearing in favor of continued education or professional advancement needs a seat in the metaphorical Relief Society room where she can feel welcome and validated on her path. We are all richer for a diversity of voices and perspectives in our teaching and fellowship. Role models for girls should depict a full range of life's possibilities, because a broad spectrum is the reality of women's lives. Retaining more young women into adulthood will probably require that we expand our ideal of what it looks like to be an adult woman participating faithfully in The Church of Jesus Christ of Latter-day Saints.

When one of my daughters graduated from high school, our stake president called her in for an interview. He invited me to join them. During their chat, he asked what she would do next in her life if she could do anything she wanted. She replied that she dreamed of earning a degree from Rhode Island School of Design, an option that was financially out of reach. The stake president responded by encouraging her to follow her dreams. He believed she could accomplish anything if she really put her mind and heart to it. That was the counsel he felt inspired to deliver. I felt he was more in tune with my specific daughter's needs than any other priesthood leader I observed in my years as her mother. That interview remains a bright spot in her church experience. She felt cared about as a whole person, not just a future wife or mother.

## Today's Young Women Bring New Priorities to Their Discipleship

As a result of the culture in which they're living, some messages we have previously emphasized no longer resonate in the same way for our youth. We have a real opportunity to harness their understanding of the world in which they're growing up, and the strengths they're developing as a result of navigating that world, to create needed change and to progress as a church.

Social issues are increasingly important to our young women, and some Church policies are difficult for many to accept, let alone embrace. They do not wish to affiliate themselves with an organization that does not reflect their personal views, even to the point that some are reconsidering their decision to be educated at Church schools.

My daughters, who have left the Church, each cited social issues as one area where they cannot reconcile current policies with their own beliefs. For Cynthia's daughters, the Church's lack of progress on LGBTQ inclusion was paramount. Her eldest daughter, who is gay, couldn't see a way forward in a church where she didn't see herself modeled among the Latter-day Saint women in her ward. At a broader level, there are few active LGBTQ women to serve as examples for young women,[11] despite there being some prominent active gay men in the Church. For Cynthia's youngest daughter, being extremely protective, seeing her older sister leave/get pushed out was decisive. In her words, "If they don't want my sister, they don't want me."

But there are more subtle improvements young women desire too, areas where they want or need something different from what we are

---

11. Peggy Fletcher Stack, "Help all women—including queer members—to feel they belong in Relief Society, LDS attendees told at BYU conference," *Salt Lake Tribune*, April 29, 2021, sltrib.com/religion/2021/04/29/help-all-women-including/. During the BYU Women's Conference on Thursday, April 29, 2021, "[Sharon] Eubank, who heads the Church's humanitarian arm, Latter-day Saint Charities, invited her friend Jessica Livier Mendoza de la Vega - 'Liv' - to talk about her experience as a self-identified queer Latter-day Saint." While this is a significant milestone—the first openly queer Latter-day Saint to speak in an official Churchwide meeting—we have a long way to go.

offering. Our messaging around modesty is but one example where a shift in focus would better fit the current attitudes and life experiences of young women. For years we have emphasized covering girls' bodies, an approach that has proven to be not only unhealthy but also ineffective. It fails to teach underlying principles in a way that empowers girls to make good decisions for their own benefit.

My daughters were dedicated competitive swimmers, which meant they spent a lot of their lives in swimsuits. For them, wearing a swimsuit was about what they could do and accomplish with their bodies, not about how they looked. At Young Women camp one year, a stake leader insisted that all girls whose shorts did not come to the knee must pin fabric around the hems to lengthen them. Besides the harmful shaming effect of such a policy, to my girls the idea of needing to be covered by fabric to their knees was laughable, if not insulting. It flew in the face of everything they knew about themselves. As a mother devoted to providing full support for pursuit of their personal goals, I saw it as a damaging message completely at odds with the principles I wanted them to internalize about their strength, potential, and worth. They deserved better.

In his talk "Come, Join with Us," Elder Uchtdorf urged listeners to "Come and add your talents, gifts, and energies to ours. We will all become better as a result." Later in the talk he added, "Your background or upbringing might seem different from what you perceive in many Latter-day Saints, but that could be a blessing. Brothers and sisters, dear friends, we need your unique talents and perspectives. The diversity of persons and peoples all around the globe is a strength of this Church."[12] I hear these words as a prophetic message in our current world, a call for those who might hesitate to join us because they feel they don't fit, but perhaps more importantly, a call to those of us already in the pews to make space, make more space, and then make even a little more space. Our children demand it.

12. Dieter F. Uchtdorf, "Come, Join with Us," October 2013 general conference, churchofjesuschrist.org/study/general-conference/2013/10/come-join-with-us.

Flexibility has historically not been our hallmark, but it's possible to turn weakness to strength with focus and effort. Our continued growth as a church, but more importantly our discipleship, will depend on our ability to welcome differences and stretch beyond our current comfort zone. I truly believe that the gospel of Jesus Christ is big enough for all, and if we're willing to listen to a diversity of women's voices, look around with eyes tuned to possibilities, and think creatively about ways we might progress together, the future Church can accommodate every woman in every stage of her life.

## Seeing the Unique Contributions of Women

**Richard:** I'm grateful for my friends Cynthia and Susan, who have helped me to better value women's voices and see their unique contributions.

I would like to add some additional comments. In doing this, I worry that I am adding to the culture that men should have the last word. But perhaps I can share some thoughts that support these insights and suggestions offered by Cynthia and Susan. These women have helped me in my journey to work to set aside the massive iron gate of what I thought I already knew,[13] some of which was internalized sexism—so that I can better be like the Savior and, more importantly, do my part to help our congregations feel that all are welcome, included and valued.

During a training as part of my YSA assignment, it was suggested that we ask the women's point of view in all ward council issues, including those that affect only the men's organizations. It was part of President Ballard's vision of the importance of councils and that hearing all voices helps us make better decisions.[14] In thinking about this, I realized it never occurred to me to ask the women leaders for input in ward council when we discussed the

---

13. Uchtdorf, "Acting on the Truths of the Gospel of Jesus Christ."

14. President Ballard's book *Counseling with our Councils* (Salt Lake City: Deseret Book, 2012) has been particularly valuable to me in learning how to coordinate and participate in all kinds of councils and honor all contributions.

elders quorum needs, such as how to help a brother, or who should be considered as a new instructor.

In the next ward council, as we were talking about an elders quorum issue, I asked the Relief Society president for her opinion. At first, she said she was guarded because she felt that it was not her place to speak about an elders quorum issue—but her thoughtful insights gave us important perspective to make a better decision.

In our YSA ward council, we only had one woman (the Relief Society president) among all the men (elders quorum president, Sunday School president, ward mission leader, and bishopric). In a family ward, there are usually three women, representing Relief Society, Young Women, and Primary. I love the idea of women presidents chiming in on all issues, instead of staying within the boxes of our respective organizations. When we each bring our varied perspectives and counsel together, we make better decisions. I believe it is the responsibility of the priesthood leader to create this culture by talking about the goals of ward and stake councils, including the importance of women sharing their insights on all agenda items.

In that same training, I also learned that the priesthood leader should speak last. Once the priesthood leader has stated his opinion, it usually shuts down the discussion for both women and men, while everyone gets in line behind his decision. However, the leader's job is to hear all the voices to help him make the best-informed decision, often taking that input in prayer to Heavenly Father. This means the priesthood leader needs to listen and ask questions before voicing his opinion. This principle also applies in other presidencies—including those led by women.

One of the women I once visited with sent me an email: "You are the very first and only man who has ever asked me, a younger woman in the Church, to offer insight or counsel for priesthood authority. I'll never forget how impactful that was for me to feel seen after nineteen years of feeling less-than." I share this not to draw attention to myself but to illustrate the importance of listening to and asking for counsel from women. It is such a simple thing—something we all can do—but it is powerful. Not only is it helpful and healing for them, but we receive needed input to make better decisions in our wards and stakes.

In closing, my brother David Ostler shares this impactful story that helped me better understand these issues that Cynthia and Susan are teaching. In his book *Bridges: Ministering to Those who Question,* David recounts:

> With permission, I share the experience of an auxiliary president in a stake in the United States. Ashley's story demonstrates the need for us to include women in our decisions and to recognize their authority. During a recent stake council meeting, a discussion ensued about the schedule of a ward conference and how it would impact each organization in the stake. The meeting was conducted in the style of a lecture, not a council; everyone was told what had already been decided by the stake presidency. Then the discussion moved on to implementing changes associated with the newly announced two-hour block. Ashley had prepared for the council meeting by identifying issues she wanted to discuss with the council. As they were reading through the details of the changes, Ashley raised her hand and presented a few concerns she had. One of the counselors interrupted her and responded harshly that the stake presidency had already met and decided how each ward should do things, even though the strategies they were referring to were not proscribed by the Church. She pushed back, uncertain they fully understood her concerns. The stake president and counselor were visibly annoyed and patronizingly said that they just need to move forward and trust God.
>
> I want to pause here and ask us to reflect on what we would do in this situation. I think stake councils are particularly difficult for women. The usual stake council has eighteen or so men and only three women. The overwhelming majority of men at the meeting can be daunting for a woman. Imagine being in Ashley's shoes—that we had prepared for the meeting and advocated our point of view and that we had been called and set apart and had the priesthood authority to help make a decision regarding the issue at hand—but instead of receiving the respect of having someone listen to our ideas, we get shut down

and told that no one wants to hear from us. In this situation, many of us would probably defer to the power and authority of those men leading the meeting and would become silent and accept the status quo.

Ashley, like most of us would in this situation, felt vulnerable after speaking up and getting shut down. She knew if she said any more, she would be seen as a disruptor. Ashley recounts:

*I could acquiesce, tone it down, hold back, try to blend in. . . . My heart was beating, pounding through my chest all the way to my face. This felt wrong inside of me and I need to confront it, to understand it. Suddenly, the faces of all the capable, strong women I work with in this church came to my mind. The ways I have witnessed them seek and follow divine inspiration. Their faithful, humble desire to love and serve flowed into my heart and calmed the jitters in my intensity. This suddenly became a bigger deal. I had to speak for them.*

She did. She spoke kindly, but firmly, saying,

*That's easy for you to say. You speak from a place of "authority" where you can have the final word and inspiration. But what about me? Do we get to lean into our own inspiration, trusting God? The truth is, the women have thought so much more about this than you have, and yet decisions are constantly being made without them. This is my specific responsibility, and yet, if I say something different, I'm expected to yield my concerns or inspiration to you. It's hard to figure out what my role or purpose is if my voice never really has the same weighted value.*

The moments following her comment were filled with tension and discomfort. She even saw one of the male leaders roll his eyes. They discussed the matter some more, and Ashley expressed love as they concluded the discussion. They moved on without a firm resolution on the issue. She was shaking and squeezed the hand of another female stake leader and steadied herself. A few minutes later, the stake president stopped before concluding the meeting and said, "I had the wrong approach earlier, and I am so grateful we could counsel together so I can improve and be better with others." The meeting ended, and Ashley received support from others as she walked to her car.

The next day, Ashley received a voicemail from the other counselor, who had sat silently throughout the exchange. He told her,

*I have not been able to stop thinking about that meeting and what you expressed. I found myself praying for you as you spoke, completely sympathetic to your concerns and hoping you could express them clearly . . . then cheering as you did.*

Later that week her stake president met with her and told her he needed every word she shared. She felt his sincerity. They cried, they laughed, and Ashley said, "I felt the fulness of the gospel."

When I first heard this story, I was amazed. I have time and again seen Church leaders shut down comments from women in councils in similar ways, but I had never heard someone assert themselves in such an articulate yet forceful way. As I heard this story, I found myself, like the silent counselor, praying for it to resolve positively. I have seen similar situations resolve otherwise. Ashley was confident in her authority and her right to receive inspiration, and she saw the value she had in contributing to the discussion. Ashley's point was right; she has priesthood authority and is entitled to fulfill the responsibilities of her calling. She is a member of a council in which each person's opinion is valued. She has experience and understanding that others around the table need to hear and consider. She wasn't called to silently affirm; she was called to contribute her unique viewpoint and share the inspiration she has received while studying important issues. If we can create an environment where women's voices are heard and supported, without the risk and vulnerability that Ashley experienced, more women would make valuable contributions to our discussions. More women would participate. More women would feel like they belong. We would come a step closer to having women fully participate in church meetings and decision-making.

If Ashley had remained quiet, she may have left the meeting discouraged, perhaps becoming cynical. If her stake president hadn't responded the way he did, she may have left feeling defeated. In either of these alternative scenarios, what would the other female auxiliary presidents have learned about their roles?

Ashley and the stake president patterned behavior that other Church members and leaders can learn from and follow: we can talk about difficult issues, create discomfort through honesty, and make better decisions at the end. The challenges of faith we have today requires engaging and hearing each voice in our councils.

Reflecting back on the meeting, I wonder what would have happened if the silent counselor had, instead of remaining silent, affirmed his support for Ashley in the meeting, or if all those people who encouraged her in the parking lot had verbally supported her in the meeting. Perhaps her experience can inspire us to do better—we can be the ones who support future Ashleys, whose voices are being silenced. When we see something that devalues women in the Church, we need to say something and enable the voice that isn't being heard.[15]

Ashley's story really changed me and helped me better understand the things Cynthia and Susan are teaching. I realized that devaluing women's voices amounts to dismissing fifty percent of the world's intelligence, ideas, and inspiration. I also realized the importance of expressing support in the moment when I see a woman being silenced, instead of waiting until later to express encouragement.

Furthermore, listening to women's voices not only pays immediate benefits, but sets a great example for men in all areas of their lives. When unmarried men see their priesthood leaders actively seek out women's voices, they will likely remember it in their own church assignments and even down the road when they become husbands and fathers. They may even listen differently to the women already in their lives—their mothers, sisters, and women friends. It will help them in professional and academic interactions. For those who are already husbands and fathers, setting that example of actively involving women in Church councils sends a message about how

---

15. David Ostler, *Building Bridges: Ministering to Those Who Question,* (Salt Lake City: Greg Kofford Books, 2019), 147–150.

they should value women's voices in their lives. The ripple effect continues.

Everyone benefits when we include women's voices in all levels of family and church participation. Women have unique insights that help everyone as we counsel together to make better decisions.

# CHAPTER 4

# ENDING PORNOGRAPHY USE

When I was set apart as a YSA bishop, there was a line outside my office door, waiting to meet with me. The subject of my very first interview was pornography use.

For my entire assignment, helping others end pornography use was a major part of my service. Some of my YSAs had started to view pornography before they were ten years old. They often felt so much shame, leading to feelings of low self-worth, making it more difficult to solve the problem. It became a constant cycle of low self-worth, triggers, acting out, and shame. That is a difficult whirlpool to escape without the help of others, practical tools, and the Atonement of Jesus Christ.

As I left the bishop's office that first day, I knew I needed to learn as much as I could. I fasted, prayed, attended the temple, counseled with other leaders, reviewed available resources,[1] attended addiction recovery meetings,[2] and learned from those working to find recovery. Since my

---

1.  One of my favorite books on the subject is Dr. Donald J. Hilton Jr., *He Restoreth My Soul: Understanding and Breaking the Chemical and Spiritual Chains of Pornography Through the Atonement of Jesus Christ* (San Antonio: Forward Press Publishing, 2011). Many have reported to me that this book was key to resolving unwanted pornography use.

2.  "Addiction Recovery Program," The Church of Jesus Christ of Latter-day Saints, accessed June 30, 2021, addictionrecovery.churchofjesuschrist.org. See this webpage for the twelve-step program information, videos, locating in-person and virtual meetings, testimonials, and more. Many report success using these resources.

release, I have continued to develop more skills to help others end pornography use.[3]

How big is this challenge? I do not speak for the entire Church, but more than 40 percent of the active men and more than ten percent of the active women in my YSA ward were working to end pornography use. I heard similar reports from my peer YSA bishops. I share these numbers not to normalize or encourage it, but to help those working to end pornography use know they are not alone. I personally believe pornography use is peaking with this group, since they are the first generation managing unlimited internet access in the privacy of their own room (a huge difference from when I grew up in the 1970s). This generation will become the parents and leaders of tomorrow, equipped with added insights and skills needed to guide the next generation.

This chapter is not about never viewing pornography, though to be clear, I strongly invite everyone to not start in the first place. For children and youth, the primary message is to establish safeguards and systems to avoid pornography. But in today's world, parents can't entirely prevent their children from being exposed to it. Unintentional exposure is likely to happen, but children can be taught to not seek it out.

I hope parents create relationships in which their children can share any pornography exposure (unintentional or intentional) without shock, judgment, or shaming. Parents can tell their children in advance that they will respond with love, listening, and kindness if they tell them about viewing pornography. Doing this does not increase the chance their child will view pornography; in fact, quite the opposite. The Church website, in a section titled "How do I talk to my child about healthy sexuality?" makes this observation: "Let your children know they can ask

---

3. The Church has provided resources to leaders and families about ending pornography use at "Pornography Use," Counseling Resources, The Church of Jesus Christ of Latter-day Saints, churchofjesuschrist.org/study/manual/counseling-resources/pornography (may be accessible to only members of ward and stake councils).

you any questions, and then try not to overreact or attach shame to their questions or confessions. Celebrate that they are talking to you, show them love and support, and do your best to keep communicating."[4]

Jill Manning, former BYU professor and marriage and family therapist, agreed. In her book, *What's the Big Deal about Pornography? A Guide for the Internet Generation*, Dr. Manning said,

> Many adults are hesitant to communicate openly and clearly about pornography for fear that it will spark curiosities and backfire on them. But we know from various social science studies that when parents openly discuss sexual topics in age-appropriate ways and share their values about what is right and wrong, that youth are less likely to experiment, and are more likely to adhere to a parent's value set and remain abstinent in adolescence.[5]

When parents talk honestly and openly with their children about these topics, parents can remain a trusted partner through the adolescent years. Children can know that the parents' love for them is not conditional on any specific behavior or outcome, so they will feel safer confiding in them. When parents know what is going on in their children's lives, they can walk with them and help them overcome the challenges they face.

For the purposes of this chapter, we will focus on ending pornography use with a review of tools, gospel insights, and stories from others. This chapter is dedicated to the good men and women

---

4. "How do I talk to my child about healthy sexuality?" Life Help: Pornography: Help for Parents, The Church of Jesus Christ of Latter-day Saints, accessed July 25, 2021, churchofjesuschrist.org/study/manual/help-for-parents/talk-about-healthy-sexuality.

5. Jill C. Manning, PhD, *What's the Big Deal about Pornography? A Guide for the Internet Generation* (Salt Lake City: Shadow Mountain, 2008). Dr. Manning appears with Dr. Jason Carroll, also a BYU professor, in a series of short videos with transcripts for parents about how to teach their children about healthy sexuality and pornography prevention. See "Family Conversations: Talking About Healthy Sexuality," Video Collections, The Church of Jesus Christ of Latter-day Saints, accessed July 25, 2021, churchofjesuschrist.org/media/collection/family-conversations-talking-about-healthy-sexuality-video-collection.

courageously trying to end pornography use, and those who love them, trying to better understand how to help.

First, some comments about masturbation, which is almost always part of the pornography cycle—but can also occur without pornography use. As a bishop, I was surprised to learn some YSAs had concluded it was a major sin, that they were the only one with this sin, and they were almost beyond the Atonement of Jesus Christ. This caused them to isolate themselves, full of shame—one of Satan's greatest tools to separate us from our Heavenly Parents. All of this increased the chance they would continue to act out, as they were trapped in whirlpool of shame and self-loathing. My heart broke for them, that they had been carrying this burden alone for so long, making their spiritual journey more difficult.

A few of the YSAs were so weighed down with this sin that it took them either a long time or a few visits before they could finally confess—it was so difficult to even get the words out. I felt I was preparing myself to hear the confession of an Alma the Younger type situation (son of a prophet, but leader among the unbelievers, wicked, and doing all he could to destroy the Church in Mosiah 27:8–9). I sensed their near-broken hearts, feelings of shame, and low self-worth—a place I don't believe their Heavenly Parents want them to be. This experience, along with many others, taught me that we need to do a better job of talking about this subject, because *not* talking about it can cause more problems than the sin itself.

I told the YSAs that this sin is not listed as a major sin in the handbook, so we should conclude it is a minor sin—a far cry from an Alma the Younger situation. I invite parents to teach their children factually about what masturbation is,[6] with a clear understanding

---

6. When I was around age thirteen, my bishop asked me if I had a problem with masturbation. I said yes but I incorrectly understood masturbation to be having a wet dream (involuntary nocturnal emission). I confessed to something that is not a sin.

of how this sin ranks with other sexual sins that are more serious,[7, 8] and focusing on the power of the Atonement of Jesus Christ to align their behavior with God's guidelines. Since it is a minor sin, I am not sure it needs to be confessed to a bishop, as the handbook does not directly spell this out.[9] I told the YSAs that if they felt confession to me would help them, then I was glad to visit with them—but I wanted them to know they could work directly with God if they felt that was their best path to solve it. This may be especially true for YSA women who have the added challenge of talking with a man about this sensitive subject. I also told the YSAs I would not proactively ask them about masturbation during an interview. All these efforts were not to minimize the sin but to reduce shame to help the YSAs move forward in a positive and healthy way.

In family wards, I suggest that bishops work with parents to decide the appropriate role for them in talking with youth about masturbation and pornography. That role will be different for each family, depending on the needs of each youth. I believe parents need to know and feel good about what questions are going to be asked of their children—and some parents may feel more comfortable with a bishop talking to their sons about these topics than their daughters.

In YSA wards, I believe bishops should talk about this subject in elders quorum and Relief Society so everyone is on the same page. Clear definitions and expectations help the YSAs understand Church teachings about these sins and what needs to be talked about with their bishop. Anxiety of the unknown is reduced. Any needed visits to the bishop can focus on solutions and moving forward.

I want to share seven hope-filled ideas to end pornography use, from what I learned as I walked with the YSAs on their journey.

---

7. Richard Ostler, "Content Warning: This post is about masturbation and is for an LDS audience." Facebook, August 21, 2016, facebook.com/richard.ostler.5/posts/10209126875962171.

8. *Listen, Learn & Love* podcast episode 13.

9. There are times, such as preparing for a mission call, when a priesthood leader may feel impressed to discuss this subject.

These ideas are the basis of an article that I wrote for the *Ensign* magazine.[10] I have expanded on that article below, to bring more understanding to this critically important topic. Further, I have included insights from some who have bravely been on my podcast[11] to talk about their own pornography use, and therapists working with them to help end this behavior. They are some of my heroes for being on the podcast and including their journey in this chapter.

## 1) Know that you are a child of Heavenly Parents who love you.

As you work through this challenge, you may believe that you are not worthy of love or help, and subsequently pull away from your Heavenly Parents. Satan wants to convince you that you must resolve this issue entirely on your own and that you are outside of your Heavenly Parents' love and help until you end pornography use. I believe that this is a lie intended to isolate you from the Spirit.

We are all children of Heavenly Parents. We all have a divine nature and inherent value. Everyone is worthy to receive hope and personal revelation from Heavenly Father, and the healing power of Jesus Christ. Do not pull away from Them or the people who love you.

Sister Joy D. Jones, Primary General President, said:

> Let me point out the need to differentiate between two critical words: *worth* and *worthiness*. They are not the same. Spiritual *worth* means to value ourselves the way Heavenly Father values us, not as the world values us. Our worth was determined before we ever came to this earth. . . . On the other hand, *worthiness* is achieved through obedience. If we sin, we are less worthy, but we

---

10. Richard Ostler, "7 Tips for Overcoming Pornography Use," Ensign, October 2020, churchofjesuschrist.org/study/ensign/2020/10/young-adults/7-tips-for-overcoming-pornography-use.

11. See listenlearnandlove.org/solving-porn-use for episodes focused on ending pornography use.

are never worth less! We continue to repent and strive to be like Jesus with our worth intact. . . . No matter what, we always have worth in the eyes of our Heavenly Father.[12]

When I reflect on Sister Jones's words, I see worthiness as something that we *do* and is earned, such as having a temple recommend. I see worth as something that we *are*—beloved children of Heavenly Parents. Our worth is set. It is not something that comes and goes. This is reflected in the first paragraph of the Young Women theme: "I am a beloved daughter of heavenly parents, with a divine nature and eternal destiny,"[13] and the Aaronic Priesthood quorum theme: "I am a beloved son of God, and He has a work for me to do."[14] Remembering this doctrine is key to understanding that divine help is always there to help you end pornography use.

## 2) Remove shame.

In chapter 5, we will discuss the principle of hope-filled repentance, including the difference between shame and guilt. That concept should be applied specifically to pornography use. Feeling remorse or guilt for something you have done is part of the repentance process and can help you change behavior. It is a response to an action—you *did* something wrong. It is positive in nature and points you forward with hope. Shame, however, is believing that you *are* something wrong—inherently bad, broken, damaged, and beyond the help of the Savior. It keeps you in a whirlpool of self-loathing caused by lies.

---

12. Joy D. Jones, "Value Beyond Measure," October 2017 general conference, churchofjesuschrist.org/study/general-conference/2017/10/value-beyond-measure.

13. "Young Women Theme," Youth, The Church of Jesus Christ of Latter-day Saints; accessed June 30, 2021, churchofjesuschrist.org/study/manual/young-women-theme/young-women-theme.

14. "Aaronic Priesthood Quorum Theme," Youth, The Church of Jesus Christ of Latter-day Saints; accessed June 30, 2021, churchofjesuschrist.org/study/manual/aaronic-priesthood-quorum-camp-guide/quorum-theme.

## ZACH SPAFFORD[15]

As a member of The Church of Jesus Christ of Latter-day Saints, I looked like the perfect husband. When my friends were handing off their young babies to their wives to be changed, fed, or put down for a nap, I was elbow deep in wipes, spit-up, and snuggles. I was living up to my duty to provide for my young family, climbing the ladder at work, receiving bonuses, and being promoted.

I was that husband that we hold up as a model in the Church.

Except that I viewed pornography in secret. That made me the worst kind of hypocrite, scumbag, and failure anyone could imagine.

Sociologist Dr. Brené Brown is credited with saying, "Guilt equals I did something bad. Shame equals I am bad."[16] When it comes to pornography, we have a huge problem: shame.

As Christians and members of the Lord's restored Church, we too often stand firmly on a mountain of judgment and disgust when we see the wounds of men and women who have been engaged in viewing pornography.

We speak about pornography with phrases that conjure up a mythology of inescapable lust, self-abuse, and irredeemable loss. We tell stories of those who have habitually used pornography, filled with warnings of how their actions destroyed their families, caused them to lose their jobs, and made them outcasts in our society. We use fear to teach about pornography.

As a youth, I recall lessons in which young women were warned to "run the other way" if they found out someone they were dating was involved with pornography. Imagine what that means for any young man who has viewed pornography. It means they are unlovable for the rest of their life and can never repent. Imagine what that means to a young woman who cannot run from herself if she has been viewing pornography.

We have not acted like the body of Christ in succoring those who are lost from the fold. We have offered shame and fear as substitutes for unconditional love, acceptance of agency, and the unmatched capacity of the Atonement of Jesus Christ.

---

15. *Listen, Learn & Love* podcast episode 376.
16. Dr. Brené Brown, "Shame v. guilt," *Brené Brown* (blog), January 14, 2013, brenebrown.com/blog/2013/01/14/shame-v-guilt/#close-popup.

When I was deep in my struggle to remove pornography from my life, I also took professional promotions, moving from place to place. I met with multiple professional therapists, members of stake presidencies, and bishops. One stands out to me. Bishop Keith D. Ward was a man who embodied Christlike love.

Other bishops took away my temple recommend.[17] Bishop Ward took me to the temple with him. Other bishops said, "You need to pray more." Bishop Ward prayed with me and for me. He showed me that I was worthy of his time, his talents, and his effort. He was not afraid to talk about my struggles.

The Apostle Paul tells us, "For God hath not given us the spirit of fear; but of power and of love, and of a sound mind" (2 Timothy 1:7).

As members of Christ's church, we are given power. We are filled with love. We have greater understanding in our minds. How can we use these gifts to improve our conversation around pornography? We can begin by being open about the struggles that some among us face.

My wife, Darcy, eventually began to share with trusted friends what was going on in our lives, as a way for her to deal with what we both understood as "my pornography problem." This lifted an enormous burden off her shoulders as it was shared with our surrounding community.

It was also an opportunity for me to see that I was not irredeemable, and that I could repent and become clean again. Those friends loved us despite what they knew about my behaviors and habits. They treated us kindly. They never once rejected me or made me feel as though I were unacceptable to them. The Bailio and Barrus families created a space that helped me recognize that I was lovable, and the shame began to fade into the background.

Recently, one of them said to me, "The key, from my perspective, is that you were never our project, you were and are our friend. We wanted you to succeed because we love you."

My struggle began moving into the open, into the clear light of day. It became a topic of discussion. It also became secondary to my friends' concern for how I was doing. Rather than asking,

---

17. When I was a YSA bishop, I did not have a set rule on temple attendance for those working to overcome pornography use, nor did the handbook state one. I learned to pray and counsel with each individual for the right approach regarding temple attendance. See chapter 5, "Hope-Filled Repentance."

"Have you looked at pornography?" my wife began asking me, "How are you doing?" Rather than hiding in my home and feeling sorry for myself and lonely while Darcy was visiting her parents, my friends invited me to have dinner with them, join them on walks, and checked in with me during the day.

They asked the bishop, "How can we help the Spaffords? We know what is going on with them."

They demonstrated love, not fear. They drew on the power of heaven, rather than avoiding me. They saw me as a son of God.

If we are going to eliminate shame from those who struggle, we need to live up to the gospel's clear and direct teachings. We need to support those around us like my friends and Bishop Ward did with me.

Love is the antidote to shame. Let us practice it liberally. In doing so we will leave behind the fear and shame. We will come into the open and we will feel the love of others, of God, and love for ourselves.

## 3) Don't be quick to use the label of "addiction."

People who struggle with pornography are not necessarily addicted. They might be, or they might not. Various medical professionals, including within the Church, have differing opinions and analyses.

*Addiction*, in the medical field, is a complex neurological condition. Whether a person is or is not addicted to anything, including pornography, is for a doctor or psychologist to diagnose and guide them through. But we should not automatically assume that a person is addicted to pornography, because using this diagnosis incorrectly may make it more difficult to end its use due to the correlated shame. It might become a self-fulfilling prophecy.

Dr. Cameron Staley joined us on the *Listen, Learn & Love* podcast[18] to talk about his research and counseling efforts to help others overcome unwanted pornography use. He is a clinical psychologist at Idaho State University who completed his psychology residency at Brigham Young University's Counseling and Psychological

---

18. *Listen, Learn & Love* podcast episode 345.

Services. In his education, he learned Acceptance and Commitment Therapy (ACT) as an effective treatment for unwanted pornography viewing. I wish I understood his insights back in 2013 when that first young adult walked into my office, especially about being cautious before labeling pornography use an addiction.

### DR. CAMERON STALEY

I completed my psychology residency at Brigham Young University's counseling center, which offered an approach known as Acceptance and Commitment Therapy (ACT) that has been found effective in treating compulsive behaviors that are often driven by uncomfortable emotions or urges. ACT is a mindfulness-based treatment that has been helpful for more than thirty years in managing many mental health concerns including depression, post-traumatic stress disorder (PTSD), chronic pain, and anxiety.

In 2016, researchers from Utah State University and McLean Hospital/Harvard Medical School published the first randomized clinical trial on ACT as a treatment for decreasing unwanted pornography viewing. Their participants were able to reduce their pornography viewing on average over ninety percent after twelve weeks of ACT. ACT is the only therapy I have found with published research demonstrating its effectiveness in reducing pornography viewing.

Over the last decade, I have published several studies on pornography and worked with many individuals in counseling to reduce unwanted pornography viewing using mindfulness-based ACT principles.[19] I often find that individuals spend more time trying to overcome their "pornography addiction" than time spent actually viewing sexual images. For many, the battle to overcome "pornography addiction" has actually become the "addiction."

Researchers and clinicians have discovered common traits among individuals struggling with unwanted pornography viewing that help us better understand this concern. First, individuals with compulsive sexual behaviors tend to be less aware of

---

19. Cameron Staley, "Changing the Narrative Around the Addiction Story," TEDx Idaho State University, 3 December 2019, youtube.com/watch?v=mNGg5SMcyhI. Cameron has online resources titled "Life After Pornography" on Facebook, Instagram, YouTube, and *The Life After Series* podcast.

their emotions and less comfortable experiencing natural sexual urges. Often individuals do not realize that they are lonely, sad, overwhelmed, or bored, prior to an impulse to view pornography. Helping individuals identify what they may be struggling with or recognize their emotions prior to an urge to view pornography is a helpful first step in overcoming this challenge.

Individuals who attempt to avoid, escape, or otherwise control uncomfortable thoughts, emotions, or sexual urges struggle more with compulsive behaviors. When we try to *not* think about something, like a "warm jelly donut," we still think about, well, a "warm jelly donut." Spending your time trying not to think about pornography, counting days since you last viewed, or trying not to notice sexual urges tends to amplify these experiences. Our minds *cannot not* think about something. I know that wording sounds strange, but the principle holds true. What we resist tends to persist.

Instead, it is more helpful and productive to focus on things your mind can do. Attend to your emotions. Enhance your connections with others by sharing your experiences instead of reporting whether or not you have viewed sexual images. When appropriate, church and temple attendance can be a powerful way to better manage sexual urges. Devote your energy to meaningful pursuits in education, recreation, physical health, friendships, family, and faith. Living consistently with your values is building your legacy! We want to be known for the good things we have accomplished instead of the things we have tried to avoid.

Instead of focusing on pornography as an "addiction," I have found it more helpful to think about unwanted pornography viewing as the "cough" or symptom of an underlying "cold." The "cold" is often stress, depression, anxiety, trauma, loneliness, limited awareness of emotions, or shame. Fixating on getting rid of the "porn cough" does not treat the cold. Pornography is a coping strategy many use for dealing with underlying emotional difficulties. Address the cold, and the coping strategy of viewing porn becomes obsolete.

Everyone engages in unhealthy coping at times. Many people do not struggle with unwanted pornography viewing but turn to food, social media, video games, shopping, or hours of sports instead of addressing important and complex emotional experiences. Finding a way to relate to others increases understanding, compassion, and fosters connection, which is the antidote to unwanted pornography viewing.

Importantly, we have learned that individuals who are religious are more likely to *perceive* themselves as "addicted" to pornography, even when they are not viewing at higher rates than less religious individuals, and their behaviors are inconsistent with what the medical community considers "addictive" patterns. Perceiving yourself as an "addict" may lead to increased pornography viewing over time.

I encourage individuals to identify themselves in ways that enable agency such as being a disciple of Christ or a child of God. Labels like "pornography addict" often erode our sense of self-worth and limit our ability to see our value and true potential.

We may not be able to control the experience of a particular emotion or a sexual urge, but we can choose how we respond to these inner experiences. Mortality provides us an incredible opportunity to better understand and exercise our agency. Constructing your identity around labeling yourself an "addict" may interfere with this process and mask our true identity as children of loving Heavenly Parents who want us to do our best to learn and develop.

Most men and women I've worked with who struggle with unwanted pornography viewing are some of the kindest, most hardworking, religiously devout individuals I've ever met. They also tend to have unrealistically high expectations for themselves, are less aware of their emotions, have difficulty managing stress, and are overwhelmed with intense feelings of shame. They see themselves as the most unworthy, dangerous, disgusting person imaginable. These unhelpful fear-based messages around pornography can have a greater impact on individuals than the actual viewing of sexual images.

We all struggle in this life. Some deal with depression, some battle anxiety, many have experienced abuse, and some struggle with compulsive behaviors. All of us can make a difference by being kinder, more understanding, and open to offering our love and support. We are all brothers and sisters. I hope we can all support one another on this wonderfully challenging journey of life together!

## 4) Create a written personal prevention plan.

As we counseled together, sometimes young adults in my ward shared concepts with me that they had learned from therapists, teachers, mentors, and leaders to overcome the challenge of ending pornography. The idea of a written personal prevention plan especially resonated as I saw how it helped others. This is not your regular journal. Rather, it is something private to you and others in your circle who are helping you to solve pornography use. Here is a general outline of a written personal prevention plan:

### PART 1: LIST YOUR TRIGGERS

Triggers are the first step in the cycle to view pornography. One YSA described it as a small chemical spill in the brain as hormones are released. I believe that part of our brain is focused on the long-term, and another part says, "Give it to me now." The prevention plan works to keep the long-term part of your brain in the game when you are triggered, at the moment the "now" part of your brain wants to take over. The chemical spill is normal, so do not feel shame for being triggered as there is no sin in that initial small chemical spill. There are several types of triggers:

- Situational—an environment, such as a specific location or time of day.
- Emotional—stress, anxiety, loneliness, or traumatic events.
- Visual—inadvertent exposure to something not pornographic but triggering images in social media, movies, photos, and so on.

### PART 2: PLAN TO REDUCE TRIGGERS

A situational trigger could be avoided by turning off your phone before being in a specific situation. Could an emotional trigger of stress or anxiety be alleviated by exercise or appropriate medication? Might enrolling in a class or spending time with friends reduce loneliness? Consider the available options, including spiritual tools. Prayer, scripture study, service, church, and temple worship are vital in helping you withstand temptation.

### PART 3: PLAN TO RESPOND TO TRIGGERS

Redirect your thoughts. As Dr. Staley pointed out, our minds *cannot not* think about something. You can't block a thought with a void of nothing, so be proactive in deciding what you will focus on instead. You could text or call a confidante, go for a walk, read or memorize verses from the Book of Mormon, or other positive actions that pull you out of the moment. Plan responses that work for you!

### PART 4: UPDATE YOUR PREVENTION PLAN

What worked or didn't work, and how can the plan be modified to be more effective next time? Use a slip-up as a learning experience. What happened? Why was this trigger different? Did three days of stress finally catch up to you? Did four days of no scripture study weaken you? Did your exercise or eating change? Write down the learning and improve your prevention plan. This is a work in progress; you do not have to be perfect today. I believe you can be square with your Heavenly Parents if you are doing all you can to resolve any issue in your life.

Newly returned missionaries, especially those with some pre-mission history of pornography use, should write a prevention plan in the final weeks of their mission. The first six months after a mission are critical, and a prevention plan is key.

### 5) Understand "lapse" versus "relapse."

A *lapse* is when you fall back but quickly recover and use it as a learning experience to improve your trigger-response plan. A *relapse* is when you give up, binge, and do not care.

A lapse is part of improving, so do not conclude that you have lost all progress when you do. Satan wants you to think you are back to square one. Jesus wants you to understand you are one day closer to ending pornography because His Atonement provides hope and healing. This is when updating your prevention plan is useful: review triggers, examine what happened this time that was different, and assess your response. Then recommit to moving forward with a positive attitude, knowing you are another day closer to recovery.

My friend Hayden Paul has been on the *Listen, Learn & Love* podcast three times: by himself,[20] with his wife Savannah,[21] and

---

20. *Listen, Learn & Love* podcast episode 328.
21. *Listen, Learn & Love* podcast episode 340.

with his therapist, Bo Buchi.[22] Below you will read Hayden's story and how he *lapsed* but did not *relapse*. He quickly got back on track and agreed to commitments, which enabled him to access the healing power of Jesus Christ. Hayden eventually overcame his pornography use. He just kept trying.

### HAYDEN PAUL

I just couldn't stop.

At seventeen years old, looking at pornography had become a daily habit. I knew it was wrong. I knew I needed to stop, but the shame of my problem kept me from seeking the help I needed. Even after serving a full-time mission, I could not kick the habit.

My ten-year struggle with pornography started when I was thirteen years old. I was curious about female bodies specifically and sex generally. I took my curiosity to the internet, and it was not long before I found a pornographic website. What I saw was not just a picture of a scantily dressed woman, it was the "real deal." It shocked me, and I hurried to shut off the computer.

It was not long before the images and videos that originally scared me became enticing, and I began viewing pornography purposefully. I had no idea what I was truly getting into and the impact these seemingly small decisions would have on the rest of my life.

Whenever pornography was talked about in church or with my family, the focus was always on how bad it is. There was such an emphasis on the destructive nature of pornography on families and relationships and how wrong it was that when I became caught up in it, I did not tell anyone for fear of being viewed as a "pervert" and sinner.

While preparing for a mission, my ecclesiastical leaders directly asked me if I viewed pornography. They even told me that many young men struggle with it, so there was no reason to feel ashamed if I did. But I was so worried about what other people thought of me that I lied. I lied to go to the temple, and I lied to go on my mission. I thought that if I could slow the frequency of porn use, that would be sufficient.

It did not take much time in the MTC before I realized I needed to be honest. The first person who heard about my

---

22. *Listen, Learn & Love* podcast episode 347.

struggle with pornography was my MTC branch president. When I told him, I felt peace and confidence before God that I had craved for years. When I looked at myself in the mirror, I no longer saw a pervert and sinner but an honest disciple who, although still imperfect, was capable and worthy of preaching the gospel. And that is what I did.

For two years, I dedicated myself to the work. I had limited access to technology. I was with a companion constantly and engaged in such spiritual work that I did not have issues with porn. By the end of my mission, I felt the immense joy that came from living a life without pornography and lust controlling my actions. I wanted that to never be a part of my life again.

My first time in the temple after I returned home, I prayed in the celestial room. I thanked God for the incredible experience of my mission and asked, "What is the one thing you want me to focus on now that I'm home?" It might sound funny, but I closed my eyes, opened the scriptures randomly, and pointed my finger. The verse hit me hard: "Stand fast therefore in the liberty wherewith Christ hath made us free, and be not entangled again with the yoke of bondage" (Galatians 5:1).

I knew exactly what it meant. I had felt that yoke of bondage, and I had also felt the liberty that Christ had given me. I committed that day to never entangle myself in pornography again.

It is normal that after a mission, old habits started to creep in. It was only about three months later that I visited a pornographic website. Had I already forgotten the warning that God gave me in the temple? Was the conversion I experienced on my mission even real? As these questions ran through my head, I received a prompting from the Spirit: "the yoke of bondage" was lashed on by lies and deceit. This one misstep did not have to define my life if I would be honest and turn to the Lord.

I met with my bishop, but soon became frustrated. Despite my honesty and sincere desire to repent and change, I continued to seek out pornography more and more. I had awesome bishops but felt like I was never truly understood. The advice they gave was along the lines of, "Just continue to pray and read your scriptures, serve in your calling, and go to the temple. Eventually, this will go away." I felt like I was drowning in the ocean and they were standing on the deck of a boat cheering for me to keep swimming, but what I needed was a life preserver.

I later moved to a new stake and told the new stake president my entire history with porn. He encouraged me to continue developing my relationship with God through prayer and

115

scripture study, and gave me specific commitments that helped immensely. He held my temple recommend for a while, which gave me something to work toward.

The commitments I agreed to included telling my parents about my struggle with porn, attending a twelve-step recovery program, and participating in family history by indexing one name a day (transcribing digitized records helpful for genealogy and temple work). These efforts were crucial in my recovery. Therapy was also extremely helpful in addressing deeper, underlying issues that caused me to turn to porn as a coping mechanism. Daily prayer and scripture study provided a foundation that I needed to receive more personal direction from God. I finally felt like someone had handed me a life preserver.

It was not that the checklist itself healed me, but by keeping those commitments, I gained access to the grace of Jesus Christ and learned lessons that eventually led me to true healing. After three years, I was once again free from pornography.

My road to recovery was long and challenging, but I became very confident in my standing before God and in my goals of overcoming pornography use. It was easy for me to be open about my struggles, because I knew I was heading toward a life of freedom. I did not need to hide this part of myself anymore. Instead of feeling like a helpless sinner, I felt hope and forgiveness from my Savior.

## 6) Believe in the Savior's healing power.

Jesus Christ has the power to enable your growth and repentance process and is waiting to ease your burdens. Do not think that turning to Him adds to His burden. He has already paid the price for you. Instead, do your best to draw closer to the Savior; ask Him to help you heal and give you strength to change your desires and move forward.

Elder Ulisses Soares taught, "As we continually strive to overcome our challenges, God will bless us with the gifts of faith to be healed and of the working of miracles. He will do for us what we are not capable of doing for ourselves."[23]

---

23. Ulisses Soares, "Take Up Our Cross," October 2019 general conference, churchofjesuschrist.org/study/general-conference/2019/10/55soares.

In the April 2021 general conference, President Nelson reminded us of the Savior's love that encompasses all of us:

> Internalize the truth that the Atonement of Jesus Christ applies to *you*. He took upon Himself *your* misery, *your* mistakes, *your* weakness, and *your* sins. He paid the compensatory price and provided the power for you to move *every* mountain you will ever face. . . . The more you learn about the Savior, the easier it will be to trust in His mercy, His infinite love, and His strengthening, healing, and redeeming power.[24]

## ZACH SPAFFORD

The Atonement of Jesus Christ is possibly one of the least understood principles of the gospel. I have heard "the Atonement changed me" so many times, as if the healing power of Christ through His infinite Atonement was the thing that made our decisions different.

As a pornography user, I was constantly pleading with the Lord to remove this burden, to make it so I would not return to pornography, to eliminate the urges that drove my habitual use of this forbidden media.

What I misunderstood was the relationship between repentance, agency, and the Atonement. These three principles must be combined together to effectuate the change that each of us wants and needs to progress through life and become the best versions of ourselves.

But to get to a place where we can use them, we need to better understand what each is and how they interact together.

When I ask people what it means to repent, they often offer a list of actions that must be completed, for instance:

- Stop the behavior.
- Confess your sins.
- Remunerate or pay back anything you can.
- Suffer the consequences of your actions, including accepting any punishment.

---

24. Russell M. Nelson, "Christ is Risen; Faith in Him Will Move Mountains," April 2021 general conference, churchofjesuschrist.org/study/general-conference/2021/04/49nelson. Emphasis in original.

This is, in my view, the wrong way around.

The Book of Mormon talks about a mighty change of heart in Mosiah 5:2. The root of the word repentance—the Greek word *metanoia*—speaks of having a new mind. This indicates that the core of what must change is in our beliefs, thoughts, or souls.

Imagine a bank robber who loved robbing banks but had stopped doing so, confessed their actions, paid back all the money, and even spent time incarcerated for their crimes. If they still believed "I love robbing banks," they would remain unrepentant even if they never robbed a bank again.

Often, especially when it comes to pornography, we are insistent on stopping the behavior above all else. Instead, what we are truly looking for is a fundamental shift in our beliefs about who we are and why we choose not to engage in that activity.

This takes us to agency. I have countless experiences with men and women who believe that they "can't view pornography" and that they "should be better" than they are. I once believed this myself. These phrases are abdications of our agency. This perspective seeks to place the onus of our choices on an external set of rules that we believe we must embrace as our own without equivocation. I believe this is why we tend to label pornography use as an addiction. What else could it be if we are out of control and incapable of stopping our viewing? Agency is the antithesis of addiction and "can't, should, or shouldn't."

Latter-day Saints often defend our choice to not drink alcohol or coffee with the phrase, "I can, but I choose not to." Similarly, we must exercise our God-given agency with pornography use. I know it might seem counterintuitive to believe "I can view pornography." It is, however, in line with the reality of our full exercise of agency.

I remember distinctly the first time I thought, "I can look at pornography, and maybe I'm going to choose that today." As I thought of all the times I had struggled to fight away the urge to view, and how I disappointed myself and my spouse if I didn't succeed, I realized this simple truth: I had agency, I could look at pornography, and if I did, it was my choice. It was no longer a rule that my bishop had laid out. It was not something my wife told me I couldn't do. It was not because my church said so. It was MY choice.

That realization took me from, "I can, and maybe I will today" eventually to, "I can, but I choose not to." A place I stand today. That exercise of agency imbues us with power, allows us to take responsibility, and ultimately brings us closer to the principles and priorities we actually want in our lives.

Finally, as we look back on our exercise of agency, we can readily find examples of choices we aren't proud of which were the catalyst of suffering, struggle, and sorrow. Christ's Atonement, a power immeasurable and immutable in our lives, is there to make up for those mistakes which have alienated us from God and the person we are striving to become.

The Bible Dictionary says, "The purpose of atonement is to correct or overcome the consequences of sin. . . . By transgression man loses control over his own will and becomes the slave of sin and so incurs the penalty of spiritual death, which is alienation from God."[25]

The Atonement provides incentive to change and allows us to know we are not lost forever because of our actions, and supports us in our efforts, but does not change our behavior directly. That is our part.

Imagine you are on a boat, travelling from the place of your birth to the place of your death. Anytime you get off the boat to swim, you are disobeying God's law. You can stay in the water as long as you want. You can get out of the water whenever you want. That is your agency. When you get out of the water, you are still wet. The effects of your actions remain with you. You can dry yourself with towels, but you aren't completely dry until the sun warms your clothes and removes the last of the water from you.

That part is the Atonement: the part that you can't complete without something outside of you. The Atonement won't keep you out of the water. It won't make you use a towel to dry off. The Atonement gets you dry but can't keep you dry if you exercise your agency to get in the water again.

In this example with the warmth of the sun and the cool of the water, there is no wrong choice. The scriptures, however, make it clear that in the battle for your eternal happiness, there is a bitter and a sweet, a right and a wrong, bondage and freedom.

They also make it clear that we all must choose. "And to bring about his eternal purposes in the end of man . . . it must needs be that there was an opposition; even the forbidden fruit in opposition to the tree of life; the one being sweet and the other bitter. Wherefore, the Lord God gave unto man that he

---

25. "Atonement," Bible Dictionary, The Church of Jesus Christ of Latter-day Saints, churchofjesuschrist.org/study/scriptures/bd/atonement.

should act for himself. Wherefore, man could not act for himself save it should be that he was enticed by the one or the other" (2 Nephi 2:15–16).

So, when you say to Heavenly Father, like I did and I'm sure many others have as well, "Please take this sin away from me, make it so I never have to deal with it again," you are missing the point.

The point is getting out of the water and drying off as best you can. The point is choosing to stay in the boat. The point is having faith enough to keep trying even when you aren't sure how to move forward. The point is to stop worrying about whether you can be forgiven and just start working on the things you have control over. These things are repentance and agency. On the rest, the Atonement of Jesus Christ has you covered. It is all encompassing. He has paid for your past mistakes and will pay for the ones you make going forward.

The love of Christ and His Atonement have made it possible to heal and to believe in ourselves and our capacity to change and grow. He has given us hope of a better world, one where we no longer turn to sin to sustain us in difficult moments. His Atonement is the anchor which leads us to do better and do what is right.

It has made all the difference to me to exercise these three principles together: repentance, agency, and the Atonement of Jesus Christ. It can make all the difference to you. It can heal the wounds of your past and give your future its best chance of being what you want it to be, free from pornography.

## 7) Do not do this alone.

Satan tries to use the trap of pornography to separate you from your Heavenly Parents (see point 1), *and* he hopes to isolate you from the support of family and friends. He wants you to believe that you must overcome this challenge entirely on your own. But this is not true. Connection and friendship give you power and will help you succeed. Seek counsel from Church leaders or family members, and if necessary, a professional therapist or mental health counselor.

An accountability partner can see you through your best and worst days, offering support without judgment. You could also provide the same support to them. It is usually better if the accountability partner is not one's spouse or dating partner because that can define the relationship. A third person can often provide the ongoing needed support. I am an accountability partner for some people right now. When they face a challenge, I can just be there for them. It is easier because it does not affect our relationship.

Each married or dating couple needs to prayerfully find the right approach to being honest about pornography use.[26] For some, a daily accounting may be needed; for others, a weekly or monthly discussion may be the right approach (especially if there is a separate active accountability partner).

In the dating process (once a couple is exclusive but before they are engaged), I encourage a discussion about current or past pornography use. Honesty is one of the basic building blocks of a healthy relationship, and not sharing current pornography use damages that trust. It is difficult to be so vulnerable, but in my experience, disclosing this information ends up bringing the couple closer most of the time. Such conversations often open the door for both partners to share sensitive issues that may be uncomfortable, such as personal debt, a family member with legal challenges, serious illness, education or employment setbacks, or others. Sharing about these issues can bring the couple closer together as vulnerability brings authentic connection and enables the relationship to be built on a foundation of accepting each other for who they truly are—instead of what our checklist culture often dictates what one should be. I encourage both partners to bring an open mind to these conversations.

Every person should give their partner full permission to end the relationship once pornography use is disclosed. The partner should feel totally justified if that is what they choose. However, this is a

---

26. The Church has provided resources to leaders and families at "Support for Spouses of Pornography Users," Counseling Resources, The Church of Jesus Christ of Latter-day Saints, churchofjesuschrist.org/study/manual/counseling-resources/spouse-support-pornography (may be accessible to only members of ward and stake councils).

highly individualized decision. I have seen some of the best men I know disclose a current pornography problem to a girlfriend, and—usually after some time, thought, and prayer—she stays in the relationship. Why would she do this? Sometimes she sees beyond the behavior to the purity and goodness of his soul, his understanding of the Atonement of Jesus Christ, and how he applies those principles in his own life and in teaching others.[27] The couple sometimes concludes that the pornography is really a symptom of deeper challenges, such as loneliness, stress, or anxiety. Maybe they can work together during the dating process to address those feelings. That is not to say that the partner takes responsibility for the problem or tries to become the other person's rescuer—that is the Savior's role. In almost all cases, pornography use predated the current relationship. But a romantic partner can be supportive while the person deals with their triggers and develops healthier responses than pornography use.

I have seen people end pornography use as they move into a healthy relationship, with their future spouse feeling at peace in continuing the relationship. I have also seen people end a relationship because of pornography use, as it became clear that was their best path forward. Continue or leave the relationship—both are possible and appropriate outcomes. Only the individuals and their Heavenly Parents know which outcome is right for each person. Further, we shouldn't hear someone's else's story and make it our story. We need to finish our own story—but others' stories help us make a more informed decision as we seek personal revelation.

These same principles extend to disclosing during the dating process about repented sexual history or being a survivor of sexual abuse (the latter is of course not a sin, so I hesitate to even mention it in the same sentence). Discussing this is a highly personal decision.

---

27. While I have used the example of a man using pornography, the reverse also happens. In fact, there may be more shame for women who view pornography because we usually talk about it as only a challenge for men.

I believe your Heavenly Parents will guide you to make the right decision about whether or when to discuss it with a potential spouse.

I have heard some people say they will only marry a virgin. I strongly encourage men and women not to focus on the virginity status of their future spouse, but rather look for virtue. This is the Christlike attribute you are seeking.[28] That checklist mentality requiring your future spouse to be a virgin (or other checklist items) could keep you from considering someone who could be a wonderful eternal companion for you and parent to your future children.

If you have a current problem with pornography, should you date now or wait and solve the problem first? This too is a highly individualized decision. I have seen both roads work, but I worry that too many take themselves out of a social life altogether because of current pornography use. I believe that dating can help reduce the isolation and loneliness that contributes to this problem. If you are not dating and are viewing pornography, perhaps a middle ground is to participate in social activities with larger groups instead of pairing off. Also, I have met with many people who no longer feel worthy of their "dream spouse" because of a prior or current issue. I discourage this type of thinking. Do not rule out anything. Do not let your current situation limit your future hopes and dreams. Let your Heavenly Parents guide you. They have a plan for you.

I believe in you. You are some of our Heavenly Parents' finest sons and daughters. They will help you. Hang in there, make progress, have hope, and you will join the many others I know who have ended pornography use.

Savannah Paul, Hayden's wife, tells the following beautiful story about receiving personal revelation for what was right on her path. As Savannah says, her path is not everyone's path.

---

28. See Molly Oswaks, "Elizabeth Smart Is Standing Up for Rape Victims—And Tearing Down Purity Culture," Vice.com, September 1, 2016, vice.com/en/article/mbqjka/elizabeth-smart-is-standing-up-for-rape-victimsand-tearing-down-purity-culture.

## SAVANNAH PAUL

I don't know that it was explicitly taught while I was growing up, but I thought I needed to marry someone who had never used pornography. I considered it a deal breaker. During dating relationships, I sometimes wondered if pornography use was at play, but it wasn't ever an open topic of conversation. It wasn't until I met Hayden that a guy was open with me about the subject so early in our relationship. He shared with me his past struggles with pornography and how he was still on the path of recovery. It didn't scare me like I thought it would. He was really open with me, and it was easy for me to trust him.

When we were engaged, Hayden told me over the phone that he'd had a lapse with pornography. I could tell it was hard for him to tell me about this, and we were both emotional. My first thought was, "I have no idea what to do about this." I wondered if this was a red flag that I should break off our engagement. I wondered if pornography would destroy our marriage if we went through with it. I felt very uncertain, but I realized the importance of waiting to react until I could pray and receive God's insight first.

I thanked Hayden for being open with me and told him I needed some time to think about it before saying anything else. He understood and we ended the call. I immediately got on my knees and told Heavenly Father my fear, worries, and uncertainty. I laid out my own past experiences and insecurities, knowing that God would take every part of both our hearts into account.

The answer I received brought a lot of peace. I knew instantly that God knew Hayden much better than I did. The Spirit reminded me that I wanted to marry a man who knew the Savior very personally, could testify of the Atonement of Jesus Christ, and was willing to repent when he made mistakes. I was not looking for someone who was perfect. I also had the thought that the Lord would use my naturally forgiving nature to bless Hayden's life in this situation. I couldn't "fix" him, but I was comforted to be able to play a forgiving role. My job was to love him, pray for him, and encourage him. I liked that.

I also felt some insecurities that I talked to God about. I wondered if I wasn't attractive enough to Hayden and that was why he'd looked at pornography again. It's important to know that the feelings I had, and any others that result from conversations like ours, are completely valid. Betrayal, anger, fear, and insecurity are normal reactions. But those natural emotions shouldn't dictate the choices and actions that follow. The Spirit reminded me that it was a temptation to think negatively about myself. I was comforted. When I mentioned those insecurities to Hayden, the Spirit helped me believe him when he told me his lapse had nothing to do with me or my body.

My answer that night was specific to our relationship and gave me the courage to move forward with our engagement and marriage. The conversations that resulted brought us closer together. The whole experience strengthened my testimony that God knows each of us personally.

Hayden and I communicate openly about pornography in our marriage. He is honest when he feels tempted or when he accidentally comes across pornographic material. I am not afraid anymore because I trust my husband and I trust the answers I got from the Lord.

Sometimes I hesitate to share this experience, because I am not suggesting that this is the exact answer that God will give you. I don't think the answer I received applies to every situation. God will give you specific revelation that will help you know which steps to take when someone you love struggles with pornography.

## "I have flooded the earth with temples to help them"

For those who compulsively view pornography, feeling worthy enough to access spiritual tools is a challenge and takes some deprogramming (please review what I shared in point 1). Many who are dealing with sin think that they will turn back to God and the Church *after* they have solved their problem, feeling unworthy until then. I believe just the opposite. I encourage everyone to read, pray, and attend church *while* they are changing their behaviors and hearts. There is no belief or behavior hurdle required to attend church or to have a close relationship with our Heavenly Parents.

During my service as a YSA bishop, I sought divine guidance to help people overcome pornography more than any other subject. Some of the best people in my ward were diligently working to put it behind them. While pondering this one night alone in the bishop's office, I asked Heavenly Father, "Did you know so many of your best children would struggle with this?" It was as if He underestimated the depth of this challenge, maybe even miscalculated how difficult it would be to stay free from it in today's world. I quickly realized that my thinking was flawed. Of course He knows everything, so He must have a plan for His children to overcome this. A clear impression came into my mind: "I have flooded the earth with temples to help them."

I consider this one of the most direct revelations of my life. I believe the temple is key to helping our youth avoid pornography. My wife and I loved seeing our children (who are now adults) frequently performing baptisms for the dead. I love that my wife displays pictures of the temple in our home. I love noticing a picture of the temple as a screen saver on our children's phones and computers. I love talking about the temple in our family discussions. I love serving in the temple and the added spirit it brings into our home. I love the temple covenants and the spiritual power those covenants bring into our lives.

Further, I believe temple worship can be part of the process to help some permanently put pornography use behind them—especially those deeply committed to solving it and doing the hard work required as outlined in the stories above from Zach and Hayden. As I mentioned, I am not advocating unrestricted temple attendance for everyone working to solve this, but I do believe temple attendance can be part of the solution. I recognize part of Hayden's path to ending pornography use was having his priesthood leader "hold his temple recommend" for a while which gave Hayden "something to work toward."

I encourage those working to overcome unwanted pornography use and their leaders to counsel together and with the Spirit to seek the best individual approach. For those currently without a temple recommend, I encourage walking the temple grounds or visitors' center. There is power in and around temples.

## Christ's Power Is Stronger

I believe that pornography is one of Satan's last, best weapons to bring down God's children in the last days. But never forget that Christ's power is stronger. Pornography is no surprise to Jesus Christ, and His grace is sufficient to overcome it if we meet Him through our best efforts, day by day. Those efforts may be halting at first, and we will need to dust ourselves off and try again when we fall. But over time, with Christ's help, full recovery *is* possible.

# CHAPTER 5

# HOPE-FILLED REPENTANCE

One of my greatest honors during my service as a YSA bishop was to facilitate the repentance and forgiveness process as my ward members changed their lives and drew nearer to the Savior. Over the course of my assignment, my approach to this process significantly changed, while the core doctrine of repentance through the Atonement of Jesus Christ stayed the same. I wrote about the principles of repentance in the August 2020 *Ensign* article, "How the Savior's Healing Power Applies to Repenting from Sexual Sin."[1] This chapter is an expanded version of that article.

While this chapter is generally focused on the YSA age group, I believe the principles apply broadly. Further, I hope these thoughts will be helpful for all of us, since everyone needs to repent, as well as to local Church leaders, members, and parents seeking to teach repentance principles. I also believe we can improve our understanding of repentance, shifting it from the perception of punishment to a more positive experience of change as taught by President Nelson:

> Too many people consider repentance as punishment—something to be avoided except in the most serious circumstances. But this feeling of being penalized is engendered by Satan. He tries to block us

---

1. Richard Ostler, "How the Savior's Healing Power Applies to Repenting from Sexual Sin," *Ensign*, Young Adult digital section only, August 2020, churchofjesuschrist.org/study/ensign/2020/08/young-adults/how-the-saviors-healing-power-applies-to-repenting-from-sexual-sin.

from looking to Jesus Christ, who stands with open arms, hoping and willing to heal, forgive, cleanse, strengthen, purify, and sanctify us. . . .

When Jesus asks you and me to repent, He is inviting us to change our mind, our knowledge, our spirit—even the way we breathe. He is asking us to change the way we love, think, serve, spend our time, treat our [spouse], teach our children, and even care for our bodies.

Nothing is more liberating, more ennobling, or more crucial to our individual progression than is a regular, daily focus on repentance. Repentance is not an event; it is a process. It is the key to happiness and peace of mind. When coupled with faith, repentance opens our access to the power of the Atonement of Jesus Christ.[2]

## Checklist Versus Principle-based Repentance

When I started my YSA assignment, I assumed the bishop's handbook had a "repentance grid" where I could look up a sin and it would list the two-part penance: restrictions, and duration of those restrictions (for example, three months of no temple attendance). The grid might include other factors such as being temple endowed. This idea parallels our criminal justice system, in which judges have sentencing guidelines within the laws of their jurisdiction (such as six months in jail for a specific offence). I thought similar "sentencing guidelines" existed in the handbook.

I quickly learned our inspired Church leaders provided no such grid. Further, the Spirit taught me to understand principle-based repentance, unlike the rules-based criminal justice system which is not based on the Atonement of Jesus Christ. This was a paradigm shift for me as I began to understand that the measure of true repentance is "godly sorrow" (2 Corinthians 7:10) and a "mighty change of heart" (Alma 5:12-14, 26), not the conclusion of time-based restrictions—which are the means, not the end, of complete repentance.

Godly sorrow and a change of heart capture the central elements of the repentance process. Godly sorrow means recognition

---

2. Russell M. Nelson, "We Can Do Better and Be Better," April 2019 general conference, churchofjesuschrist.org/study/general-conference/2019/04/36nelson.

of the sin, confession (to God, to anyone harmed, and when needed, a bishop), and restitution. Change of heart means giving up the sin, with a deeper resolve to move forward.

## Customized Repentance Plans

For serious sins, I worked with each person to develop a customized repentance plan that worked best for them. The process usually included a list of things to do and possible restrictions. I tried to be sensitive to the Spirit and treat each situation as unique.

### List of Things to Do

The list of things to do might include increased scripture study, prayer, or reading conference talks or passages of books (my favorite is chapter 17, "The Blessing of Repentance," from the book *The Infinite Atonement* by Tad R. Callister).[3] In some cases, I hesitated to make a long list of reading material, because I sensed that the individual did not connect with the Spirit in this way. Failure to complete the list might cause them to conclude that they could not be forgiven. Often the individual and I counseled together in a team effort, instead of the authoritative judicial method that does not allow for collaboration.

Also, I did not want to lose sight of the fact that the objective is godly sorrow and a change of heart, with any list items as the means to accomplish this goal. In some cases, a person completed a list but we both felt they had yet to experience godly sorrow and a full change of heart. In other cases, godly sorrow and a change of heart came well before a list was completed.

### List of Restrictions

The restrictions depended on the sin, the Spirit, and discussions with the person. I usually went slowly to decide restrictions. In many cases, we both felt that pausing temple attendance or partaking of the sacrament would be a positive thing to help the person. Other times, I

---

3.   Tad R. Callister, *The Infinite Atonement* (Salt Lake City: Deseret Book, 2000).

felt that restrictions would not be helpful—that partaking of the sacrament and attending the temple (if they could pass the recommend questions) would give them added spiritual strength. I have always believed that taking the sacrament is about looking forward and committing to do better, rather than *not* taking the sacrament as a penalty for the past. Many can honestly take the sacrament because they make those covenants looking forward. Further, for some people, abstaining from the sacrament creates shame that is particularly unhelpful to the repentance process, especially for youth in a family ward.[4] There is a higher worthiness standard for attending the temple or performing an ordinance such as *blessing* the sacrament, but I believe it is a much lower hurdle for *taking* the sacrament—which is open to even nonmembers and children younger than eight years old.[5]

## Church Discipline

There are many sins that *may* result in a membership council,[6] but it is not *required*. (Please see the General Handbook[7] for complete information.) Unless it was a serious sin in which a membership council was required, I was hesitant to convene such a council. During my service as bishop, I was never in a situation where a membership council was required.

---

4. Several teenagers have told me they are grateful to work in confidence with their bishop to resolve sin but feel shame and embarrassment to not take the sacrament. They are likely seated with their parents in sacrament meeting, who may be unaware that their child is working with the bishop. This could make it harder for youth to have needed talks with their bishop.

5. See "Can Nonmembers Take the Sacrament?" *New Era*, March 2012, churchofjesuschrist.org/study/new-era/2012/03/to-the-point/can-nonmembers-take-the-sacrament.

6. In February 2020, the wording changed from disciplinary councils to Church membership councils. "A Look Inside the New General Handbook for Church Leaders and Members," *Newsroom*, The Church of Jesus Christ of Latter-day Saints, February 19, 2020, newsroom.churchofjesuschrist.org/article/new-general-handbook.

7. See chapter 32, "Repentance and Church Membership Councils," *General Handbook: Serving in The Church of Jesus Christ of Latter-day Saints*, (Salt Lake City: The Church of Jesus Christ of Latter-day Saints, 2019), churchofjesuschrist.org/study/manual/general-handbook/32-repentance-and-membership-councils.

When serious sins were involved, I explained the process of a membership council, and then we discussed together whether this would be helpful to them. Although I as bishop had priesthood keys for a final decision, the input of the person was valuable as I prayed to Heavenly Father for direction. After this process, I sometimes concluded that a membership council would make the process to completed repentance more difficult[8]—and we could get to godly sorrow and a change of heart without it. In other cases, while a membership council was not required, I felt it would be helpful, especially if the YSA felt it would help them end a behavior pattern or put an experience behind them.

I also generally felt that a membership council (unless required by the handbook) would only be helpful if someone wanted to return to full activity—for example, have a temple recommend and a calling. In these situations, a membership council was a positive step to help them return to full participation, a goal we both shared. I never felt prompted by the Spirit to initiate a membership council with a YSA who did not want to return to full activity. My feeling was it would drive them further away.

Some YSAs were sexually active (both straight and gay) who had no immediate desire to change their behavior or get a temple recommend, but they wanted my help with other aspects of their life, such as overcoming addiction, difficult family situations, self-reliance, or emotional health issues. We both knew the Church's teachings on the law of chastity, but I felt impressed to not define our relationship by this commandment. I did not call for a membership council but simply offered support in areas of their lives that they wanted to improve. I wanted to be a trusted person in their lives. Yes, I invited them to keep the commandments. I also invited them to attend

---

8. In most of these situations, the YSA felt embarrassed to know that more people would become aware of their circumstances. It added to their shame. This was especially true for women, since membership councils are composed of only men.

church so they could feel the Spirit. All of our Heavenly Parents' children should feel welcome at church.

The Spirit also taught me that confession might be the thing that *starts* the repentance process, but in some cases could be the thing that *completes* it. Some people had already achieved godly sorrow and a change of heart and were keeping the commandments. All they needed to do was to confess serious sins to their bishop. I learned to be sensitive to the Spirit in responding to the individual nature of each situation and not react with a mechanical checklist process. I needed to deprogram myself from my two years as a missionary, teaching repentance with a flip chart outlining a numerical step-by-step process. Yes, those steps are part of the process, but the order may be different in some situations.

## Brother Russell Trammel

The story of Russell Trammel,[9] shared with permission, illustrates the principle that confession may not come at the beginning but can come near the end of the repentance process.

On January 24, 2016, Russell Trammel (age twenty-six and a priest in the Aaronic Priesthood) walked into our singles ward—his first time in church in nearly a decade. I met him at the beginning of church and welcomed him to the ward. He stayed the whole three-hour block—a little unusual for someone who is not used to church.

At the end of the three hours of church, I asked him if we could meet during the week. He responded, "Can we meet right now?" Wow—that said something about Russell Trammell! We did meet that first Sunday, and I learned Russell is a remarkable man who had completely turned his life around and wanted to return to a life of following Christ.

I learned that Russell, living in California, had fallen into a life of drugs and other challenges. In June 2014, Russell knew he had to

---

9. Richard Ostler, "The amazing story of Russell Trammell," Facebook, July 3, 2016, facebook.com/richard.ostler.5/posts/10208733772494830.

leave California to put this life of drugs behind him. Showing tremendous courage and faith, he moved to Utah. This enabled him to put his challenges with drug use permanently behind him. I believe a loving Heavenly Father has been carefully guiding His dear son Russell—and knew this move to Utah would help him.

Russell and I met a second time a few days later on January 27, and I learned more about his life story. As we spoke, I felt this was someone who had gone to enormous lengths to align himself with Heavenly Father before walking into church three days earlier. Russell told me that he stopped smoking that day—his last hurdle to living the Word of Wisdom. During that visit with Russell, I had one of the strongest impressions I have ever felt from Heavenly Father. God told me to invite Russell, if he could go another week without smoking, to receive his limited-use temple recommend and go to the temple. The impression was, "This is my dear son. He has come so far on his own. He needs to be in the temple to receive the strength to permanently put his past behind him and to see his future. Don't create some drawn-out process to receive his temple recommend. He is at the finish line and is ready." Acting on this clear message, I extended this invitation to Russell and gave him a priesthood blessing.

I believe the steps of repentance are not always in a set order. Everyone is different. Sometimes confession is the last step in the repentance process, as some have already completed the core of repentance with the Lord, which is godly sorrow and a change of heart.

Seven days later, on February 3, Russell and I met next. Russell reported that he had continued to live the Word of Wisdom. He said it was difficult, but he knew he could do it and the Lord would help him. I went through the temple recommend questions. When Russell answered "yes" to living the Word of Wisdom, we both just stopped. Neither of us said anything and took in the moment with tears in our eyes. This was far from a routine temple recommend interview. I signed his temple recommend—his first in about ten years.

What did Russell do once he had a temple recommend? He bolted from my office that evening and went straight to the Salt Lake Temple to do baptisms for the dead. Wow! What did he do the next day? He took the day off work and went to every temple in the valley, texting me several times during the day about how great he felt and the healing feelings of being in the temple. To me, this was evidence of his godly sorrow and change of heart.

Russell never looked back. He changed his living situation to be in a more positive environment. He was laser-focused on becoming an elder and receiving his endowment.

On February 25, Russell downloaded Tinder (works for some, does not work for others, and gets some in trouble). He met Becky Jump the next day. On their first date, he knew she was the one. Wow! Heavenly Father had a plan for Russell and Becky. Knowing that they'd found their eternal companion, they both deleted Tinder the day after they met.

On March 23, Russell proposed to Becky on the grounds of the Oquirrh Mountain Temple. Becky enthusiastically said yes, ultimately setting a date of July 1. I have come to know Becky, a returned missionary, as one of the kindest and most loving people I've ever met, a true disciple of Christ. Becky and Russell make a great couple, both lifting and helping each other to become better, both so loving to each other.

Soon it was time for Russell to become an elder and receive his endowment. Russell's family came into town from California for his priesthood ordination on Friday, April 29. It was the first time I met Russell's parents, Duane and Darlene Trammell. As I looked into Darlene's eyes, I imagined this dear mother and all the time she (and others) spent on their knees praying for her son, all the times she put his name on the temple prayer roll.

There were many tears of joy as Russell's family saw their son, brother, and friend aligned with Heavenly Father and met his wonderful fiancée, Becky. Russell's dad, Duane, performed a wonderful ordination to the Melchizedek Priesthood. The next day, Russell went to the Oquirrh Mountain Temple to receive his endowment.

Russell and Becky were married on Friday, July 1, in the Draper Temple.

I share this story to bear testimony that the Lord is behind this work. He has a plan for each of us. Our plans are all unique. Many of His very best sons and daughters will spend a period of time not fully connected to the Church. If you are walking this road, maybe you can use the example of Russell and come back, knowing the Atonement of Christ can make you clean and take pain out of your life. However, most importantly, when you return, you bring all the learning, perspective, and experiences that make you a better person and can lead you to help others. How cool is that?

I love Russell Trammell, this incredible, faithful man who bravely walked back into church on the last Sunday in January 2016, and then walked out of the Draper Temple on the first day of July 2016 with his stunningly beautiful new bride, sealed for time and eternity, both wonderful disciples of Christ with a great future ahead of them.[10]

## Iceberg Concept

Christine Holding, a wonderful LDS therapist, taught me the principle of the iceberg,[11] which can be helpful to better understand the totality of a situation for someone who is working to fully repent.

The iceberg concept means that what is visible above the waterline is only part of the story. Sin occurs above the waterline, but there may be something more underneath. Those who sin and those who are guiding someone through the repentance process (priesthood leaders, although family, friends, and therapists can be key members of a support team) may need to learn what is at the bottom of the iceberg to understand the full situation. Understanding the entire iceberg results in a more comprehensive and customized plan

---

10. Russell and Becky became the parents of a beautiful baby girl in June 2021.
11. Richard Ostler, "Sin, Shame and the 'Iceberg' Concept (LDS Audience)," Facebook, October 6, 2016, facebook.com/richard.ostler.5/posts/10209526826840693.

to both complete repentance and solving underlying issues that make recurrence less likely.

When I met with a person working to overcome sin, if the Spirit prompted me, I drew a picture of an iceberg and asked what was below their waterline. I listened and listened, sometimes over multiple visits. The person was often surprised that I did not want to immediately address the repentance steps needed to overcome the sin.

One example of the bottom of the iceberg is the inherent need to be loved, wanted, and desired—a deficit that some women attempted to meet with sexual activity. Some had experienced this gap their entire lives, never feeling valued or loved, sometimes compounded by abuse and trauma. All these factors could leave a wonderful sister more vulnerable to sexual activity because of her emotional needs for love and validation. Often the relationship ended when the male partner made it clear that he was not looking for a long-term relationship, leaving her even more emotionally injured, compounded by the shame of being sexually active.

While less common, I found that the same circumstances could occur with men who were sexually active. The Spirit prompted me to be less black-and-white in my thinking and seek to understand the reasons behind their choices, so I would know how best to help. I realized that most people did not just wake up one day and think, "I want to disappoint my Heavenly Parents by sinning, so I'm going to be sexually active today."

While sexual sins at the top of the iceberg are generally the same, the bottom of the iceberg can be much different. At the beginning of my YSA assignment, I would have given everyone the same repentance plan because the sin was the same. By the end of my service, the Spirit had taught me to develop customized repentance plans based on the totality of each individual situation. I recognized that the wrong repentance plan could further wound a person and make it harder for them to access the Atonement of Jesus Christ to be healed.

Another example is pornography. Yes, pornography is a sin. But as discussed in chapter 4, the underlying problem is often about how pornography has become a coping mechanism to find connection or to deal with stress or anxiety.

If I felt that there were emotional issues at the bottom of the iceberg, I would often suggest to the YSA that they might get a therapist involved to work through the issues. In some cases, and with permission, I shared a situation with a therapist, without disclosing the person's name, to give me insights. My education, training, and professional career are in business, and I recognized the need to consult experts in areas in which I have no training to give me needed perspective. I often found that I had blind spots that kept me from effectively ministering. Clinically trained therapists often had valuable insights that were key to connecting the dots to the full situation at the bottom of the iceberg. The result was a hope-filled, customized repentance plan to help the person move forward.

At times, I felt that the sin was a coping mechanism for emotional health issues such as poor self-esteem, stress, or anxiety—not because of a heart that wanted to turn from our Heavenly Parents through sin. Yes, the sin was still a sin, but the path to healing could be less about typical repentance steps (such as no temple attendance for three months) and more about improving one's emotional health.

I have always wondered about the woman taken in adultery, whom Jesus told to "go thy way and sin no more" (John 8:3–11). With His perfect understanding, Jesus knew the totality of her situation and acted with understanding and compassion.

## How Serious Is Sexual Sin?

One of the ideas I have heard over the years is that being sexually active before marriage is ranked next to murder. Perhaps this is because of the words of Alma to Corianton, his missionary son:

> And this is not all, my son. Thou didst do that which was grievous unto me; for thou didst forsake the ministry, and did go over into the land of Siron among the borders of the Lamanites, after the harlot Isabel. Yea, she did steal away the hearts of many; but this was no excuse for thee, my son. Thou shouldst have tended to the ministry wherewith thou wast entrusted. Know ye not, my son, that these things are an abomination in the sight of the Lord;

yea, most abominable above all sins save it be the shedding of innocent blood or denying the Holy Ghost? (Alma 39:3–5)

Before we conclude that Alma's words to Corianton are the
same words he would use with one of our YSAs, we should
pause to remember that Corianton was a missionary on a sacred
assignment to the Zoramites. It seems he was the face of the
Church to this people. So his sin was more than sexual immor-
tality; it also included the serious sin of leaving his ministry
as he abandoned the people with whom he was entrusted. I
sense that Alma's heart was heavy with not only his son's sexual
sin, but also the negative impact of Corianton's example on the
people.

I also worry that if someone is sexually active before marriage
and feels their sin is next to murder, they may falsely conclude their
situation is so hopeless that the Atonement of Jesus Christ doesn't
apply to them and their future is forever ruined. These are two of
Satan's biggest lies.

After meeting with many YSAs who had been sexually active
before marriage—sensing their core goodness and desire to follow
Jesus—I do not feel their sin is of similar seriousness to Corianton's
because they are not in his situation. They haven't forsaken a mission to engage in sexual activity. Yes, I strongly encourage everyone
to keep the law of chastity. But as I read Alma 39, much of that
chapter is still filled with hope for Corianton's repentance through
the Atonement of Christ.

Moreover, the scriptural record shows that Corianton's repentance was complete. Perhaps chastened by his father's strong words,
he turned his heart around and resumed the ministry (Alma 43:1–2,
49:30, 63:10). In fact, Alma 48 extolls the virtues of Moroni and then
includes all of the sons of Mosiah and Alma, including Corianton, in
the same category!

> Yea, verily, verily I say unto you, if all men had been,
> and were, and ever would be, like unto Moroni, behold, the
> very powers of hell would have been shaken forever; yea, the
> devil would never have power over the hearts of the children

of men. Behold, he was a man like unto Ammon, the son of Mosiah, yea, and even the other sons of Mosiah, yea, and **also Alma and his sons, for they were *all* men of God.** Now behold, Helaman and his brethren were no less serviceable unto the people than was Moroni; for they did preach the word of God, and they did baptize unto repentance all men whosoever would hearken unto their words. (Alma 48:17–19; emphasis added)

If Corianton's repentance was complete, ours can be too. Yes, we should avoid all sins, including sexual sins. These concepts do not give permission or encourage us to let down our guard. Everyone I met with wishes they had not sinned in the first place.

## Shame Versus Guilt

When I started my bishop assignment, the words *shame* and *guilt* were synonyms in my mind. However, I learned they are different. I love how Dr. Brené Brown explained it:

> Shame is a focus on self; guilt is a focus on behavior. Shame is "I am bad." Guilt is "I did something bad." How many of you, if you did something that was hurtful to me, would be willing to say, "I'm sorry. I made a mistake"? How many of you would be willing to say that? Guilt: I'm sorry. I *made* a mistake. Shame: I'm sorry. I *am* a mistake.[12]

No one should feel they are a mistake.

The Apostle Paul wrote to the Corinthians about the difference between godly sorrow, which I call healthy guilt, and worldly sorrow, which I call unhealthy shame: "For godly sorrow worketh repentance . . . but the sorrow of the world worketh death" (2 Corinthians 7:10).

Elder Uchtdorf further explained this scripture:

> *Godly sorrow* inspires change and hope through the Atonement of Jesus Christ. *Worldly sorrow* pulls us down, extin-

---

12. Dr. Brené Brown, "Listening to Shame," TED talk, March 16, 2012, 20:39, youtube/psN1DORYYV0.

guishes hope, and persuades us to give in to further temptation. *Godly sorrow* leads to conversion and a change of heart. It causes us to hate sin and love goodness. It encourages us to stand up and walk in the light of Christ's love. True repentance is about transformation, not torture or torment. Yes, heartfelt regret and true remorse for disobedience are often painful and very important steps in the sacred process of repentance. But when guilt leads to self-loathing or prevents us from rising up again, it is impeding rather than promoting our repentance. . . . True heartfelt repentance brings with it the heavenly assurance that "we can do it now." My dear friends, no matter how many times you have slipped or fallen, rise up! Your destiny is a glorious one! Stand tall and walk in the light of the restored gospel of Jesus Christ! You are stronger than you realize. You are more capable than you can imagine. You can do it now! [13]

While a painful feeling, guilt is positive in nature as we look forward with hope, armed with an understanding of the doctrine of the Atonement of Jesus Christ to become clean. We know our worth is set because we are beloved children of Heavenly Parents and always within the circle of divine love, as taught by President Thomas S. Monson:

> Your Heavenly Father loves you—each of you. That love never changes. It is not influenced by your appearance, by your possessions, or by the amount of money you have in your bank account. It is not changed by your talents and abilities. It is simply there. It is there for you when you are sad or happy, discouraged or hopeful. God's love is there for you whether or not you feel you deserve love. It is simply always there. [14]

---

13. Dieter F. Uchtdorf, "You Can Do It Now!" October 2013 general conference, churchofjesuschrist.org/study/general-conference/2013/10/you-can-do-it-now.

14. Thomas S. Monson, "We Never Walk Alone" (general Relief Society meeting, Salt Lake City, September 28, 2013), churchofjesuschrist.org/study/general-conference/2013/10/we-never-walk-alone.

Yes, we regret any sin, but we pragmatically realize that we are not asked to be perfect in mortality. We know that the real test of our character is what we do after committing a sin. Are we able to learn from it? Will the repentance process make us a better, more Christlike person? Are we one day closer to solving this challenge? Will this journey allow us to help others working through similar challenges? If so, we are using the gift of repentance to grow.

Shame, also a painful feeling, is different. Instead of looking forward with hope, it looks backward into a whirlpool of lies and self-loathing about your character and worth. It creates the impression that you are a broken, damaged, or flawed person. Believing these negative ideas can keep you trapped in the cycle of sin. I believe Satan is real and wants to destroy us. He wants us to sin, but his real victory is when he can convince you of the lie that your mortal and eternal future is permanently altered, that you are outside the love of your Heavenly Parents, causing you to forget you are Their child. Please stay off the shame road. You are never beyond the reach of the Atonement of Jesus Christ.

I am grateful for the prophet Nephi's honesty with his own human weaknesses in the Psalm of Nephi (see 2 Nephi 4:17–35). Nephi's vulnerability has only increased my love and respect for him, and his humanity draws me toward him as a beloved prophet. His authenticity causes me to rally for his success. Nephi talked in first person about his shortcomings ("groaneth" because of his sins), but he was filled with hope—not shame—and faith in God "in whom I have trusted" (verse 19). Nephi's words can give us hope, as we realize that this prophet-teacher is also human. He was once on the same road we are on, yet he still did wonderful things despite his "valley of sorrow" (verse 26). We do not need to wait to get to the other side of that valley to feel our Heavenly Parents' love and to help others.

## The Prodigal Son[15]

Knowing my love for the parable of the prodigal son, my wife Sheila, commissioned a painting from Michael Malm[16] about that parable as a Christmas gift. That beautiful painting of the father hugging his son hangs in the entry of our home. Each time I see it, I am reminded of the way we should love each other, no matter what—emulating our Heavenly Parents' unimaginable love for each of us, whoever we are, whatever we have done.

This parable is a dramatic example of multiple sins. The prodigal son first sinned against his father by wasting his inheritance, compounded by choosing to engage in riotous living. I imagine the prodigal as a young man, unmarried, on his own for the first time—out of control. Because of his wealth, he had access to all the things he thought would bring happiness. I think Christ set up the parable to be dramatic to help us understand that His Atonement applies even in the worst-case scenario, to give us hope in our individual journeys.

My wise institute teacher, S. Michael Wilcox, pointed out that the story of the prodigal son is introduced in the scriptures by two mini parables: the lost sheep and the lost coin. I believe the key to these mini parables is what the man and woman do once they find what they are looking for: they go out and tell everyone! "And when he cometh home, he calleth together his friends and neighbours, saying unto them, Rejoice with me; for I have found my sheep which was lost" (Luke 15:6). "And when she hath found it, she calleth her friends and neighbours together, saying, Rejoice with me: for I have found the piece which I had lost" (Luke 15:9). Why would Christ include these two mini parables? I believe the core message is that our Heavenly Parents and our Savior rejoice when we are found.

---

15. Richard Ostler, "The Prodigal Son: For those who need to feel forgiven," Facebook, November 3, 2016, facebook.com/richard.ostler.5/posts/10209802682896922.

16. See mikemalm.com.

The Savior rejoices when someone accepts His greatest gift to mankind: His Atonement. He does not turn us away, resent us, or get angry with us. We do not add to His burden when we repent—He has already paid the price. By contrast, when we humans are offended, we may make it harder for the offender to receive our forgiveness. We might make the other person grovel for a time while we have "control" of the relationship because of their offense or mistake. We might even relish the power it creates—something I have been guilty of. However, Jesus Christ loves to forgive and is glad when people are "found." I can see our Heavenly Parents and our Savior rejoicing, just like the man who found the sheep and the woman who found the coin.

Back to the prodigal son: he went into the "far country," lived a "life of riotous living," and eventually "came to himself" (Luke 15:13, 17). Those last three words are critical in the parable. This is the point when he knew he needed to change. It is that honest self-reflection when we realize we are not where we want to be. I think these moments are God-given as we sense our divine nature and truly desire to improve. I have met with so many people after these moments. They are my heroes for acting on their "came to him/herself" moment. There is no shame, just hope. I wish I could have met the prodigal son at this point. I bet I would have felt his goodness, sincerity, and desire to move forward. I have had these "came to myself" moments. I think the test of my character is how I respond.

The prodigal son's response was to return to his father. But he no longer saw himself as a son. He concluded in advance that he would return as a servant, stating, "I am no more worthy to be called thy son: make me as one of thy hired servants" (Luke 15:19). Why did the Savior put that in the parable? In my mind, it reveals the core meaning of the parable: when we are leaving our own far country, do we return as a son or servant? The Savior knows our natural human tendency. He also knows that Satan's voice would cause us to see our future as forever changed for the worse—in this instance, the prodigal son concluding that he would be a hired servant instead of a son.

Then comes my favorite part of the parable: the prodigal made his way home alone while considering his fate. I wonder how long that journey was and how many times the son played out in his mind the conversation he was going to have with his father. I cannot imagine the pain he felt having to face his father, having sinned against both his father and God, wondering how his father would respond. He would have to see firsthand the pain of his complete failure in his father's eyes—maybe the worst pain to face.

But then the miracle of the parable happens, opening our eyes to our Heavenly Parents' feelings when we return. The father sees his son "yet a great way off" (Luke 15:20). It is interesting that the Savior put this in the parable. The father could have first seen the son as he walked in the door of the house. Or the son could have returned during the night and climbed into bed (that would have been my plan). But the father sees his son during daylight, still approaching.

Look at what the father does. Does he hide in his home and make his son grovel? Does he give him the cold shoulder for a while? Is he bitterly angry, reminding him of all his mistakes? Does he disown him? I wonder how I would have handled this if I were his father.

I imagine the prodigal's father and mother praying for weeks, months, and years that their son would return. I imagine the day the prodigal returns. His father working alone in his field under a hot sun, missing his son who used to work alongside him, with a hand plow turning the soil. Leaning on the plow, he looks up to catch his breath, innocently gazing over the horizon and seeing someone. Looking closer, considering whether it could be his son—maybe recognizing something familiar in his stride or his clothes—squinting his eyes, with his heart rate increasing as he wonders and then fully realizes that this is his beloved son.

Then I imagine the father dropping the plow and running across the rows, leaving the outer perimeter of the farm, across the open land, and finally embracing his son. And what an embrace! The father "had compassion, and ran, and fell on his neck, and kissed him" (Luke 15:20). I have tears in my eyes as I write these words. The response of the father stunned the son. Once that healing embrace ended, the son, probably sobbing as he received this love and acceptance, looked into his father's eyes and said, "I have sinned against heaven, and in thy sight, and am no more worthy to be called thy son" (Luke 15:21). I think the son is saying, "I'm not worthy of your love, compassion, and acceptance. I am not worthy of the way you are treating me." But the father was not done.

Remember that the son wanted to return to a different position in the household: not as a son but as a servant because he felt unworthy. The parable forever answers the question, "When we are in our own far country, do we return as a son or a servant?" The father answered that critical question without hesitation. "Bring forth the best robe, and put it on him; and put a ring on his hand, and shoes on his feet" (Luke 15:22). Wow! The robe, ring, and shoes were more than accessories. They gloriously symbolize his return as a son. The Savior uses the very best visual imagery to communicate to our minds and hearts that when we return, we return as full sons and daughters of Heavenly Parents. They stand ready to embrace us as we make our way back to Them, just like the father of the prodigal son. As Brother Wilcox said, "I don't think religious literature gets any better than that."

I believe Satan knows we are very vulnerable when we have our "came to ourselves" moments. Satan can lure us to the "far country," but he only wins if he keeps us there. He does not want us to act on this God-given impression to "come to ourselves" and return home. He wants us to feel shame and hopelessness from our sins. He wants us to believe that our mortal and eternal trajectory are permanently changed. Even if we return, he tries to convince us that we have forfeited our right to still be a child of Heavenly Parents, and will only be a servant. He tells us we are not good enough. The parable of the prodigal son refutes all those lies in striking visual imagery.

As a bishop, I met with many who had the courage to act on their "came to him/herself" moments and walk into my office. I wanted to be like the father in the parable, symbolically representing that first tender interaction with the same healing spirit the prodigal experienced. My Heavenly Parents want me to universally love and build up the YSAs. When we talked about their "far country" sins, I tried to make the conversation an uplifting and positive experience, focusing on what they had learned, what direction they wanted to move in, and the hope of the Atonement of Jesus Christ to become clean.[17]

## Pink Latter-day Saint

Isaiah 1:18 teaches, "Come now, and let us reason together, said the Lord: though your sins be as scarlet, they shall be white as snow." A pink Latter-day Saint[18] is someone who has sinned but falsely concludes this scripture does not apply to them and they cannot become fully clean. They think that "with a lot of repenting on my part and a lot of forgiving on the Savior's part, He can get my soul to a light shade of pink but not totally white or clean."

They have "pink Latter-day Saint thinking" such as, "No one will want to take someone like me to the temple. I will never be able to effectively teach the law of chastity to my own children because I messed up. I will not be a good missionary since I need to wait a year to serve. I won't be as effective in my calling as so-and-so because I bet they never messed up like I did."

Please do not be a pink Latter-day Saint. If you do this, you are not taking full advantage of the gift of the Atonement of Jesus Christ and His promise in Isaiah 1:18. C. S. Lewis agreed: "If God forgives us, we must forgive ourselves. Otherwise it's like setting up ourselves as a higher tribunal than Him."[19]

Perhaps this is similar to Elder Uchtdorf's talk[20] about living below our privileges, like the person on the cruise who didn't

---

17. Please read Ethan Bakker's story on page 191 for his positive repentance experience with his second bishop and stake presidency.

18. The concept of "a pink Latter-day Saint" was taught to me by Brother S. Michael Wilcox.

19. C. S. Lewis, *Collected Letters of C. S. Lewis,* (San Francisco: Harper, 2006).

20. Dieter F. Uchtdorf, "Your Potential, Your Privilege," April 2011 general conference, churchofjesuschrist.org/study/general-conference/2011/04/your-potential-your-privilege.

understand that the food on the ship was already paid for as part of the ticket and needlessly denied himself joy.

## Repentance as a Spiral Staircase

My friend Hayden Paul (who talked about resolving pornography use in chapter 4) shared these excellent thoughts about repentance:

> I don't see repentance as an action with a start and end. It should be an ever-present attitude, a constant desire to improve and reconcile oneself with God. It is a hunger to be closer to Him and more like Him.
>
> Without conscious thought, it's easy to separate things into black and white categories—good or bad, positive or negative, healthy or not healthy, and the list goes on. Sometimes our minds use this as a coping mechanism to avoid intricacies about ourselves or the world that we don't fully understand. We like to have answers, and we save our brains a lot of energy by creating simple, distinct categories. It's easier than trying to figure out the gray area.
>
> However, this can be detrimental to progression, especially when we make the same mistake repeatedly. It can be frustrating to "relapse, repent, repeat," and easy to fall into a good/bad mindset: "Well, I messed up again. Obviously, nothing I've done works, and I'm starting from the beginning AGAIN."
>
> Instead of viewing this effort as an all-or-nothing endeavor of being a complete success or a complete failure, try viewing your recovery as a spiral staircase. Sure, you're moving in circles, but with every cycle, you also ascend higher and higher. You're looking for progress, not perfection.
>
> At its core, the gospel of Jesus Christ is a single, never-ending cycle. The doctrine includes faith in the Lord, repentance, baptism, receiving the gift of the Holy Ghost, and enduring to the end. We are not repeatedly baptized and confirmed, but we sincerely partake of the sacrament to renew our covenants and be forgiven of the mistakes and sins of the previous week. We implement these basic principles over and over again, allowing the grace of Christ to slowly change us. The cycle may feel repetitive, and it is. But it is the only way to ascend.

# CHaPTeR 6

# CREATING BETTER UNDERSTANDING OF MENTAL ILLNESS AND SUICIDE

At times, faithful Latter-day Saints can experience mental illness[1] and even feelings of suicide. Our Church culture should provide love and support—not create a feeling that mental illness is a sign of weakness or a spiritual deficit. In fact, everyone should feel that church is a safe place as they work through these difficulties.[2] Hopefully we will not look down on them, limit their chances to contribute to, or dismiss, discussions about mental health as inappropriate. Judgment can create shame and isolation, discouraging members with mental health issues from attending church and receiving the blessings of taking the sacrament and serving others.

Further, we especially need to gain a better understanding of suicide, so people with suicidal feelings can get the help they need. Talking about suicide in appropriate ways actually helps prevent suicide and saves lives.

---

1. This chapter uses "mental illness" as an umbrella term for health conditions involving changes in emotion, thinking, or behavior, or a combination of these.

2. The Church has provided resources to leaders and families about mental health at "Mental Health," Counseling Resources, The Church of Jesus Christ of Latter-day Saints, churchofjesuschrist.org/study/manual/counseling-resources/mental-health (may be accessible to only members of ward and stake councils).

## Elder Holland: "Like a Broken Vessel"

I will never forget Elder Holland's 2013 general conference message:

> Let me concentrate on MDD—"major depressive disorder"—or, more commonly, "depression." When I speak of this, I am not speaking of bad hair days, tax deadlines, or other discouraging moments we all have. Everyone is going to be anxious or downhearted on occasion. The Book of Mormon says Ammon and his brethren were depressed at a very difficult time, and so can the rest of us be. But today I am speaking of something more serious, of an affliction so severe that it significantly restricts a person's ability to function fully, a crater in the mind so deep that no one can responsibly suggest it would surely go away if those victims would just square their shoulders and think more positively—though I am a vigorous advocate of square shoulders and positive thinking!
>
> No, this dark night of the mind and spirit is more than mere discouragement. I have seen it come to an absolutely angelic man when his beloved spouse of fifty years passed away. I have seen it in new mothers with what is euphemistically labeled "after-baby blues." I have seen it strike anxious students, military veterans, and grandmothers worried about the well-being of their grown children. And I have seen it in young fathers trying to provide for their families.[3]

I thought Elder Holland would end there, with this list of general challenges. But in an extraordinary moment of vulnerability, Elder Holland pivoted and publicly revealed a personal story about his own mental health:

> In that regard I once terrifyingly saw it in myself. At one point in our married life when financial fears collided with staggering fatigue, I took a psychic blow that was as unanticipated as it was real. With the grace of God and the love of my family, I kept functioning and kept working, but even after all these years

---

3.  Jeffrey R. Holland, "Like a Broken Vessel," October 2013 general conference, churchofjesuschrist.org/study/general-conference/2013/10/like-a-broken-vessel.

I continue to feel a deep sympathy for others more chronically or more deeply afflicted with such gloom than I was.

As Elder Holland shared his journey, my love, respect, empathy, and admiration for him increased. In no way was his apostolic calling diminished—rather, I found myself praying more for his success as I knew more about his journey. Further, I knew that if I were in a situation to share with Elder Holland about my own mental health, he would be a safe person and respond with empathy and kindness.

One of the gifts of Elder Holland's talk was to normalize mental health challenges and talking about them in church settings. If an Apostle was willing to share this kind of personal challenge in a general conference talk that would be read and viewed worldwide for years to come, maybe it is okay that we have similar challenges. I hope we can talk about those trials with members of our ward, trusted friends, and family. I believe that we better realize as a Church that mental health issues are not spiritual weakness, since we obviously do not consider Elder Holland in this category. I believe we also more fully understand and accept the role of therapists to manage and resolve these kinds of health challenges.

Another gift is to help us see our leaders as human, which allows all of us to be more human in our church assignments and everyday lives as well. I worry that our culture has created an expectation that our leaders have reached a point in their mortal journey that they are almost knocking on the door of perfection. No leader I know feels that they are near-perfect, but our culture sometimes elevates them to this place. When we do this, it can make them less relatable and approachable for ordinary members.

This is one of the reasons I love the Psalm of Nephi in 2 Nephi 4, mentioned earlier. Nephi's prophetic ministry was not diminished as he opened his heart to his readers, the people of our day, exclaiming in anguish, "O wretched man that I am! Yea, my heart sorroweth because of my flesh; my soul grieveth because of mine iniquities. I am encompassed about, because of the temptations and the sins which do so easily beset me. And when I desire to rejoice, my heart groaneth because of my sins; nevertheless, I know in whom I have trusted" (2 Nephi 4:17–19).

## Trials Can Help Us Help Others

When Elder Holland opened up about his own mental health issues, he became a "wounded healer." He can authentically talk about a "desert" that some experience, as taught by Catholic priest Henri Nouwen: "A minister's service will not be perceived as authentic unless it comes from a heart wounded by the suffering about which he speaks. The great illusion of leadership is to think that others can be led out of the desert by someone who has never been there."[4]

Since Elder Holland knows about mental health challenges, we can trust him to lead us out of that specific desert. He can also relate to and help others in similar deserts, such as physical illness or financial loss. His experiences, while painful and discouraging at times, have enhanced his mission to bless others. We too can reflect on our difficult experiences and become "wounded healers" to help lead others out of their deserts. This is one of the greatest gifts I know—that our trials can be used in a uniquely positive way to bless others.

I have been to a therapist twice in my life for my mental health—during my early teenage years, and later while serving as a YSA bishop. My diagnosis as an adult is dysthymia, which is still part of my life.[5] The song lyrics "Hello darkness, my old friend,"[6] remind me of my ongoing journey with this mental health issue. I am grateful for my dear wife, Sheila, who is always at my side to provide hope, prayers, and encouragement, and my brother Steve who gave me a book called *Deliverance from Depression*,[7] which reframed my understanding about depression. The authors, three members of the Vandagriff family, taught me how brain chemistry

---

4. Henri J. M. Nouwen, *The Wounded Healer: Ministry in Contemporary Society* (New York: Doubleday, 1972).

5. Dysthymia is a mild but long-term form of depression. See hopkinsmedicine. org/health/conditions-and-diseases/dysthymia.

6. Paul Simon, "The Sound of Silence," recorded by Simon and Garfunkel, *Wednesday Morning, 3 A.M.*, released October 19, 1964. Also performed by Disturbed, Pentatonix, and other artists.

7. G.G. Vandagriff, Greg Vandagriff, David P. Vandagriff, *Deliverance From Depression* (American Fork UT: Covenant Communications, 2008).

can lead to depression and how the right medication(s) can resolve brain chemistry issues and help to manage depression. Further, they teach about finding hope and healing through the Atonement of Jesus Christ.

To be honest, I felt shame wondering if the YSAs in our ward would think their own bishop was "so weak" that he needed to seek treatment from a therapist. I was glad my therapist's office was in a different area of town so no one would see me walk into the building. Since being released from my calling, I have concluded I should have felt no shame for my mental health challenges. They were not because of a spiritual weakness, and my diagnosis did not impact my ability to serve the members of my ward. If I had realized this, I might have been receptive to spiritual promptings to share about my own mental health in appropriate situations, as Elder Holland did, to help others walking a similar road and let them know I am a safe person to discuss their own situation.

Further, my mental health challenges have helped me develop more compassion, empathy, and understanding for others. I believe it has made me a better husband, priesthood holder, friend, and father. On some level, I am grateful to be on this road. I love these additional insights from Nouwen:

> Over the last few years I have been increasingly aware that true healing mostly takes place through the sharing of weakness. Mostly we are so afraid of our weaknesses that we hide them at all costs and thus make them unavailable to others but also often to ourselves. And, in this way, we end up living double lives even against our own desires: one life in which we present ourselves to the world, to ourselves, and to God as a person who is in control and another life in which we feel insecure, doubtful, confused, and anxious and totally out of control. The split between these two lives causes us a lot of suffering. I have become increasingly aware of the importance of overcoming the great chasm between these two lives and am becoming more and more aware that facing, with others, the reality of our existence can be the beginning of a truly free life.
>
> It is amazing in my own life that true friendship and community became possible to the degree that I was able to share my weaknesses with others. Often I became aware of the fact

that in the sharing of my weaknesses with others, the real depths of my human brokenness and weakness and sinfulness started to reveal themselves to me, not as a source of despair but as a source of hope. As long as I try to convince myself or others of my independence, a lot of my energy is invested in building up my own false self. But once I am able to truly confess my most profound dependence on others and on God, I can come in touch with my true self and real community can develop.[8]

In many *Listen, Learn & Love* podcasts,[9] brave guests have stepped forward to share their experiences. They are some of my heroes. Hearing their stories has helped me and given me more tools and insights to help others.

One of my guests is my friend Jane Clayson Johnson,[10] who wrote the book *Silent Souls Weeping.*[11] I encourage everyone who wants to learn more about depression to read Jane's book. She is brave. She is a wounded healer. She is one of my heroes.

## Trauma as a "Scratched Record"

In July 2021, I did a podcast with Dr. Christy Kane[12] about her book *Fractured Souls and Splintered Memories: Unlocking the "Boxes" of Trauma.*[13] Dr. Kane said,

Trauma is like those old records that get scratched. On a scratched record, every time you play it, the needle goes to the scratch and kicks back. You never get to the end of the song.

---

8. "Sharing Our Weakness," *Meditations*, Henri Nouwen Society; accessed December 19, 2019, henrinouwen.org/meditation/sharing-our-weakness/.

9. See listenlearnandlove.org/depression-mental-illness-podcasts for episodes focused on depression and mental illness.

10. *Listen, Learn & Love* podcast episode 100.

11. Jane Clayson Johnson, *Silent Souls Weeping: Depression, Sharing Stories, Finding Hope* (Salt Lake City: Deseret Book, 2019).

12. *Listen, Learn & Love* podcast episode 429.

13. Dr. Christy Kane, *Fractured Souls and Splintered Memories: Unlocking the "Boxes" of Trauma* (Springville UT: Cedar Fort Publishing, 2021).

Trauma scratches the brain. That pain and those difficult emotions stay trapped. Therapy helps you play it through to the end of the record. It doesn't erase the memories or make them go away, but it takes the pain and the darkness out. It brings the darkness into the light and allows it to heal.

When I heard this analogy from Dr. Kane during the podcast, it immediately resonated with me as a tool to get past some of the scratches on my own record, to help me get to the end of my song.

## Suicide[14]

A few with major mental health challenges die by suicide. Sister Reyna I. Aburto of the Relief Society General Presidency was surprisingly frank about mental illness in her family during her 2019 general conference talk:

> Untreated mental or emotional illness can lead to increased isolation, misunderstandings, broken relationships, self-harm, and even suicide. I know this firsthand, as my own father died by suicide many years ago. His death was shocking and heartbreaking for my family and me. It has taken me years to work through my grief, and it was only recently that I learned talking about suicide in appropriate ways actually helps to prevent it rather than encourage it. I have now openly discussed my father's death with my children and witnessed the healing that the Savior can give on both sides of the veil. . . .
>
> Sadly, many who suffer from severe depression distance themselves from their fellow Saints because they feel they do not fit some imaginary mold. We can help them know and feel that they do indeed belong with us. It is important to recognize that depression is not the result of weakness, nor is it usually the result of sin. It thrives in secrecy but shrinks in empathy. Together,

---

14. In conversations about suicide, I've learned that most experts use the term "died by suicide" rather than "committed suicide." That is because "commit" is a word frequently associated with blame, such as commit a crime or commit a sin. "Died by suicide" is a more neutral and compassionate phrase.

we can break through the clouds of isolation and stigma so the burden of shame is lifted and miracles of healing can occur.[15]

I am grateful for Sister Aburto's inspired words to help normalize talking about suicide and mental illness. She has helped us understand that talking about these subjects brings us together in ways that build empathy and understanding. Even more important, her words help reduce suicide and bring more support to families that have lost someone to suicide.

## Talking about Suicide

Suicide is an unimaginable tragedy for the person and their family and friends. It is one of the most devastating trials a family can experience, and we should all do everything we can, individually and collectively, to help keep our friends and loved ones from making this choice. In 2018, the Church updated its online video library[16] and included a section on better understanding suicide. Elder Dale G. Renlund made several important statements in three short videos within this collection:

> There's an old sectarian notion that suicide is a sin and that someone who commits suicide is banished to hell forever. That is totally false. I believe that in the vast majority of cases we'll find that these individuals have lived heroic lives and that that suicide will not be a defining characteristic of their eternities. What we need to do as a church is to reach out in love and caring for those who have suicidal thoughts, who have attempted suicide, who feel marginalized in any way. We need to reach out with love and understanding.[17]
>
> This is now beyond that they need to read the scriptures or

---

15. Reyna I. Aburto, "Thru Cloud and Sunshine, Lord, Abide with Me!" October 2019 general conference, churchofjesuschrist.org/study/general-conference/2019/10/31aburto.

16. "Suicide," Gospel Media, The Church of Jesus Christ of Latter-day Saints, accessed January 2021, churchofjesuschrist.org/media/collection/suicide-topic.

17. Dale G. Renlund, "Understanding Suicide," The Church of Jesus Christ of Latter-day Saints, 2:22, churchofjesuschrist.org/media/video/2018-06-0020-renlund-understanding-suicide.

pray more fervently, or exercise more faith. Those things will become important, but right now, you need more help. The best thing is if you genuinely love the person, then you're willing to sit there with them and you're willing to cry with them and you're willing to hold them. And you do that in concert with health-care professionals and with ecclesiastical leaders, with friends and family support.[18]

The Lord will help us. There's this particular verse that Isaiah gives that is remarkable. He says, when you are weary, He, the Savior, "wakeneth morning by morning" (Isaiah 50:4). He's there every day. He neither slumbers nor sleeps. So if the best you can do is to get up and out of bed in the morning, just know that He's there with you. He's there to help you. The Savior will sanctify to you your deepest distress.[19]

When families and congregations watch these videos together and have needed conversations on this sensitive topic, we help heal families who have lost a loved one to suicide and reduce the chance that someone will choose to die by suicide.[20]

## Asking Someone If They Are Suicidal

I have learned to ask if someone is suicidal. I am direct when I ask this question. If they say yes, I ask them if they have a plan. I ask them the details of the plan. I ask if they have a specific date. Experts in the field have taught me that doing this helps reduce the chance that someone will die by suicide. It also allows me to connect them with appropriate mental health resources.

---

18. Dale G. Renlund, "Talking About Suicide," The Church of Jesus Christ of Latter-day Saints, 1:45, churchofjesuschrist.org/media/video/2018-06-0040-renlund-talking-about-suicide.

19. Dale G. Renlund, "Grieving After a Suicide," The Church of Jesus Christ of Latter-day Saints, 2:06, churchofjesuschrist.org/media/video/2018-06-0050-renlund-grieving-after-a-suicide.

20. The Church has provided resources to leaders and families at "Suicide," Counseling Resources, The Church of Jesus Christ of Latter-day Saints, churchofjesuschrist.org/study/manual/counseling-resources/suicide (may be accessible to only members of ward and stake councils).

I started doing this during my YSA assignment when someone confided in me about their mental health or made general comments about "not feeling very good." I have continued to ask this question when visiting with LGBTQ Latter-day Saints. I have asked this question hundreds of times and have never had anyone report being offended because I asked.

Further, I have learned that when I ask more general questions, such as, "Could you hurt yourself?" they may not feel safe enough to fully disclose their true thoughts or plans. They may conclude that it is only safe to talk with me in general terms about hurting themselves and not about suicide. In my experience, people who are suicidal are looking for safe people with whom to share the totality of what they are feeling and/or planning. I believe all of this is consistent with the words of Elder Renlund: "It's completely safe, *completely safe* to ask someone if they're having suicidal thoughts. . . . A great way is to just reach out and hold them by the hand, look them in the eyes and ask. . . . And if they pause for a long time and say, 'Maybe,' that should raise the red flag."[21]

Sister Aburto also taught this principle: "I learned talking about suicide in appropriate ways actually helps to prevent it rather than encourage it."[22]

## Podcasts about Suicide

The *Listen, Learn & Love* podcast has many episodes focused on suicide prevention.[23] We also have podcasts from those who have lost a family member to suicide, including Leanne Tressler,[24] who lost both her husband and son to suicide; Heidi and Eric Swapp,[25] who lost their son to suicide; and many others who bravely share

21. Renlund, "Talking about Suicide."
22. Aburto, "Thru Cloud and Sunshine, Lord, Abide with Me!"
23. See listenlearnandlove.org/suicide-podcasts for episodes focused on suicide prevention.
24. *Listen, Learn & Love* podcast episode 176.
25. *Listen, Learn & Love* podcast episode 121.

their stories. Some were close to suicide themselves, including my dear friend and ward member Joseph Cramer.[26] Joseph had a successful medical career (residency at Duke University, over thirty years as a successful pediatrician, and president of the Utah Medical Association) and a great family (wonderful wife, five children, and thirteen grandchildren), but was suffering with mental health challenges. We discussed how he got to the point of considering suicide and what led him away from the path of making that choice. We also have interviewed experts working to solve suicide, including Dr. Jeff Case, clinical psychologist,[27] and Dr. Scott Braithwaite,[28] BYU associate professor of psychology.

## The Joiner Model of Suicidality

Both Dr. Case and Dr. Braithwaite talk about a model developed by clinical psychologist Dr. Thomas Joiner. As a person without any training in this area, I have found this model very useful to better understand why someone might be suicidal.

1. **Perceived burdensomeness:** the view that one's existence burdens family, friends, and/or society. This leads to the idea that "my death will be worth more than my life to family, friends, society, and so on." It is important to emphasize that this view represents a potentially fatal misperception.

2. **Low belonging/social alienation:** the experience that one is alienated from others, not an integral part of a family, circle of friends, or other valued group.

3. **Acquired ability to enact lethal self-injury:** While feelings of burdensomeness and low belongingness may instill a desire for suicide, they are not sufficient to ensure that desire will lead fully to a suicide attempt. Indeed, for this to occur, a third element must be present: the acquired ability for

---

26. *Listen, Learn & Love* podcast episode 220.
27. *Listen, Learn & Love* podcast episode 86.
28. *Listen, Learn & Love* podcast episode 193.

lethal self-injury. This aspect of the theory suggests that suicide entails a fight with self-preservation motives. Fighting this battle repeatedly and in different domains instills the capacity to stare down and override the self-preservation instinct, should an individual develop the desire to.[29]

This model helped me better understand the unique road of LGBTQ Latter-day Saints in particular, and why some consider suicide. In point 1, some **incorrectly conclude** that their existence is ruining their eternal family and their family would be better off without them. In point 2, some feel they do not belong—that they are not welcome or needed in our church community, family, or society. I believe helping someone genuinely feel they belong is one of the greatest gifts you can give. President Ballard invited us to do just that in his April 2021 general conference talk:

> The Quorum of the Twelve Apostles have counseled together in a spirit of prayer and with a yearning to understand how to help all who feel alone or feel they don't belong. We long to help all who feel this way. Never forget that you are a child of God, our Eternal Father, now and forever. He loves you, and the Church wants and needs you. Yes, we need you! We need your voices, talents, skills, goodness, and righteousness. The gospel of Jesus Christ has the power to unite us. We are ultimately more alike than we are different. As members of God's family, we are truly brothers and sisters.[30]

Dr. Brené Brown captures the overwhelming feeling of not belonging and being powerless to change the situation:

> The most terrifying and destructive feeling that a person can experience is psychological isolation. This is not the same as being alone. It is a feeling that one is **locked out of the possibility**

---

29. Dr. Thomas Joiner, "The interpersonal-psychological theory of suicidal behavior: Current empirical status," *Psychological Science Agenda*, American Psychological Association, June 2009, apa.org/science/about/psa/2009/06/sci-brief.

30. Ballard, "Hope in Christ."

**of human connection and of being powerless to change the situation**. In the extreme, psychological isolation can lead to a sense of hopelessness and desperation. People will do almost anything to escape this combination of condemned isolation and powerlessness.[31]

This is particularly relevant to LGBTQ Latter-day Saints. Just like those with red hair or blue eyes did not choose those attributes, LGBTQ Latter-day Saints did not choose their sexual orientation or gender identity—so there is no path to "unchoose" this attribute to belong in a heteronormative world.[32] Indeed, the Church states that "a change in attraction should not be expected or demanded as an outcome by parents or leaders."[33] Similarly, Elder Holland also taught this in his October 2015 general conference address when he spoke of a missionary with same-sex attraction and his wonderful mother.[34] After describing their challenges, Elder Holland commented, "And, I must say, this son's sexual orientation *did not somehow miraculously change—no one assumed it would*."[35]

Furthermore, LGBTQ Latter-day Saints not only cannot change their sexual orientation or gender identity, but they also generally feel powerless to change Church culture in which they often do not feel fully accepted. They may see no way out of the

---

31. Dr. Brené Brown, *Daring Greatly: How the Courage to be Vulnerable Transforms the Way We Live, Love, Parent, and Lead* (New York: Gotham Books, 2012), 140.

32. Please see chapter 3 of Richard Ostler, *Listen, Learn & Love, Embracing LGBTQ Latter-day Saints* (Springville UT: Cedar Fort Publishing, 2020), 35–39. "False Statements on Why People are LGBTQ" includes responses from LGBTQ individuals about the allegation that they "choose" to be gay.

33. "Same-Sex Attraction," Gospel Topics, The Church of Jesus Christ of Latter-day Saints, accessed February 19, 2021, churchofjesuschrist.org/topics/gay/individuals, emphasis added.

34. The missionary in Elder Holland's talk is Preston Jenkins, who shared his story on *Listen, Learn & Love* podcast episode 237.

35. Jeffrey R. Holland, "Behold Thy Mother," October 2015 general conference, churchofjesuschrist.org/study/general-conference/2015/10/behold-thy-mother; emphasis added.

psychological isolation and consider suicide. They are a square peg in a world of round holes with no path to either become a round peg or create square holes.

Dr. Brown explains the powerful difference between belonging and fitting in: "Fitting in is about assessing a situation and becoming who you need to be in order to be accepted. Belonging, on the other hand, doesn't require us to change who we are; it requires us to *be* who we are."[36] The Joiner model and Dr. Brown's insights can be foundational in discussions with our families and congregations to create holes of every shape, so LGBTQ members feel they belong in our church, families and society.

Coming out for LGBTQ Latter-day Saints can strengthen belonging as people accept them for who they are. We should work to create an environment so that those who wish to come out can do so with confidence that they will be met with love and support. However, there should be no universal requirement for our LGBTQ members to come out. I'm sure there are closeted LGBTQ members who do not feel a desire or need to come out, and I do not see those individuals as weak or inauthentic. I believe they are working with their Heavenly Parents to receive personal revelation for their best path forward.

## To Those Considering Suicide

If you are considering suicide, please stay. Please. Even if it feels like there is no light at the end of the tunnel, I promise it will get better. I also promise you that your older self will be glad you stayed. In March 2020, I asked on Twitter for those who were once suicidal to give advice to those who are currently suicidal. Here are some of their responses:[37]

---

36. Brown, *Daring Greatly*, 232.

37. @Papa_Ostler (Richard Ostler). "For those of you that have been suicidal and are now OK, what would you say to those reading this thread who are suicidal? Please stay." *Twitter*, March 23, 2020, 1:52 p.m., twitter.com/Papa_Ostler/status/1242147102773243904.

- Take things one day at a time. Every day you make it is another victory. You are loved by those around you. You'll look back down the road and be so glad you stayed.
- No matter what, no one is ever better off without you. Even if you've made huge mistakes. The world needs what YOU have to offer.
- Breathe. Take a walk. Play with puppies. Do anything but get out of your head. Reach out. Please stay. Someone needs you. You need you.
- It's worth it. There are brighter days ahead amidst the darkness.
- I'm glad I didn't do it. It took about 2 months after that day for life to start improving and another 3 years for things to become something approaching normal, but I have a really, really good life now.
- Get a psychiatrist, be brutally honest.
- Depression lies. Life gets better. It gets better. Hold on. These words seem so simple, but every time it gets too hard, I just hold on a little longer.
- I still struggle with suicidal thoughts, but I'm glad to still be here. Tell people how low you are so you can get help. Staying is worth it.
- If you are feeling a wave of suicidal thoughts right now - get up, jog in place, crank up the music and dance the biggest dance you can. If you can't stand - wave your arms above your head, roll your eyes around your head, blink and open, blink and open. Deep breaths.
- Something my dad told me: don't make a permanent solution for a temporary problem. It's always stuck with me.
- Text "help" to 741741 to talk to a crisis counselor, 24/7.
- Whatever motive you need to stay alive is worth it. It can be something like family or pets, but it can also be spite, or you want to see what meme the internet comes up with next week. It doesn't need to be big and meaningful because living is living no matter the reason.
- I tried. I'm so glad I failed. It was hard. At first, I thought it was just something else I'd failed at. Over time, I learned that I was loved. You too are loved. All of you. You are enough. You are complete. You are exactly who God designed you to be.

- You may think that no one will miss you or even care that you're gone. That's what I thought. Then one of my friends took his life last year and I got to see the other side. It sucks. You're NOT alone and people WILL miss you! Reach out before you give in.
- You are loved by so many people you haven't met yet.
- We can choose 2 live 4 the sake of loved ones & the small joys of life. The waves of despair r real, but they also subside. Please stay 2 witness the rest of ur life's painting. There r deep shades, but countless beautiful colors await as well. Ur going 2 b alright! Ur not alone.

Elder Renlund provides hope in these comments: "In most cases, people continue to have a burden, but the burden can be made lighter. And as that happens, joy can fill their soul again."[38]

I close with a story from my good friend, author Drew Young:

> In The Church of Jesus Christ of Latter-day Saints, mental health and suicide can be very touchy subjects. I don't know that either was publicly addressed by a General Authority until Elder Holland's talk, "Like a Broken Vessel," in the October 2013 general conference.
>
> I grew up with separation anxiety, experiencing panic attacks, fear, and homesickness for much of my childhood. This led to incessant bullying from peers within church, school, and Scout groups during my middle school years. Kids thought I was a baby and couldn't handle being away from home. When I reached high school, my anxiety subsided enough for me to play sports, make friends, and prepare to serve a full-time mission.
>
> At the MTC, I experienced anxiety again, but this time was different. It wasn't the usual "homesick" separation anxiety that caused me so much grief as a child. I literally felt ill. I gained an unhealthy amount of weight, and I was sleeping too much or not at all. My anxiety would not subside no matter how much I prayed, read the scriptures, exercised, etc., and I believed that nothing I

---

38. Renlund, "Talking about Suicide."

did was good enough. These symptoms led me to seek medical and therapeutic help for the first time in my life. I was prescribed anti-anxiety medication and visited the therapist at the MTC once a week. I knew I was emotionally and mentally unstable.

Every time I wrote home to my parents or talked to the MTC leadership, the answers were always the same: "Don't worry, we'll fast for you to get better." Or, "Elder Young, you just need to forget yourself and go to work." Or, "Spend less time worrying and more time praying." Or, "If you come home early, Satan will have won."

They were well-intentioned, but woefully misinformed and harmful. Due to my severe mental health challenges, I was sent home after only nine weeks of service.

The following four years consisted of medication changes, bi-weekly therapy visits, family and Church members telling me to suck it up, frequent panic attacks, nights of soul-crushing depression that left me on my bedroom floor reeling in emotional pain, and the occasional thought that ending my life would be better than continuing it.

One particular night, I thought, "I can't do this anymore." I planned to take my own life, but just before I was going to execute my strategy, I called a friend who helped me realize what I was about to do.

I have now found the medication that I will take daily for the foreseeable future, and I LOVE IT.

I have now found the therapist that I will see once a month for the foreseeable future, and I LOVE IT.

I have now become a strong mental health, suicide prevention, life advocate, and I LOVE IT.

If I could share any message, whether you believe that mental illness is "fake" or "all in your head," or you experience emotional trauma and suicidal thoughts, please take this to heart:

Mental illness is NOT mental weakness.

Mental illness is NOT a personal failure.

Emotional trauma or suicidal thoughts do not make someone "crazy."

The stigmas must stop. The judging must stop. The unrealistic expectations we put on our families, friends, and colleagues must stop. It's time to show compassion, educate ourselves about mental health, and come together to love one another and be there for each other when hard times come.

I am grateful for all the lessons my mental health challenges have taught me, and for the opportunity I have now to help others make it through their trials, knowing they are more than enough to overcome and triumph.[39]

---

39. Drew B. Young, *Stand Guard at the Door of Your Mind* (Springville UT: Cedar Fort Publishing, 2021). Drew has published two books, is a life coach at @mrdrewbyoung, and has been interviewed on the *Listen, Learn & Love* podcast episodes 276, 325, and 419.

# CHapTeR 7

# OVERCOMING SCRUPULOSITY (RELIGIOUS OCD)

In chapter 6, we talked about improving our culture to better understand emotional health. This chapter continues the discussion with a specific emotional health challenge called *scrupulosity*. I wanted to dedicate a full chapter to this topic so that more Latter-day Saints understand scrupulosity. I wish I had known about it before I became a parent and before I had any Church assignments. It would have given me better tools to end needless suffering in others.

I would like to introduce this topic with a story that is very meaningful to our family about our son Ben, the youngest of our six children and our fourth missionary. As Sheila and I dropped him off at the Missionary Training Center in July 2019, we were confident that he would, like his older brothers, have a wonderful and positive experience to help people come unto Christ. We felt Ben was prepared—he had the benefit of his older brothers' examples, missionary experiences, and influence. He had wonderful and experienced ward and stake leaders assisting him in preparation.

Further, Ben had a track record of doing hard things. One example was his experience with football. Ben played Little League football but "hung up his cleats" at age eleven and donated his jersey, with *Ostler* printed on the back, to Deseret Industries. As a side story, two years later, that same jersey was spotted in western Africa.

Ben's uncle and aunt, David and Rachelle Ostler, were presiding over the Sierra Leone Freetown Mission when they saw a young man walking on a backroad, wearing a football jersey with *Ostler* on the back. They were astonished to see their name on a shirt worn by a young man in Africa. It felt like a tender mercy, a literal sign that our Heavenly Parents were aware of them. (The story was shared by the local Utah media, including pictures of the jersey.[1]) Our entire family's testimony was strengthened of the Savior's love and reassurance of our Heavenly Parents' concern for each of us.

When Ben was in high school, he sat in the stands and cheered on the football team, which was shorthanded and experiencing difficult seasons. After his junior year and with the encouragement of friends like quarterback Hunter Workman, Ben courageously decided to put back on those "hung-up cleats" as he walked on to his high school football team as a senior. Ben played offense, defense, and special teams, and worked through injuries and a difficult season. Not one to quit, Ben was committed to his team, coach, and school to the end. That commitment paid off in the last play of the last game of the season, as Ben caught a touchdown pass—his only touchdown catch. His quarterback friend Hunter called an audible—overriding the coach's instructions—for a Hail Mary pass to Ben. I think Coach Bart Bowen—a great coach, mentor, and human being—forgave the boys. Ben was also the field goal kicker and successfully kicked the ugliest extra-point kick I have ever witnessed. Sheila and I joined Ben and his teammates on the field for the celebration, and as he earned First Team[2] regional honors as a wide receiver.

---

1.   Nkoyo Iyamba, "Boy's donated jersey creates connections across the globe," *KSL News,* March 21, 2014, ksl.com/article/29158959/boys-donated-jersey-creates-connections-across-the-globe.

2.   James Edward, "High school football: All-region teams announced for 6A, 5A, 4A, 3A," *Deseret News,* December 17, 2018, deseret.com/2018/12/17/20661411/high-school-football-all-region-teams-announced-for-6a-5a-4a-3a. See also Brian Shaw, "Cottonwood football wraps up 2018 season with marked statistical improvement," *South Salt Lake Journal,* November 26, 2018, southsaltlakejournal.com/2018/11/26/184591/cottonwood-football-wraps-up-2018-season-with-marked-statistical-improvement.

Ben had many Polynesian friends among his teammates and spent the previous summer doing humanitarian work in Samoa. So our entire family was delighted with his mission assignment to Samoa. He felt deeply connected to the Polynesian people and culture, and would be serving a people and an area he already loved.

While not perfect, Ben was faithful and righteous with a strong testimony of the Church and a love for our Savior and for others. He was leaving his long-time girlfriend, Summer, who was headed out on a mission to Australia.

All these experiences gave us peace, hope, and confidence that Elder Ostler would be a successful missionary as Sheila and I drove home from the Missionary Training Center after dropping him off. While we prayed for Ben's success to find people and be protected, it never crossed our minds that his experience would expose his personal struggle with scrupulosity.

That began to change in the MTC. Elder Ostler reported having a hard time feeling the Spirit and feeling worthy to be a missionary. No serious sins, just a general feeling of unworthiness. We encouraged him, chalked it up to normal homesickness, and believed that everything would be fine once he got to Samoa.

However, after the initial excitement of being in Samoa, Elder Ostler opened up to us in his emails and video chats. He spoke about not feeling the Spirit, not feeling worthy, not feeling like he belonged there, and being in a dark place. As his parents, we were worried. This was a complete surprise. We were pleased that Elder Ostler told us his actual feelings, but we were stumped. We realized this was different from normal homesickness.

Things continued to go downhill for Elder Ostler. He talked openly about coming home rather than completing his time of service. We were supportive if that was his decision, especially since we were genuinely concerned about his emotional well-being. Our normally happy and positive son was in a dark place, which was totally new territory for all of us.

In counseling with our bishop, Jim Campbell, we learned that Elder Ostler frequently emailed him from Samoa to re-confess minor sins from before his mission, sins that did not even require speaking with a bishop. Then our stake president, David Sturt, got involved as well. These priesthood leaders reassured him that he was worthy; there was no belated confession at the root of this situation. But the cycle repeated itself in a way that I had never witnessed. We all realized something different was happening that we did not understand.

There were pieces of the puzzle that we were not seeing, and our combined life experiences did not give us the tools to find what was missing. Sheila and I fasted, attended the temple, and prayed. We are forever grateful to Bishop Campbell, President Sturt, and Ben's mission president (President and Sister Ho Ching) for going slowly, not overreacting, and trying to understand his unique situation before deciding the correct next steps. Importantly, along with his leaders, we felt Elder Ostler was emotionally stable enough to continue to serve while making decisions about his future.

During this time, while my wife and I were praying for more personal revelation for our missionary son, I had lunch with my friend Kent Griffiths, a well-respected marriage and family therapist in Salt Lake City.[3] Sheila and I had kept the situation confidential, but I felt impressed to make an exception and confide in Kent. After about five minutes of listening, Kent typed something into a search engine on his phone and handed it to me. There was the description of *scrupulosity*. The definition fit Ben's situation perfectly. We will be forever grateful for Kent and his inspired expertise to point us to the path of healing for Elder Ostler. We were hopeful that we had finally found the missing piece of the puzzle.

## Unexpected *Ensign* Article

I shared this information with Sheila. She found an *Ensign* article on scrupulosity by Dr. Debra Theobald McClendon that had been published just one month earlier—the first article ever in a Church publication on this subject. Dr. McClendon wrote: "Do you

---

3.   See riverside-chats.com/about.

constantly obsess about living the gospel the "right" way? Do you feel an urgency to repent for the same mistake or sin over and over again because you doubt whether you have repented "properly"? Do you feel perpetually guilty? If so, you might be struggling with a form of obsessive-compulsive disorder (OCD) known as scrupulosity."[4]

As we read that article, we learned that this is not a spiritual weakness, but an emotional illness. More specifically, it is an anxiety disorder. This particular anxiety disorder requires OCD treatment—not just a greater level of personal worship activities (such as more prayer, more confession, more scripture study, and so on) or even getting some "general" counseling. While not clinically trained, we felt reasonably confident that we had an accurate diagnosis. We shared the information with President Sturt, who worked with President Ho Ching in Samoa to get our son access to a therapist. We were blessed to learn that Elder John and Sister Becky Edwards, full-time welfare self-reliance missionaries, were serving on the same island as Elder Ostler. Sister Edwards has a master of social work degree from BYU and is a marriage and family therapist.

Sheila pointed out that Heavenly Father was in the details—Sister Edwards, an experienced therapist with expertise in this area, was on the same island as Elder Ostler and able to meet with him in person.[5] Prayers are often answered through others, and this was certainly the case with the Edwards coming into Elder Ostler's life.[6] We will be forever grateful to this couple.

We contacted Sister Edwards so she was aware of the tentative diagnosis as she helped Elder Ostler. We also contacted Dr. McClendon and interviewed her on the *Listen, Learn & Love* podcast as a follow-up to her *Ensign* article so that we and others

---

4. Dr. Debra Theobald McClendon, "Understanding Scrupulosity (Religious OCD)," *Ensign*, September 2019, churchofjesuschrist.org/study/ensign/2019/09/young-adults/understanding-scrupulosity-religious-ocd.

5. Becky Edwards was later on *Listen, Learn & Love* podcast episode 458 to share the experience from her perspective."

6. Elder John Edwards, a respected Utah orthopedic surgeon, also helped Ben with a nagging football injury.

could become more connected with her important work. In a labor of love, my wife transcribed the entire podcast and sent it to Elder Ostler. Here are some particularly insightful excerpts about anxiety from that podcast:

> What is anxiety? Why do we have anxiety? Anxiety is a normal emotion, and there are ways that anxiety is helpful to us. We are always going to get little bits of nervousness before a performance, for example. If we don't have any anxiety before we take a test, if we think the teacher is lax and the test isn't that important, then we don't study because there's no anxiety. There is nothing pushing us, and we don't do well on the test. So a mild or moderate level of anxiety helps us perform better and is helpful in our lives. With a little bit of anxiety before you give a church talk, you're probably going to perform better because you've prepared better and there's some motivation there. But if you think, oh, I'm not worried about it, I'm going to wing it, I'm going to go up there without any notes—unless you're an expert speaker, you might not do so well.
>
> How do we understand when anxiety has gone from that normal range to a pathological range? It is when our anxiety gets to a very high level that it becomes problematic. And these are the kinds of people that I end up working with in my own practice. But at a low level, anxiety helps all of us and it is going to continue to be with each of us. We need to all work to create a healthy relationship with anxiety.[7]

It was very helpful to understand that anxiety is actually useful when it stays in the mild to moderate range. But Elder Ostler's anxiety had reached that unhelpful range, where it was full-blown scrupulosity.

## Scrupulosity Defined

Scrupulosity is spiritual obsessive-compulsive disorder. It is an incorrect belief that one is not spiritually worthy, with confession

---

7.  *Listen, Learn & Love* podcast episode 191.

being the compulsion that provides short-term relief—but reinforces the cycle. Confession, for those with scrupulosity, is the opposite behavior to healing. For me, this was both mind-blowing and made total sense. Sheila and I were filled with compassion for our son, who was worthy in every way to serve a mission, but had concluded he was not worthy. Scrupulosity attacked the thing that was most precious— feeling worthy to represent the Savior among the people of Samoa.

## Another Person Experiencing Scrupulosity

On November 9, 2019, Tim and Aubrey Chaves were in our home recording a podcast about their great work at Faith Matters Foundation,[8] including how to navigate a faith crisis. I felt impressed to share with Tim a little bit about the situation with our missionary son. Tim shared that he also had undiagnosed scrupulosity for many years. The last twenty minutes of our podcast consists of Tim bravely discussing his journey with scrupulosity, which closely mirrors that of our son Ben:

> I think the first place that scrupulosity reared its head was on my mission, really. Missions are sometimes difficult. They can be pressure cookers in a lot of ways. From my perspective, at the time, it was so important to be perfect because there were literally spiritual lives at stake, right? So, if I wasn't perfect, then I wouldn't have the Spirit and if I didn't teach with the Spirit, then people would not feel the truth of what we were preaching. Their own eternal destiny could be lost because of mistakes that I had made.
>
> And scrupulosity took that to a whole new level for me. It's OCD. OCD is a bigger umbrella and can manifest itself

---

8. See faithmatters.org. "Faith Matters Foundation aims to create a space in which an expansive, radiant approach to the restored gospel can be considered and discussed. Our goal is to provide a powerful and widely engaging platform for exploring ideas, practices, and initiatives that provide deeper engagement with our faith and our world. All who are involved with Faith Matters share a deep commitment to the restored gospel tradition, and a profound desire to see it thrive and remain vital and relevant to rising generations."

in different ways. A lot of people think of OCD as needing to line up the pencils perfectly or have your bed made or excessive vacuuming or whatever it is. In scrupulosity, you need to follow the rules, perfectly. And, like I said, a mission is just the perfect place for that, unfortunately, to manifest itself.

In the MTC, what starts to happen is, you'll think of something that actually happened in your life, and start to assign new and nefarious meaning to it. So I looked back on things that I had done in high school, saying, "Oh my gosh. I can't believe I forgot that I had done that thing. I should have confessed this before I came out. I need to make an immediate confession and hopefully, get the Spirit back. Or maybe I'll just be sent home."

In reality, we're talking about very, very minor infractions from anyone else's point of view. But scrupulosity—you get into this chain of thinking where you build it up into something much, much bigger than it ever needed to be. I got into a cycle of constantly confessing to my leaders. This happened with branch presidents at the MTC, and it happened with my mission president for the duration of my mission. Eventually it got to the point—I guess it was mostly thoughts that I had—that I would start to confess it to my mission president and he would say, "You know what, Elder, if it's a thought, then don't worry about it. Just move on." And I would say, "Okay, I guess that's how it's going to be." But the scrupulosity and the OCD, it doesn't let that go.

At the time, I didn't have any vocabulary for this whatsoever. So it was this crazy cycle of guilt and confession, which brought momentary relief. After I'd confessed something, I'd feel good for probably just that day. By the next day, I'd have some new thought I thought was terrible, or I would remember something else in my past that I thought made me unworthy; and it would be this new cycle of guilt until I was able to confess again and release the pressure.

It got so absurd with that cycle. I had worked certain things into such a big deal that I believed I was beyond saving. I was very much a straight arrow, now that I see it with a more normal perspective. But at the time, my belief was, "I've gone so far down this path of sin that I'm never going to be able to get married, I'm never going to have an eternal family, or worst case, some of these things that I've done are so severe, that I'm going to hell and there's nothing I can do about it at this point. I'm beyond anything that can reasonably be repented of."

I decided that the only thing I could do was help others not suffer my fate. So that meant sticking it out on my mission, doing the best work that I could, and just saying, "Hey, yeah, I'm a lost cause, but I still know and have the truth and I'm going to share it with other people so they can live the life with an eternal family that I won't ever be able to have."

That was the entirety of my mission and it was very, very difficult. My mission president was a fantastic guy. If he'd had any real training on this sort of thing, I think my first interview with him, he would have known immediately what he was dealing with and probably would have had some better tools for it.

It didn't go away, obviously, once I came back because I wasn't dealing with it. It came to a head a few years later. I worked through certain things enough to get married, and I was applying to graduate school (Harvard MBA). After the whole application process was over and I was accepted, I was hit with this thought from OCD: "You cheated on your essays. You don't deserve to have gotten in."

This is the terrible thing about scrupulosity: it attacks whatever matters to you most at the time. On my mission, what mattered to me most was worthiness, so it attacked that. At that moment, what mattered to me most was fulfilling my dream of going to grad school, so it attacked that. I thought about confessing to the admissions committee that I had cheated on my essay. The real background was, just like everybody, I had sent my essay out to be edited by my friends. I accepted some of their editing suggestions. Based on that, I felt like those hadn't been truly my words in my essay, so I'd gotten into the program on false premises. The cycle is to confess to relieve the pressure, but at the same time, I realized how weird that would be for a potentially admitted student to call the admissions committee and say, "Hey, I cheated on my essays, I'm going to leave this in your hands." So my proposed solution, instead, was to take myself out of the mix. I was not going to go to grad school after all, even though it was really a lifelong dream.

At this point, I'd been having this discussion with my wife, Aubrey, and she said basically, "Like heck you're not going. I'm making you an appointment." We had figured out that it was OCD, but I'd never truly addressed it. She literally called a therapist, an OCD specialist, and made an appointment. I started going regularly those next few months, and it was a total life-changer.

There are scientifically proven ways of dealing with this stuff and it doesn't work the same for everybody, but the methods that therapists use, like exposure/response therapy, actually work. For me, the conclusion to most of that exposure is saying, "Maybe I did cheat. Maybe I did sin," or whatever it is. And the response prevention is saying, "However, I'm not going to confess that." That's incredibly painful, and you just feel torn inside because with OCD, and scrupulosity in particular, you want to be so perfect. You want to be so upright. You want to be so honest. And you feel like by not confessing, by not airing the laundry out for everybody to see and decide that you're worthy, that you're being dishonest in a lot of ways.

But once you've practiced that skill, you start to see things from a high level again and say, "Wait a second. What I'm going through—what I did on my essays—is totally normal." Or, on the mission, the thoughts that I'm having are totally normal. So when you accept that it's normal, and accept that uncertainty, then that thought kind of goes away. It was not easy dealing with it. But I luckily did get to the point where I was okay. I didn't call the admissions committee and we went to grad school and had the time of our lives.

It has been a long journey, and I feel for anybody out there who has OCD or scrupulosity or anything, that's causing them to tear at themselves on the inside. It is very difficult. It's been probably the most significant trial of my life and I'm just grateful that now there are professionals who know how to deal with it and that the Church is taking strides to educate leaders on how to help members with that as well.[9]

---

9.  *Listen, Learn & Love* podcast episode 199.

I wish everyone could read these words from Tim, which bring tears to my eyes every time I read them. No one should spend the years on their mission feeling they are beyond salvation but resolving to stay to save others. I wish Tim could go back and talk to his younger self on his mission and help him understand. I hope his words are healing to anyone with scrupulosity. I am so grateful for Tim and Aubrey for sharing this story and for Tim's positive role in Ben's life during his mission. That podcast episode is estimated to have over 30,000 listens, which tells me how much it resonates with many.

Knowing what I know now, I recognize that some of my YSAs had scrupulosity. They would confess and leave my office feeling lifted and peaceful that they were clean and worthy. However, within a short time, they were back in my office re-confessing the same sins. In hindsight, I recognize that I was reinforcing the cycle and adding to their spiritual OCD. If I had known about scrupulosity, I would have connected them to a qualified therapist on this subject to help them recognize that their path to healing was managing scrupulosity—not more visits to the bishop's office.

## The Outcome

With Sister Edwards' help, and family and priesthood leader support and prayers, Elder Ostler's emotional health stabilized. He saw hope in his future and understood that he was worthy to be a missionary. He no longer set dates to come home. He reported feeling happiness as a missionary and said to Sheila in a call home that if COVID-19 shut down his mission, he hoped he would be the last missionary standing. We, with the undeniable guidance of the Lord, had found the missing piece and the correct people were put into place to give Elder Ostler the tools to be emotionally stable and understand that he was worthy to serve a mission.

In March 2020, because of COVID-19, all the foreign missionaries were evacuated on a charter flight out of American Samoa. Elder Ostler's girlfriend, Summer, also came home from Australia because of COVID-19. Once home, Ben chose to participate in exposure response therapy with Dr. McClendon, where he learned tools to manage his scrupulosity. After a few months home, Ben and Summer felt their path was to not return to their respective missions but to get married. They were sealed in the Jordan River Temple in August 2020—a pair of nineteen-year-old returned missionaries starting their lives together. It was a wonderful day for our family.

I am grateful to Ben for allowing his story to be shared so it can bring hope and healing to others. I encourage you to listen to more of our podcasts on this topic[10] and connect with Dr. McClendon's resources.[11] Our hope as a family is that individuals, parents, and local leaders will learn to recognize the patterns of scrupulosity and help their loved ones find a path of hope and healing, and improve our culture to better understand and support those with OCD.

---

10. See listenlearnandlove.org/depression-mental-illness-podcasts for episodes focused on scrupulosity, including episodes 191,199, 204, 240, 258, 336, and 343.

11. To learn more about scrupulosity, see Dr. Debra Theobald McClendon's resources at debramcclendon.com. Dr. McClendon also published an article in the academic journal for institute and seminary teachers published by Brigham Young University. See Debra Theobald McClendon, "A Church Educator's Guide to Identifying and Helping the Scrupulous Student," *Religious Educator*, 22 (2), June 2021, 136–161.

# CHAPTER 8

# VARIATIONS IN MISSIONARY SERVICE

It is a beloved tradition in our church to gather with family and friends when a young adult receives their mission call. Many people guess a range of locations before the large white envelope is opened, or—more recently—before the email is opened on an electronic device. Often cameras and livestreaming are used to record the event, and there are cheers and tears of joy when the mission call is read by the prospective missionary.

We know the language of the call: "You are hereby called to serve as a missionary of The Church of Jesus Christ of Latter-day Saints. You are assigned to labor in the ____ Mission. It is anticipated you will serve for a period of [eighteen or twenty-four] months."

Following the mission call, there is preparing and packing, a farewell talk in sacrament meeting, perhaps an open house, and airport goodbyes as the set-apart missionary representing Christ leaves their home to help others learn the healing doctrines of our restored Church. See you in a couple of years!

But what about when it doesn't happen like that? What if they return sooner? Or what if there is no airport goodbye at all, and we still see our missionary every Sunday at church? I would like to discuss two variations in missionary service: "early release" and service missions. I will conclude with some thoughts about committed Latter-day Saints who feel their path is not to serve a mission.

This chapter examines this aspect of our culture and applies Sister McConkie's words shared earlier: "The gospel of Jesus Christ does not marginalize people. People marginalize people. And we have to fix that."[1] Our culture can view anything other than completing a full-time teaching mission as less acceptable. The Savior taught us differently with the parable of the vineyard workers:

> For the kingdom of heaven is like unto a man that is an householder, which went out early in the morning to hire labourers into his vineyard. And when he had agreed with the labourers for a penny a day, he sent them into his vineyard.
>
> And he went out about the third hour, and saw others standing idle in the marketplace. And said unto them; Go ye also into the vineyard, and whatsoever is right I will give you. And they went their way. Again he went out about the sixth and ninth hour, and did likewise. And about the eleventh hour he went out, and found others standing idle, and saith unto them, Why stand ye here all the day idle? They say unto him, Because no man hath hired us. He saith unto them, Go ye also into the vineyard; and whatsoever is right, that shall ye receive.
>
> So when even was come, the lord of the vineyard saith unto his steward, Call the labourers, and give them their hire, beginning from the last unto the first. And when they came that were hired about the eleventh hour, they received every man a penny. But when the first came, they supposed that they should have received more; and they likewise received every man a penny.
>
> And when they had received it, they murmured against the goodman of the house, Saying, These last have wrought but one hour, and thou hast made them equal unto us, which have borne the burden and heat of the day. But he answered one of them, and said, Friend, I do thee no wrong: didst not thou agree with me for a penny? Take that thine is, and go thy way: I will give unto this last, even as unto thee. Is it not lawful for me to do what I will with mine own? Is thine eye evil, because I am good? (Matthew 20:1–15)

---

1. McConkie, "Lifting Others."

Our Heavenly Parents love *all* of Their willing servants, no matter how long they serve, and each will be blessed for their service. Jesus judges us based our hearts and commitment to Him. Our worth and worthiness are not tied to how long we spend in the vineyard.

For Latter-day Saints who feel their path is not a church mission, there are other ways to serve in the vineyard, blessing the lives of others and gaining personal spiritual growth. At the end of this chapter, a few share their stories.

## Early Release Missionaries

Many of the *Listen, Learn & Love* podcasts have focused on stories from returned missionaries who did not complete the full term of eighteen or twenty-four months.[2] These brave Latter-day Saints have shared their experiences in part to improve our culture so all returning missionaries will be welcomed home and can feel the peace of belonging in our congregations, regardless of the length of time served.

Elder Holland addressed the topic of missionaries who did not complete a full term of service. He had received a letter from a person who served for only four months and went home due to mental health, and now felt like a failure. Elder Holland responded:

> Commendation to you, and the love of the Lord to you, and the blessings of the Church to you, for trying to go, for wanting to go, and for the fact that you successfully served for four months. It obviously wasn't a full term, but it was missionary service. It was honest. You were loyally participating and testifying, and I want you to take credit for that. I want you to take the appropriate dignity that you deserve from that, and to know that the Lord loves you and the Church loves you for serving. . . .
>
> I want you to be appropriately proud. I want you to take the dignity and the strength and the faith that came from your four

---

2. See listenlearnandlove.org/early-release-missionaries-podcasts for episodes on early release missionaries.

months and cherish that forever. I don't want you to apologize for coming home. When someone asks you if you've served a mission, you say Yes. You do not need to follow that up with, "but it was only four months." Just forget that part and say yes, you served a mission and be proud of the time you spent. . . .

Cherish the service you rendered. Be grateful for the opportunity to have testified, to have been out in the name of the Lord, to have worn that missionary name plaque. Because you were honorable, and because you did give your very best service to the degree that you could, please, please do not relive this. Do not rehash it. Do not think you're inadequate or a failure. Please just consider yourself a returned missionary who served and was faithful and will continue to serve and you'll continue to be a great Latter-day Saint.

I want all of you, anyone who would wrestle with this issue to have that feeling of self-worth and a successful mission, honorably offered to the Lord, regardless of the period of time involved. I encourage that and want you to feel that way forever.[3]

Hearing Elder Holland's comments and stories of those who returned home early from their mission, my empathy and love for this group of Latter-day Saints increases. I want to extend an extra measure of kindness, love, and acceptance instead of passing any kind of judgment. I don't want to go down the road in my mind or with my words to create a feeling my generation could do hard things but somehow this generation is different. I think they are the finest generation yet. Walking into their congregation after returning home early should not be one of the most difficult days of their life. Instead, they should be enveloped in love and support.

We can start now—before anyone else returns home early—to improve the culture in our congregations by sharing Elder Holland's remarks. We can also study the Counseling Resources section of

---

3. Jeffrey R. Holland, "Elder Holland's Counsel for Early Returned Missionaries," The Church of Jesus Christ of Latter-day Saints, 7:39, churchofjesuschrist.org/media/video/2016-05-012-elder-hollands-counsel-for-early-returned-missionaries.

the Church's website focused on ministering to those who return home early.[4] We can talk now in our congregations and families about the kind way we would respond if someone comes home early from their mission. Let's not wait to improve our culture until someone returns early. They should know before they leave the kind and loving way they will be treated.

I have worked to mute my curiosity on *why* someone returns home early. That inhibits my ability to love and support them. Our love and support should be unconditional, not proportional to the reason they returned early. Culturally, we seem to be more understanding when someone returns early because of a physical challenge (such as a broken leg needing surgery) versus a belated confession or a worthiness issue in the field. We can and should be mature enough to reallocate our mental energy away from "why are they home" to "how can I support" by demonstrating unconditional love and acceptance. In my experience, the first weeks home—with the support of loving families and wards—can make all the difference for the future of that returned missionary's long-term participation in the Church.

My friends on social media give these suggestions of things *not* to say to missionaries who are home early, and alternative thoughts.[5]

---

4. The Church has provided resources to leaders and families about missionaries at "Missionaries Who Return Home Early," Counseling Resources, The Church of Jesus Christ of Latter-day Saints, churchofjesuschrist.org/study/manual/counseling-resources/early-returned-missionaries (may be accessible to only members of ward and stake councils).

5. @Papa_Ostler (Richard Ostler). "Dear Friends, Give me a list (for my next book on improving LDS culture) of the things not to say to an early-release missionary. And things to say." *Twitter*, January 2, 2021, 6:36 pm, twitter.com/Papa_Ostler/status/1345514379836473345.

## What NOT to Say to a Returned Missionary Who Did Not Complete a Full Term of Service (with Possible Responses)

Here are some questions to avoid asking the newly returned missionary. Further, for the returned missionary, included are possible responses. These responses are not a script, but ideas that you can prepare ahead of time for potential questions and comments. You may want to say more to some people than others. As always, you can be guided by the Spirit.

- "What are *you* doing here?" ("I'm home from my mission. I'm figuring out what God has in store for me next.")
- "When are you going back?" ("My mission was done when I came home. I'm figuring out what God has in store for me next.")
- "How long did you serve?" ("I served for XX months, which apparently is how long the Lord wanted me to serve. I'm figuring out what God has in store for me next.")
- "Why did you come home? You'll get back out there; God still loves you." ("Yes, He does love me. I know He loves us all. I'm figuring out what God has in store for me next.")
- "What happened? Are you sick? Did you get hurt?" ("I prefer to look forward to the future. I'm glad I got to serve the Lord.")
- Don't refer to their mission as a "partial mission." ("I'm really happy for the time I had in the mission field. Like Jesus's parable of the laborers in the vineyard, some people serve longer than others, but their efforts are rewarded equally.")
- Don't minimize the service they did contribute, especially for sisters: "Oh, you didn't have to serve in the first place so it's not a big deal that you came home early." ("I'm glad I got to serve the Lord on my mission.")
- Don't ask questions about obedience.
- Don't talk about statistics. A mission is not about numbers.

- Don't react or look at me with judgment. Even though a lot of people welcomed me and said it was okay to come home early, their eyes and tone of voice said something different.
- Don't suggest that "everything happens for a reason."
- Don't rely on mission experiences to carry a conversation. We have other interesting things about us too.
- I had a bishop try to figure out "the math" of how I was home from a mission AND graduated from college by the age of twenty-two. I then had to divulge the information that I "came home early," though I didn't really think it was any of his business. So just try not to do any math, I suppose.
- Don't look at me sadly; I see you. Don't whisper about me; I hear you.

## What TO Say to a Returned Missionary Who Did Not Complete a Full Term of Service

- Welcome home! So good to see you!
- Hi, how are you? How are your parents? It's really snowing, isn't it! Have a good day!
- Congratulations! What did you learn about others in our world?
- We are proud of you and thank you for serving. We love you.
- Thank you for your willingness to serve. You were called to serve, you accepted the call, and you gave it your all. That is most important.
- Say nothing! It really helped my brother when we acted like nothing happened out of the ordinary and carried on with life like normal. If they want to bring things up, they will.
- Do say anything you would say to someone returning "on time." Don't say anything else.
- Treat them like any other returned missionary! Make sure to validate their contributions!

- "What are your plans?" Keeping a mind focused on the future makes it easier to move past this taboo point in someone's spiritual journey.
- My bishopric handled it well and treated me like I came home when I was supposed to. They asked me to give a homecoming talk, asked about school and plans for the future. When they announced I was home, they didn't mention or even imply an early release.
- One of the most healing things someone did for me was to not qualify or quantify my service. He introduced me to one of his other friends simply with: "This is my friend Kate. She recently came home from a mission."
- The best thing anyone said to me when I got home was people exclaiming genuinely, excitedly, "We're so glad you're home!"
- Don't say anything. Just put your arm around your friend and take them bowling or cow tipping or something.
- Ask what they learned. There's plenty to be learned even in a short time. It indicates their effort and helps people see the bright side. Also ask what's the next step for them on their path in the gospel? It's easy to shy away from this, but it's a sensitive time coming home early, and important to bring this up to engage in meaningful conversation and check in as a friend, so they know they still belong.
- Thank you for your service to the Lord. Would you like to go to lunch?

## Support from Heaven in the Scriptures

The Lord expressed his acceptance of our best efforts in a scripture that is tailor made for this situation:

> Verily, verily, I say unto you, that when I give a commandment to any of the sons of men to do a work unto my name, and those sons of men go with all their might and with all they have to perform that work, and cease not their diligence, and their enemies come upon them and hinder them from performing that work, behold, it behooveth me to require that work no more at

the hands of those sons of men, but to accept of their offerings. (D&C 124:49)

I think that the "enemies" that come upon us can be internal or external, seen or unseen. God assures us that He only requires our best efforts and asks no more of us. Another relevant scripture was given to Oliver Granger. Try inserting your own name:

> I remember my servant ___; behold, verily I say unto you that your name shall be had in sacred remembrance from generation to generation, forever and ever, saith the Lord; and when you fall you shall rise again, for your sacrifice shall be more sacred unto me than your increase, saith the Lord. (D&C 117:12–13)

To me, the word *increase* in this verse means "results." Our sacrifice is more sacred to Him than our results. The Savior loves our efforts, regardless of the outcome. This scripture is marvelously comforting to me. Since God approves of our efforts and appreciates our sacrifice, we need not worry what other people think.

The following are stories from and about returned missionaries. They are courageous in sharing their experiences. They have my love, admiration and respect. It is my hope that by reading these stories, we can better understand the road an early release missionary walks and what we can do to help them feel our love, acceptance, and support.

## DREW YOUNG

I spoke with my friend Drew Young on the podcast[6] about his early release from his mission. He served only sixty-two days, and the eighteen months that followed were very dark. We talked about the anxiety and depression that led to ending his mission, and how he eventually found hope and healing. He has released a book about his experience called *The Meaning of Your Mission: Lessons & Principles to Know You Are Enough*[7] with this introduction:

---

6. *Listen, Learn & Love* podcast episode 276.

7. Drew Young, *The Meaning of Your Mission: Lessons and Principles to Know You Are Enough* (Springville UT: Cedar Fort Publishing, 2020).

I was lying on the floor in my bedroom experiencing a crippling panic attack, one of many that day. I had just returned home early from serving a mission for The Church of Jesus Christ of Latter-day Saints. I felt like a failure.

The ensuing months involved bouts of debilitating depression, numerous medication prescriptions, countless therapy visits, and feelings of wanting to end it all, at times. It was in these moments that I learned a valuable lesson: we all have a mission, both in and out of the Church, and there is meaning in our missions. Regardless of what we may be going through: struggling with addiction, lack of testimony, same-sex attraction, feeling lonely, forgotten, or not good enough, experiencing mental illness and discouragement, etc., there is purpose behind our pain, and there is hope in our struggle.

It's up to us, are we going to go through life, or grow through life?

## ALEXANDRA DONNICI

My boyfriend came home early from his mission because of COVID-19, then stayed home because of mental health issues. It bothers him when people ask why he stayed or suggest that he should go back now that his mental health is pretty much back to normal. When all this was happening, I often asked, "How can I help?" or "What can I do?" It drove him nuts. I realize now that he didn't need me to *do* anything. There was nothing to change or fix. He just needed me to sit with him in his pain so he didn't have to feel so alone in it. He also hates when it's treated like a taboo subject and people avoid the topic of missions around him. He has said that he doesn't want to be treated differently or like a ward project, he just wants to be like everybody else.

Also, the fact that he came home early is not a big deal to him. It is to other people, but to him, he served the mission he was supposed to serve.

## AMANDA TILLMAUGHAN

I returned earlier than anticipated from my mission, but I decided to go home with the transfer group that occurred the same week. In the mission home, one of the other sisters asked, "I wonder if everyone from our MTC group finished their missions and is going home soon?" It hurt. I was so broken at the idea I hadn't "finished" my mission.

## DANIEL YESTERVICK

1. "You can always go back out." People think this is comforting, but it can be intensely hurtful. Some conditions never improve to the point that the missionary can return. Sometimes the missionary feels led to pursue other paths after returning home. Their decision to return home rests only between them and God.
2. "Why did you come home?" This is no one's business. Even honorable releases can cause a lot of pain to think about.
3. "Missionaries are less resilient now." A lot of older members blame the growing numbers of early release missionaries on the lack of resilience in the current generation. This is completely demoralizing.
4. "I'm sure the Church/your mission president/general authority didn't MEAN any harm." In people's rush to defend the Church, they can invalidate the painful experiences of missionaries. One of the hardest things for me was people constantly defending aspects of the missionary program that hurt me.

## ETHAN BAKKER

For the majority of my mission in South America, I really did my best and remained worthy. After well over a year, I was assigned to a new area several hours away from the rest of the mission. Gradually what was hard work and fun turned into "fun times" and some work. Eventually what was just two elders having some fun turned into both of us facing severe consequences of our actions. I was disfellowshipped for a minimum of one year. I was devastated but also so grateful to not be excommunicated.[8]

I called my dad, bawling my eyes out that I was coming home early. All he said was, "We'll be glad to have you back." I am forever grateful for a dad who loves and accepts me no matter what. He knew what I did was wrong, but he also knew that I needed to know I had a father that loves me. Even with the knowledge that my family would be happy to see me, I still felt anxiety about coming home early. How could this happen?

---

8. The term "excommunicated" is now called "withdrawal of church membership." See chapter 32, "Repentance and Church Membership Councils," *General Handbook: Serving in The Church of Jesus Christ of Latter-day Saints* (Salt Lake City: The Church of Jesus Christ of Latter-day Saints, 2019).

How will I face my family? I'm a good Mormon boy! Going home early was only for the weak. Everyone who goes home early has a weak testimony. No girl will ever want to be with me because I came home early. I felt like a loser and a complete failure.

I met with two different bishops during the repentance process. I know both wanted me to be worthy of a temple recommend, but I noticed two very different approaches. One brought up in every single interview the severity of what I had done. I knew it was wrong, so this constant reminder discouraged me and made being worthy seem unachievable.

The second bishop told me that what I had done didn't matter to him. What mattered was what I had done since then to repent. This cast a new light on my whole perspective that gave me hope for a better future. This bishop helped me to realize that holding a temple recommend was not out of reach. He made me feel loved and I was able to come much closer to my Savior.

The reconvening council with the stake presidency was one of the most spiritual experiences of my life. They did not ask questions about what had happened as a missionary; they just talked about what I had done since then to repent and draw nearer to Christ. I was reinstated to full fellowship.

Now I am grateful for this experience. It has made me realize that if someone comes home early, they do not have weaker testimonies than others. There are several personal reasons why. I learned that usually when people say offensive or rude things, they do not mean to hurt others. They are concerned, struggle with gossip, are just trying to be nice, or some other reason that should not matter to us. I learned that we all say and do things that hurt others without those intentions. I know that probably everyone who said hurtful things to me did not mean to hurt me. If someone did want to hurt me, I should follow the counsel of Moroni: "Condemn me not because of mine imperfection, neither my father, because of his imperfection, neither them who have written before him; but rather give thanks unto God that he hath made manifest unto you our imperfections, that ye may learn to be more wise than we have been" (Mormon 9:31). It is our duty as followers of Christ to not judge others, even those who may judge us.

Our church is imperfect, our leaders are imperfect, our prophet is imperfect, members are imperfect . . . We are all imperfect and should strive to not let anyone else's imperfections cause us to distance ourselves from Christ.

Our missions are not what define us, nor are our beliefs. Being a Christian is about what we do. A true Christian welcomes everyone home from their mission and doesn't think about who they were as missionaries.

## JOHN SCOVILL

I called my mission president, crying uncontrollably. He said that he could make it to our apartment in the next few hours. It seemed like an eternity for him to come. Once he and his wife arrived, he stayed in the basement apartment with me. His wife stayed outside with my companion.

"You know, there will be eternal consequences." I sat across from him, damp carpet separating us from each other, my back and chest heaving from crying so hard. "It will be hard to find someone to marry." Still that distance between him and me. I only longed for a hug or for him to be closer.

I told him I couldn't stay. I was homesick and feeling lost and depressed. There was a heaviness that I couldn't shake. That's when he said those things to me. "Everyone will look at you weird," he said in a monotone voice.

He called my parents. They decided the best thing was for me to go home. After talking on the phone, I went into the bedroom and packed my things. One suitcase. Then two. I hauled them upstairs into the bright sunlight. My companion sat on one metal chair. My mission president's wife on another. Neither talked to me.

Once home, I stayed inside and rarely ventured out. I felt like a failure. We received a visit from a sister missionary who had baptized my dad in the late 1970s. She said one thing I have always remembered: "If he goes to church, he'll be okay."

I did. I attended church. I also saw a counselor who helped me through this. As I went on with life attending college, I began to date. I always hoped my mission wouldn't come up in conversation, but I always had a rehearsed answer. I met a girl who I dated and asked her to marry me. Before I proposed, I did mention my mission experience. I was extremely nervous. What if this was her non-negotiable for marrying someone? Luckily, she told me that the greatest guy she knew had never served a mission. That guy was her grandpa. I was relieved.

## JOSEPH GIBB

I left my mission after about a year being out in the field. Prior to going home, someone I knew had gone home early and been turned out by his parents. He was forced to live with an aunt willing to take him in, but his parents stopped talking to him. I don't know what happened later to him, but the situation frightened me. I lost sleep and stopped being an effective missionary.

Deciding to serve a mission had been difficult, but I was fairly certain it was what God wanted me to do. I thought I could do a good job, obey all the rules, stay committed, and focus on the work. But I didn't. The nights leading to my return home were sad. I had nightmares of my parents hurting me or yelling at me (which they never did nor do) and I woke up crying more than once.

I arrived at the airport full of shame and guilt, but my father hugged me and told me he loved me. I had asked him to come alone as I didn't think I could bear to see my mother disappointed in me. My dad was amazing and he made me feel so at ease and even told me how excited my mom and family were to see me; no guilt, no shame, just love. When I arrived home, it was the same. My mom wrapped her arms around me and told me how much she missed me. I wept and she wept and my large family gathered around to show me love and affection.

Church that week was difficult, because my father is in the bishopric, and also because we arrived late and I felt every eye turn on me. My day was long and I received many questions but, for the most part, people were respectful. They did not say anything to hurt me but asked how I was doing and wished me well. Having suffered from serious depression, I wasn't sure if I would have been able to face this if my acceptance had not been so universal and loving. I am grateful every day that I have parents who love me and a ward family who cared enough to not get involved.

Whenever I hear stories of missionaries who returned home and were not treated this way, I am overcome with a sinking feeling, knowing that I am not as strong as they are because I can hardly handle normal days of shame, let alone weeks and months of it. Going through that made me more empathetic and has helped me to be more understanding, but it didn't free me from the guilt and shame I felt.

Having people who loved me helped me see that the way forward wasn't dwelling on the past but making a new place for myself.

## KATE TICKERBACH

My first crush and I were great friends and dated occasionally. He went on a mission and I went to BYU–Hawaii. I still remember when I called his parents to get his most recent address to send him a letter on his mission. Instead of giving me the address, his dad put him on the phone. He had come home "early." He was homesick, the mission "wasn't for him." He sounded so sad and seemed to be experiencing so much shame. I cried, not because I judged him in any way, but because I knew he would be judged by so many others. I told him I respected his decision and loved him, and this changed nothing for me. I hope he believed that. I told my mom that he came home, and she expressed that she felt no differently about him. I knew she knew his worth and would still be fine with her daughter marrying him. Her example of Christlike love over current church culture was a relief to me and felt right.

After I returned home from BYU–H, we dated and did not end up getting married, but we remain friends to this day. He has a beautiful family and is an active, believing member.

## MICHELLE FRANCIS

My husband has severe anxiety when it comes to meeting new people, making phone calls, etc. When he went on his mission, he was in the United States but assigned to another language. It didn't even have a Book of Mormon translation and, in fact, his companion was helping to translate it.

He was told by his mission president, companion, and others to just keep sticking it out, even though he was having daily debilitating panic attacks. They kept telling him to pray it away. After trying his hardest, he ended up leaving his mission in the middle of the night and getting a flight home.

He was shamed for leaving his mission early, especially because of the way he did it. One bishop from the mission area even contacted my husband and told him that his future wife would never marry him if he didn't complete the two years—it made him feel like he wouldn't find someone who'd marry him because he didn't fulfill his mission.

This was especially hard because at the time he was the only active member in his immediate family. While he was growing up, the kids in his neighborhood weren't allowed to play with him and his brothers after their parents divorced. The reaction to his mission service really added to the hurt his family felt towards the Church.

## DWIGHT BITINGERS

I returned from my mission before the usually expected period of two years. I desperately wanted to go back and had a goal to "finish" my mission. My stake president requested that we meet weekly to help me achieve this goal. He had many spiritual insights for me. He boosted my confidence. He believed in me.

Unfortunately, I was fighting an addiction and you need more than spiritual inspiration and confidence to fight that fight. He said the most damaging thing anyone told me: that I was "smarter" than my addiction. I got the impression that beating an addiction was like beating someone at chess. When it made an aggressive move, you just had to put in the brainpower to outsmart it and keep your pieces safe. The first time he said that I felt smart, like I had just been given the tool that would kill my addiction. Can you imagine how I felt after the next relapse? And the one after that? And the next twenty after that? Every relapse was followed by intense self-deprecation: *stupid, stupid, you're too stupid to ever get over this, stupid, stupid, stupid. . .* My stake president was inspired to tell me that, right? So, I really could just outsmart it, right? The guilt this added to my already guilty conscience put incredible strain on my spiritual and mental health for years.

I also received several grating and inappropriate comments from ward members. These comments usually came from members with whom I had no existing relationship. I understand now that they believed they were reaching out to someone in need. I urge members who want to reach out to early returned missionaries to consider the context of their actions. If you have already fostered a friendship with them, you may be in a unique position to support *if called upon*. If you are not already close and you do approach them, you are attempting to build a relationship with them on something they are already extremely sensitive about.

There are members of my ward that, years later, I still remember as the ones that only approached me with a sideways comment about returning home early from my mission. These exchanges were neither comfortable nor productive. When in doubt, just don't.

If you have a relationship with the returned missionary that is sufficiently strong, the correct move is still likely: just don't. Be a support and express your love for the individual that is independent from their "status" as an early returned missionary.

## LANDON YOUNG

Preparing to leave on a mission was challenging for me, even though I knew I loved God and had a testimony of the Savior and His mission. Despite these beliefs, I had great anxiety about serving a mission. I was in a serious relationship and I worried about our future if I left. At age eighteen, I thought that stepping away from the life I knew for two years would put me "behind" others my age, or that I would miss out on the experiences my friends were having. I hadn't learned to be present or to enjoy the journey.

It was difficult, but I decided to go. I made necessary changes and over time, I became more confident that I was where I was supposed to be. The Lord blessed me with needed comfort and helped me feel peace. I met incredible people and had the honor of serving my brothers and sisters alongside stellar missionaries. It was not the experience I expected, but it was the one I needed.

After one particularly impactful zone conference, I felt impressed to go to my mission president and share some mistakes I made prior to my mission that had been weighing on my mind. A couple weeks later, he let me know that I was going home. I had been out about a year.

I was devastated. I was terrified that my actions would set a poor example for my younger siblings. I was ashamed and felt like I let my parents down. The night I got back, I learned that my girlfriend had fallen out of love with me. Two weeks later, my stake president said that he didn't believe I should've been sent home, which left me feeling confused and angry.

It was all too much, and I sank into a deep depression. This was before I was formally diagnosed with anxiety and ADHD, so I had no idea how to cope with the chaotic torrent of emotions that I now had to deal with. I became a shell of myself. The next two or three years of my life were the lowest, most challenging times I had gone through so far.

I'm now thirty and happily married to a woman who completes my existence. We had our first child and our little one fills my life with incomprehensible joy. I feel no guilt or shame about coming home early anymore. I look back at the events that took place, the pain I felt, the sorrows I endured, and feel nothing but gratitude. My own mental health challenges gave me the experience I needed to empathize with and love others around me who struggle, like my angel wife and my dad. I fully accept that the consequences I endured were largely due to my own choices, but I'm not plagued with regret. Those choices set me on a path to become the person I am today, and I'm proud not only of who I am but who I'm continuing to become. I've forgiven myself and I'm so proud of that.

To anyone who might be feeling shame for returning early from a mission, regardless of the reason, I want you to know that you *can* find peace. I want you to understand that your wounds *will* heal, and the love of our Heavenly Parents can be a balm for you. You *will* feel whole again. Returning early is not a spiritual death sentence. You are not damaged goods. Your divine nature as a child of God is as valid as every other child of the Most High. Give yourself grace. Allow yourself to feel the feelings you're grappling with. Make the choice to accept these experiences for what they are—steps on your path to who you're meant to become. More than anything, know that our Heavenly Parents love you more than you can comprehend.

## RUBY BAIRD

I didn't want to serve a mission. I kept asking God if I needed to serve, and God kept giving me the wrong answer. I finally decided to trust God and His plan for me and submitted my mission papers. When I read the words, "You are called to the Alabama Birmingham Mission," I felt a fire light within me. I was nervous and scared, but I also felt deep in my soul the importance of my call.

I knew a mission would be hard, but I certainly didn't expect it to be the worst days of my life—panic attacks, anxiety, and extreme depression that would almost end my life. After a month of fighting the darkness that had overtaken my soul, I sat on my bathroom floor, wishing for the end of my life. My deepest desire was not to go home, but to no longer exist. I tried to get help, but things continued to get worse. I began to plan how I could end my life while on my mission. My once joyous life was now either painful or apathetic. Desperate for some form of control, I cut myself. It didn't seem wrong to me; it seemed like a tool to help with my challenges. I met with a therapist a few days later and somehow found the courage to tell them I was cutting myself.

I was sent home. I was lost and confused and relieved all at the same time. I felt broken and like a complete failure. The release meeting with my stake president hurt me immensely. While he had good intentions, the way he talked seemed like I had done something wrong. Instead of celebrating the mission I did serve, and acknowledging the difficulties I faced, he lectured me. He talked as if I was going to leave the Church. It felt like he didn't trust me. I had just gone through literal hell and was broken. I needed support as I healed. I needed a grace-filled plan. I did not need a long list of things I *should* be able to do.

It was as if I had just broken my leg and I was being asked to run a marathon on it. I tried to take his words to heart. I believed anything short of running that marathon meant failure. When I inevitably couldn't do it, I felt like I had failed God and He had failed me. I dealt with PTSD-like symptoms and couldn't read my scriptures or go to church without wanting to self-harm. I felt abandoned by God and forgotten by Christ.

I wanted to leave the Church, but I couldn't. Even in the depths of pain and intense anger toward God, I knew it was true. I needed heaven in my life, so I turned to my Mother in Heaven. I grew closer to Her and began to spiritually heal. I still struggled emotionally and spiraled downward. My world was dark and I started to plan to end my life again. I knew how, but I couldn't bring myself to do that to my family. So the options were that I could remain in misery and fake my way through life, or I could try to heal with faith I hardly had. Try to hope when it seemed lost. It was the hardest thing I've ever done.

Slowly, slowly, a miracle seemed to occur, and I began to heal. This miracle of healing came through the people and resources God put in my life. My sweet doctor helped me get on the right medication and my therapist helped me trust myself and God. I started dancing in the car again. I felt contentment in my life. I drew closer to God. There is still pain that I will probably carry forever, but it is nothing compared to the beauty of life. I count it a privilege to have experienced both the worst that life has to offer and the pure joy it contains.

## Service Missions

In November 2018, the First Presidency announced that young single adults in the United States and Canada could serve either a traditional teaching mission or a service mission. The program has since been expanded to other areas of the world as well.

Those eligible for a service mission are young single adults up to age twenty-five who are unable to serve a teaching mission due to health reasons. Teaching missionaries who return home early due to medical, emotional, or family situations may transfer to a service mission for the balance of their term of service.

The stated objectives of a service mission are to "provide an opportunity for all willing young women and young men to serve the Lord and increase in testimony of Him; help each service missionary prepare for a lifetime of service; provide needed and valuable service to the Lord through serving the Church and community organizations."[9]

The application process for all missionaries is the same. When the call comes, it indicates whether the assignment is a teaching or service mission, and the duration of the call to serve (six to eighteen months for women ages nineteen to twenty-five, or six to twenty-four months for men ages eighteen to twenty-five). Service missionaries live at home instead of traveling to another part of the world. They serve as close to full-time as their capability and circumstances allow. They are set apart and expected to speak in sacrament meeting at the beginning and end of their missions. They wear a name badge and are addressed as Elder or Sister while at church or on their assignments. They often have no companion, allowing for a family effort to create a home-centered, Church-supported mission experience.

Service missionaries report regularly to their stake president, rather than a mission president. They also work closely with Service Mission Leaders (SMLs),[10] which are couples who assist the younger missionaries in managing the logistics of their assignments and schedule. The service missionary doesn't necessarily choose their own assignment but counsels with the stake president and SMLs to customize their service.

I spoke with a number of service missionaries in the Salt Lake Valley and learned about their wonderful work in refugee resettlement, youth mentoring for recent immigrants, animal shelters, food pantries, homeless shelters, and grounds crews at various temples. Further, I've learned about their work with other religious organizations in interfaith efforts and in various assignments in temples and Church offices.

---

9.  "The First Presidency Enclosure to Leaders," *Service Missionary*, The Church of Jesus Christ of Latter-day Saints, churchofjesuschrist.org/service-missionary/the-first-presidency-enclosure-to-leaders.

10. My friends David and Kathleen Cook, service mission leaders in upstate New York, shared information about service missions in *Listen, Learn & Love* podcast episode 223.

Regardless of where or how a missionary performs his or her duties, the gathering of Israel is one by one. I believe that service missionaries are reaching people in a distinctive way that may not be possible in a teaching mission. Everyone has unique gifts, skills, and attributes to lift and reach the one which models the Savior's ministry.

I love the simplicity of the Savior's own mission on the earth: He taught and He served. That is so doable. We can get our arms around that and feel like we can do that too. For missionaries who cannot serve a teaching mission for a variety of reasons, this program provides a way to meaningfully contribute to building the kingdom as the Savior did. They are disciples of Christ as they serve others.

I believe that our Heavenly Parents and our Savior see everyone as equal and see their service as equal. But our culture doesn't necessarily view it that way—a teaching mission is usually held in higher esteem than a service mission. Our church culture should be more aligned with the teachings of the Savior to love and support one another on our individual paths through life. We must do our part to recognize the value of service missionaries. The Lord does not differentiate. We should say that "a mission is a mission is a mission," whether it is teaching or service.

Church leaders are explicitly clear that a service mission is not "fake" or less than a teaching mission: "A service mission is an acceptable offering to the Lord when a proselyting mission is not possible. Therefore, referring to a proselyting mission as a 'real mission,' 'normal mission,' or 'traditional mission' is inaccurate and should be avoided. All missionaries represent the Lord and carry out His work."[11]

In our wards and stakes, we can ensure service missions are seen the same as teaching missions. We can include service missionaries in a stake conference program that lists all missionaries serving from the stake. In wards that hang a mission plaque in the foyer, service missionaries should receive one as well. We should refer to them as Elder or Sister, rather than by their first name, when we see them.

---

11. "The First Presidency Enclosure to Leaders," Ibid.

These are small things but meaningful to both the individual missionary and our culture.

The following insights are from service missionaries.

## LUKE DAVENPORT

*(Luke, a dear family friend, has been interviewed for the* Listen, Learn & Love *podcast[12] twice regarding his time as a service missionary.)*

I have severe Obsessive-Compulsive Disorder, which is an anxiety disorder. Where my mental state is, I'm not able to move away from home. I've come to accept that. I've tried every type of medication to get better and nothing has really shown any difference.

I graduated from high school in 2019 and all my friends were getting their mission calls at the end of the school year. I was happy for them, but it was really rough on me and I felt really bad because I wanted to go. I did a semester at college but didn't feel like I belonged anywhere. I think the Lord prepared this path and I got a prompting that I should go on a service mission. I emailed some friends and they said, "That's a real mission, Luke. I need you to know that." That really helped me come to the decision to do a service mission.

My dad also said something really profound: "You're called where you're supposed to go." I thought it was a choice, but you're called by God. Whether it's service or teaching, you're called by God. If you're focused on comparing your mission with someone else's, you're not going to be happy. There are days when I can try harder, but others I can't do as much. It's between you and the Lord. Do your best, just trying to serve.

Maybe God knew I would have this mental illness, and maybe He called me to a service mission in Utah because there are people in need of help here, just like there are people in need of help in Samoa and Africa and Asia and everywhere in the world. It's just the same.

I worked at the Catholic Community Services (CCS) for my mission. Every faith imaginable, and it doesn't matter that there's a difference. No judgment. I love all my Muslim and Catholic friends and everyone there. I think being a missionary is just getting to know other people. I've talked with a lot of Muslims at CCS and had some deep conversations about God where I've

---

12. *Listen, Learn & Love* podcast episodes 228 and 434.

learned a lot. I know a lot of the Muslims probably won't convert to our religion and that's fine with me because they're living good lives and God knows that.

Later, I added the gardening team at the Oquirrh Mountain and Jordan River temples.

I'm sure the Savior wanted people to come back to God, but He just went in to serve. If you're going in with a one-sided objective, you're not going to gain anything from that. Missionary work is about showing love and showing who Christ is through service.

It's taken me a long time to accept my mission. I wanted to be a lot more. I finally accepted it and I love it, but I still long for the experience of teaching. It's a personal battle, but my favorite scripture is Philippians 4:13, "I can do all things through Christ which strengtheneth me."

## MADI PICKETT

I always wanted to go on a mission and serve in a foreign language. I started as a teaching missionary to Brazil in November 2019, and I knew it was where I was supposed to be at that time. I had to come home because of COVID-19 in March 2020.

I had a waiting period to go back to Brazil, and the Missionary Department told me I could have a temporary assignment here in the U.S. I did get one to Las Vegas, but I was filled with anxiety. I felt like I couldn't and shouldn't go. The Sunday before I was supposed to leave for Las Vegas, I met with my stake president. I started to cry and said, "I don't want to go. I can't go to Las Vegas." The stake president mentioned a service mission and I didn't debate it. I wanted to serve because that's what I believe in most. It was hard to teach. So that's how I ended up here and I couldn't be more thankful for how it all turned out.

I've done both a teaching mission and a service mission, and I feel the same Spirit every day. There is no difference. I wake up now as I did when I was in Brazil and I feel like I am making a contribution.

In a teaching mission or a service mission, we're all doing the Lord's work. Expanding Israel isn't just baptizing people—it's serving them and helping them in any way. There are so many, many opportunities to serve. There are missionaries who help the hungry, who work on cars, who work with cheese, who do yard work . . . We serve Muslims, we serve Catholics. We're all part of the human family and we're all on this earth together trying to make it back to our Heavenly Parents. And there are so many different ways to do that.

## SAM FOSTER

I was called to serve in the Indiana Indianapolis Mission and did the home MTC in July 2020. A few days before I was supposed to fly to Indiana, my stake president contacted me that my mission was delayed. I have asthma, and at the time, no one knew much about COVID-19 yet. So they weren't allowing missionaries with diabetes or asthma or any severe medical problems to go out.

While my mission was delayed, I registered for school so I could be doing something and attended the fall semester. In that time, I got super depressed and started having panic attacks. I didn't tell anyone because I thought they'd just go away once I went to Indiana, but obviously, that's not how it works. I left on my mission to Indiana in January 2021 but in such a terrible mental state that I knew I probably wasn't going to make it the two years. I'd be going home soon.

Sure enough, in a matter of just a few weeks, I was on the flight back to Salt Lake. My stake president brought up a service mission. I wasn't too keen on it, but the more I thought about it, the more it felt right. I decided I might as well continue to be a missionary because it's something I always wanted to do.

Recently, I was outside my house and a family was walking by. The mom asked me, "How's the mission?" There wasn't anything about what are you, what do you do, or anything like that. Just a straight up question—"How's the mission?" I've been treated with nothing but respect and everyone's been super nice to me and understanding of what I've gone through.

But the big thing is how I view myself. And that has not been the best. Another time, my mom and I were on a walk and met a family we hadn't seen in a long time, so they didn't know my situation. I said, "I'm doing a service mission, so it's still kind of a mission." My mom and the family both said, "What are you talking about? That's not *kind of* a mission. That's a *mission*." So I need to get over that and view myself as a missionary, because everyone else is already viewing me that way.

It's not that one type of person is only fit for a service mission. Every missionary just wants to serve. It's a commandment to serve God and serve our fellow brother. Service missionaries just want to get our hands dirty and get to work.

## SARAH HAROLDSEN

I started my mission on November 8, 2020, serving at Catholic Community Services (CCS) and at a local food pantry. I wouldn't change for any other mission. I love the people I've gotten to meet and serve. At the pantry, I've helped people feel comfortable accepting that they need help.

At CCS, I am a mentor to two refugee girls who are both so amazing! I feel like they mentor me! One is about to graduate high school and is at the stage of life where she is becoming more independent. I am privileged to be her friend. We have a bond of trust that I know she needs right now. I know I was meant to be matched with her, and I couldn't give her the same support if I was a teaching missionary. My other mentee is a fifteen-year-old girl with Down syndrome, who is a huge ray of sunshine. She loves day trips with just the two of us. Her personality and sass will keep you going.

I have seen the Spirit work in people through our service. It helps introduce them to Christ as they experience His love through our actions. I have witnessed people open up and welcome it in. I love getting to share about this new type of mission. I have loved the people I've gotten to meet and the experiences I've had.

At Christmas, my sisters went to Young Women and they were making packages for missionaries serving from our ward. I thought, "I'm a missionary too." When my sisters left the house to go to that activity, I didn't say anything but I hoped I would get a package.

The next day, the teachers quorum president was on my doorstep with a box that said, "Sister Haroldsen." They remembered me. I am on the same level as any other missionary. It included a bunch of letters and they all said, "Thank you for your service." I even wrote back to each of the youth, and I keep the letters. They help me remember that there are people supporting me. They see me. They even gave me a cutout of a Christmas tree to hang on my wall, and I kept it up for the longest time. It was a reminder of support.

## AARON MURPHY

I served a service mission in Portland, Oregon, March 2004–06 at Deseret Industries (DI). At the time, I was a very introverted person and my bishop felt that I would have a hard time with the social aspects of a teaching mission.

As I was serving my mission, the ward supported me by providing a bus pass for transportation to DI, and at times, members asked me how I was doing. One of the members sent me a letter, that her son wanted to serve a mission because of my example in the ward. As I finished my mission, multiple people where I served told me how I was able to help them in ways no one else was. So I know that I was where our Heavenly Father needed me to serve.

For the first couple of months, I personally felt like my mission was a second-class alternative. Because of my personality at the time, I felt I was not good enough to serve like all my friends did. But after I forgot myself and looked at my mission through spiritual eyes, it was the closest I have felt to the Holy Ghost in my life. When you serve others, you are really serving Heavenly Father and Jesus Christ.

We all need to remember that it is not what type of mission we serve, but how we serve those missions with everything the Lord has given us. A service mission requires faith in Christ and trust in His will, that He knows where we need to be more than we do. Because of my mission, I have become a stronger and better disciple of Christ.

## RACHEL CHENEY

Because of comments some Church members have made to service missionaries (including myself), it's evident that service missionaries are often considered "second-class missionaries." They are seen as not smart enough/emotionally stable enough/ physically able to serve a teaching mission. Though people may not consciously think this, it is an underlying mindset for a lot of Church members. Even some members of my own family have this mindset sometimes. I remember hearing things like, "on a *normal* mission…," implying that I am a second-class missionary. Just because someone is on a service mission does not mean they are less worthy of the missionary calling and mantle. No missionary should ever have to fight to be seen as contributing valuably to the Lord's work.

On the other hand, there are wonderful people who really do understand what a service missionary contributes, and how the Lord views their service. My stake president (who also serves as my mission president) views me as a fully contributing missionary, as do my other mission leaders. There is even written guidance for mission leaders not to refer to teaching missions as "normal" missions, or to make service missionaries feel second-class in any way. In addition, the other service missionaries I have met are lovely, friendly people who reassure me that I am making a difference in the Lord's kingdom.

## Suggestions for Improvement in Church Culture Regarding Service Missionaries

- Speak kindly, considerately, and respectfully to everyone, regardless of the mission they serve. Be careful not to compare teaching and service missions, or to assume one mission or missionary is better than another.
- Remember, it is not anyone's job to judge worthiness, except Jesus Christ's. All missions and missionaries are of equal worth in God's eyes, just like all people are worth the same in God's eyes.
- Most times when people jump to conclusions, pronounce judgment, or are biased, it comes out of ignorance. Therefore, it would be more Christlike to get educated and informed about others' experiences and see things through their eyes before forming and passing judgments.

## Personal Stories from Those Who Did Not Serve Missions

How do we treat members who feel that their path is not to serve a mission? Do our words and actions cause them to feel like second-class citizens? Do we create a feeling that there is a fork in the road where they need to either serve a mission or leave the Church? Or do we remember that serving a mission is not a saving ordinance or required for the covenant path? Do we feel that our job is to provide course correction—or do we respect their agency and personal revelation, and just love and support them?

During my YSA service, I met with a few young men who had not served missions but were still mission age. I remembered the blessings and growth that came into my own life from missionary service and logically wanted the same for these good young men. I wondered if they had families praying that I would be able to say the right words of encouragement to convince them to go on a mission.

Adrian Miller was one young man with no desire to serve a mission. Instead of shifting into "why you should go" mode, I decided to listen to Adrian's story. He recently reflected on this by writing to me:

> I found it difficult to have the desire to stay active in the Church during that time in my life. Most of my friends decided to serve missions, and I was struggling to know if that was the right path for me. I often felt like my individual worth was defined by my desire to serve. I felt I was judged by many people that I looked up to. I was lost and did not know where to turn. When I met with some of my priesthood leaders, they always wanted to discuss how they could help me serve a mission. I was told to start my mission papers, so I started some of the initial paperwork, but still felt very lost and confused. I felt that my desires, wants, or needs were not being listened to.

I asked for help from the Spirit in advising him and sensed that he was sincere and receiving personal revelation. I said something along the lines of, "If you feel your path is not to serve a mission, I'll support you. I will walk with you. I want you to feel welcome, needed and a feeling of belonging so you can continue to grow closer to your Heavenly Father and feel His love for you."

Soon, my time as bishop was up; I was released and lost track of my friend Adrian. Several years later, while serving as a temple worker, Adrian walked in to be married. I was so happy to see him! He was glad to see me and gave me a huge hug. I had the impression that he might not be in the Church if I had made our relationship solely about getting him on a mission. He shared these insightful words about that day:

> I felt so blessed to see you in the temple on my wedding day. It felt like a tender mercy, and a sign from God letting me know that He had been aware of my life the whole time. Because of your listening ear and your attention to the Spirit, I felt needed and loved, which helped me to continue to be a faithful member of the Church. I never did serve a mission, but I went to the temple and gained a greater understanding of the gospel and how the Lord is involved in my life every day. I have seen so many blessings on my unique journey. I know now

that my worth was not defined by whether I served a mission or not. It is defined by my dedication to serving and loving those around me. I have had so many opportunities to share my testimony and help others see the blessings that the gospel provides. I have also had the opportunity to help others who did not serve a mission, or who came home early, to realize they are still amazing, talented, and worthy sons and daughters of God. I am also happily married to a beautiful woman who loves me for who I am and supports me in all I do. We love being in our ward, and love to share our love of the gospel as often as we can. I know that the Lord has been blessing my life, even though my path has been different from others.

I am grateful to Adrian for sharing his feelings and making his way forward as a committed Latter-day Saint. I love his unique ability to reach out and serve others to help create Zion. Our church is better off with good members like Adrian and their contributions.

There are certainly many stories of priesthood leaders who guided a hesitant person to mission service, and they went on to be successful missionaries. I hope leaders will continue to be close to the Spirit to know the right things to say and do in these situations. I encourage leaders (and parents and friends) to do a lot of listening before responding with their impressions and suggestions.

Our culture seems to infer only two forks in the road: either serve a full-time mission or leave the Church entirely. There really is a third fork: staying active in the Church while not serving a mission, still participating and contributing and being fully valued. I am grateful that Adrian saw that third fork. In the end, it's about loving the Savior and following His path for each one of us, whether or not that path includes a mission. In fact, when we sing, "I'll go where you want me to go, dear Lord,"[13] that means staying where we already are if that's where God wants us.

---

13. *Hymns*, 270.

The following are stories that Latter-day Saints have given permission for inclusion here. I believe that hearing a variety of perspectives is key to improving our attitudes about others' decisions. Yes, some of these stories are painful. But hopefully we can learn how to improve our culture so that all can feel needed, seen, and feel that they belong in our congregations.

## JERE MILLER

My son was selected to attend the Military Academy at West Point. That was a huge accomplishment—we were not a military family. He did great at the Academy. He learned discipline, sacrifice, standing for strength, and the importance of giving of yourself. Although he was very active in his West Point branch, he subsequently didn't serve a mission. He stayed active in the church, went to Institute, and served as a stake missionary during that time and for a year afterward. However, his social standing at church severely suffered.

Our own social church circles felt sadness for us as parents. Yet, our nonmember social circles were thrilled that we had a son willing to sacrifice his life for our country. That mixed message was felt by us and our son as well: members felt he was less than valiant while nonmembers honored and complimented him. Church girls broke up after a couple of dates, while nonmember parents asked if he was willing to be set up with their daughter, niece, etc.

He sat through many sacrament meetings and Sunday School lessons in which missionaries were asked to raise their hand and identify themselves. During one Sunday School class, again, the teacher asked for people to stand if they had served as a missionary. He thought, "Well, I have been a stake missionary for three years," and he stood up. The teacher clarified that he was asking for full-time missionaries and motioned for him to sit down. My son said that was the moment he realized he would never fit in.

Although he graduated from West Point, has an MBA, and was a commander in the military . . . at church, he felt very unwelcome and unsuccessful—this church—The Church of Jesus Christ of Latter-day Saints. He easily extrapolated that members would only see him as a C- or D+ member, not the "A" person he was striving to be.

We start young with these evaluations. My son and I both remember times in Primary when children were asked to stand if one or both of their parents served a mission. Sometimes they were invited to stand in front and lead the Primary in singing "I Hope They Call Me on a Mission." Don't we realize how painful that can be for the children left sitting in the seats? He does not want his two sons to have that continued shame and identification—it isn't their fault.

I am aware of one stake conference where the presiding authority asked how many had served missions. Nearly every hand went up. While this certainly seems amazing, I wondered if every hand was up because they are the only ones who feel comfortable attending stake conferences and church.

After trying for several years and having many repeated "not a missionary" moments, my son is not in the Church. He has no desire for his sons to experience the harsh judgments of members. I certainly understand and would love to see our culture change.

We are missing the target. It could be powerful to say, "Everyone who loves serving the Lord, please stand." "Everyone who would like to find people to share the gospel with, please stand." "Everyone who has ever had an opportunity to talk about our faith, please stand." This could be such a unifying process instead of a divide/evaluate/rank process. My husband and I both served missions and I can honestly say that I don't need persistent recognition. My service was its own reward. I want everyone to feel accepted and honored.

## JACOB GUNTHERITE

I am currently active, attend church, and fulfill callings. I did not serve a mission, for a couple of reasons. First, I was dating a woman who was a single mother. Second, I wasn't worthy to serve a mission at the time.

Instead of serving a mission, I chose to marry the woman I was dating. We have now been married for more than 25 years.

At the time, my parents were very disappointed, even heartbroken, as I am sure many other family members were. However, they were very supportive. My friends were also very supportive.

My older sister gave me the most grief, mostly in her actions and animosity toward my wife. She thought it was my wife's fault I wasn't serving a mission. My sister eventually came around and is now good friends with my wife.

My best friend's dad, also a member, was perhaps the most supportive and influential. He said to me, "Your mission at this time isn't to serve a teaching mission, but to take care of this woman and her daughter." It meant the world to me and is something I think of often.

My wife was previously married, and wasn't really active in church until she married her first husband. Once she married him, she became active. She was active after her divorce and continues to be active. Her family is still not active, and due to their inactivity, none of them had any issues with me not serving a mission.

Before we got married, my wife told me that she didn't want me to regret not serving a mission. I think that was one of her biggest worries about us marrying without my going on a mission.

I often feel that I can't share that I didn't serve a mission, because of the stigma associated with it. When people share their mission stories in church, I sit quietly and listen, while hoping that I don't get called on to share anything. I think there are very few people in my ward who know I didn't serve a mission. I don't want them to think any less of me, or to have to explain why I didn't.

## ISAAC LYON

I prepared my whole life to serve a mission, but when the time arrived for me to submit my papers, I could not overcome a tremendous sense of dread and foreboding. I worked through my struggles with multiple stake presidents, three YSA bishops, and therapists but could not reconcile my mind's desire to serve with my soul's struggles. I was worthy, I was willing, and I was able; yet I could not find peace. Finally, at a low point, I found myself in my bishop's office. We were discussing missionary service when he perked up in his seat and asked me, "What if you're not supposed to serve a mission?" I felt the Spirit wash over me when he said those words, confirming their truth. With newfound clarity, I recognized that I had previously received numerous promptings that I shouldn't serve but hadn't recognized their source.

Not serving felt right, but it was still a painful decision. I felt like I was giving up, that I was disappointing my kid self, even though it was the right choice. To serve a mission is to share an experience that millions of other members have had. I don't have that shared experience and cannot relate to most members around me. That is painful sometimes. The most healing words I can hear when someone finds out I didn't serve are the words, "That's okay!" I know it's okay, but I need to hear it sometimes still. I don't know why I wasn't supposed to serve, but I experienced lots of blessings in those two years, like marrying my high school sweetheart, who (with her family) have always been supportive and understanding of my decision.

In my mind, a formal mission is only the start of a lifelong process of missionary work, and I'd like to think that I have not missed out on too much. Mine is not a traditional path, but I believe strongly that I am on the path of discipleship and will do my part to grow Zion.

# CHAPTER 9

# MANIFEST LOVE— EVEN IN POLITICS

By David L. Cook

Life experiences play a significant role in the development of one's political ideology. Those experiences may be personal or contained in the culture of our family and community. My mission in the Hispanic barrios of New York City was my first real exposure to poverty. I worked with some of the most marginalized of American society. I came to know honest, hard-working people living in deplorable conditions, most of them immigrants. They made the best of their circumstances but did not have the means nor the ability to influence their situation. Ever since, I have bristled at the implication that the poor choose to be poor or are simply lazy. For me, that was the beginning of the development of my personal political philosophy.

Political involvement throughout my adult life, in addition to consistently voting, has focused primarily on issues of alleviating poverty. I have worked to elect candidates, regardless of party, who reflect my values. As a lawyer, I have litigated poverty law issues, political asylum, and police abuse cases, and advised candidates on legal issues and policy. I have also litigated cases of voter suppression and ballot access. Most recently, I have run for office in my town on a platform of ending a system of political patronage and cronyism.

Throughout my experience, I have developed a set of principles that I believe are universal in their application. These principles may be of benefit to others as they engage in politics as a voter, activist, or candidate.

## Absolutism

No politician or no political party is perfect. Parties, for the most part, are self-interested creations. Without an effective check from an equal opposition, parties will solidify power which results in single-party domination, and not act for the best interest of the country or their constituents. Both leading American political parties are guilty of this intention. Both parties have dangerous extremes.

The Brethren understand the dangers of being aligned with only one party. No political party is favored by the Church. The Church's official statement about political neutrality states: "The Church's mission is to preach the gospel of Jesus Christ, not to elect politicians. The Church of Jesus Christ of Latter-day Saints is neutral in matters of party politics. This applies in all of the many nations in which it is established. The Church does not: Endorse, promote or oppose political parties, candidates or platforms."[1]

Political extremism leads to factionalism, and at its worst, hatred. Extremism is at the root of the worst atrocities and human rights violations in history. For Latter-day Saints, there is no support for extremism in our doctrine or history. Joseph Smith declared a universal truth when he said, "Through proving contraries, truth is made manifest."[2] This statement has universal application in politics and is the bedrock of the vision of the Founders, as expressed in the constitutional balance of power. Extremism is the province of despots and totalitarian regimes. Nonetheless, it often raises its ugly

---

1. "Political Neutrality," *Newsroom*, The Church of Jesus Christ of Latter-day Saints, accessed June 21, 2021, newsroom.churchofjesuschrist.org/official-statement/political-neutrality.
2. Joseph Smith, *Documentary History of the Church* (Salt Lake City: The Church of Jesus Christ of Latter-day Saints, 1930), 6:428.

head among the people of the world. Latter-day Saints should be on the front lines of pushing back against extremism.

## Joseph Smith's Presidential Campaign

In 1844, Joseph Smith wrote to the five candidates running for US President, asking how each would react to the crimes perpetrated against the Saints in Missouri. Only two responded. Martin Van Buren said he had no authority to prevent or redress the wrongs. Van Buren's chief rival, Henry Clay, responded that he was sympathetic but would make no commitments. Joseph, in frustration or desperation, declared his own candidacy. In my opinion, this was not an egomaniacal or quixotic effort, but an attempt to raise awareness about physical attacks on their freedom of religion. He also wanted to encourage people to vote, and Joseph's candidacy gave the Saints someone to vote for in good conscience. But Joseph knew he would not be elected president.

Having been denied Constitutional protections, Joseph wanted the nation to know the story of the Saints' persecutions and that they were deserving of the protections guaranteed to all citizens. He declared his candidacy on May 14, 1844 but was murdered six weeks later on June 27, 1844. His platform was bold and, even by modern standards, progressive. He called for prison reform, a national bank, the abolishment of slavery, and more. It is interesting that every single major plank in his then-progressive platform became the law of the land over the ensuing decades.

If one takes an historical look at the pronouncements of the Church on matters of public interest, they are very balanced across the political spectrum. Additions to the General Handbook in 2020 included a plea for stamping out racism and a warning against believing conspiracy theories and spreading misinformation on social media.[3] Counsel was also given concerning the

---

3.   Section 38.6.14 (prejudice) and 38.4.40 (conspiracies and misinformation), *General Handbook: Serving in The Church of Jesus Christ of Latter-day Saints* (Salt Lake City: The Church of Jesus Christ of Latter-day Saints, 2020), churchofjesuschrist.org/study/manual/general-handbook/38-church-policies-and-guidelines.

COVID-19 pandemic: "Members of the Church are encouraged to safeguard themselves, their children, and their communities through vaccination."[4]

## Advice for Latter-day Saints on Political Involvement

We have been counseled for years to be politically engaged. The First Presidency released a letter to Latter-day Saints in the United States shortly before the 2020 election, as they regularly do for US national elections, reinforcing this advice: "We urge Latter-day Saints to be active citizens by registering, exercising their right to vote, and engaging in civic affairs. We also urge you to spend the time needed to become informed about the issues and candidates you will be considering."[5]

Political engagement can be more than voting, and less than running for elected office as a candidate. From education to the environment, law enforcement to labor regulations, immigration to investments—we can learn about and support issues with our voices, money, and time. We can work with campaigns and non-profit organizations. There is a wide range of opportunity, both large and small, to be engaged in politics and government.

The following are some guidelines to consider in political engagement, regardless of your party affiliation or issue interest.

### Do your homework before you speak

Be sure that your knowledge of the issues is current and accurate and will bear up under scrutiny and rebuttal. Verify your facts from multiple reliable sources. Otherwise, you will be dismissed and lose

---

4. Section 38.7.13 (vaccination), *General Handbook: Serving in The Church of Jesus Christ of Latter-day Saints*, (Salt Lake City: The Church of Jesus Christ of Latter-day Saints, 2020), churchofjesuschrist.org/study/manual/general-handbook/38-church-policies-and-guidelines.

5. "First Presidency Encourages Latter-day Saints in the United States to Vote," *Newsroom*, The Church of Jesus Christ of Latter-day Saints, October 6, 2020, newsroom.churchofjesuschrist.org/article/first-presidency-letter-united-states-election-2020.

credibility. No one expects infallibility, but you must know whereof you speak, especially when you speak against the popular opinion.

We live in a time when disinformation—deliberate exaggeration or outright dishonesty—is gaining ground on truth. There are abundant resources to guide us in finding reliable information. Fact checking and media bias websites are a good place to start. Avoid any source that is rated by independent analysis as extreme, and don't fall victim to the claim that fact-checking sites cannot be trusted. Look at sources with long histories of journalistic excellence. Learn to recognize the difference between journalistic opinion and factual reporting.

## Avoid extremes

I am firmly convinced that nothing of value comes from the fringes in anything. Extremism in matters of politics and religion is dangerous and engenders a spirit of fear and anger toward other people. Christ Himself warned us about contention: "For verily, verily I say unto you, he that hath the spirit of contention is not of me, but is of the devil, who is the father of contention, and he stirreth up the hearts of men to contend with anger, one with another" (3 Nephi 11:29).

Political extremism consists of positions which are so far out on either end of the spectrum that it threatens to pull the middle apart. Like an elastic, if stretched too far to the right or left, it snaps in the center. Democracy has always been dependent upon maintaining a strong center, a solid middle ground, a place for the give and take of conflicting opinions and the marketplace of ideas.

Americans are proud to say that we are a government of laws, not of men. The Constitution—not an individual person—is the core of our government. Yet, in representative structure, we elect individuals whose intelligence and judgment we trust. We should not expect that our elected official will vote our wishes every time; but we expect that he or she will listen to reason, read our letters, study the issues, and vote in good conscience for whatever he or she thinks is in the best interest of the country or our state, not his or her own interest or that of a specific political party.

Litmus tests abound today. A litmus test is that an individual must believe a specific thing about an issue to be considered a "real" member of the political party, and they tend to be extreme positions. For example, abortion and gun access are two of the most emotionally charged litmus tests today. One party's litmus test demands a total ban in all instances, the other insists on no restrictions of any kind. The litmus test eliminates any nuance, as a registered member of either party may oppose abortion on moral grounds but recognize exceptions and oppose criminalizing abortion[6] or support weapons access within restricted parameters.[7]

In the marketplace of ideas, disagreement is legitimate, but smearing one's opponent as representing "the forces of Satan" or being anti-Christian threatens the very fabric of democracy. High-pitched name-calling is demonization of the highest order. The issue is not liberalism versus conservatism. It is a viable American pluralism versus a new form of political cannibalism, in which the exacerbation of one issue threatens to tear apart the fabric of the political order.

Instead, we should be committed to the idea of America, which is not blind patriotism or nationalism, but an open, pluralistic democracy. That concept means that groups with different interests and different points of view should negotiate with one another in the marketplace of ideas.

---

6. The Church's official stance opposes abortion but recognizes certain exceptions. Section 38.6.1, *General Handbook: Serving in The Church of Jesus Christ of Latter-day Saints*, (Salt Lake City: The Church of Jesus Christ of Latter-day Saints, 2020), churchofjesuschrist.org/study/manual/general-handbook/38-church-policies-and-guidelines. Furthermore, "The Church has not favored or opposed legislative proposals or public demonstrations concerning abortion." "Abortion," *Newsroom*, The Church of Jesus Christ of Latter-day Saints, accessed June 21, 2021, newsroom.churchofjesuschrist.org/official-statement/abortion.

7. The Church prohibits firearms by anyone except law enforcement officials in any church building, but does not appear to have made any official statement about gun control laws. Section 35.4.5, *General Handbook: Serving in The Church of Jesus Christ of Latter-day Saints*, (Salt Lake City: The Church of Jesus Christ of Latter-day Saints, 2020), churchofjesuschrist.org/study/manual/general-handbook/35-physical-facilities.

We have been counseled as Latter-day Saints many times to avoid extremism. Every generation has its doomsayers who preach a mix of religion and politics. They often claim either divine or Church approval. Despite generations of Church political neutrality, these purveyors of extremist ideologies gain adherents among some members. They have one thing in common—they "look beyond the mark." Elder Cook warned about this:

> Today there is a tendency among some of us to "look beyond the mark" rather than to maintain a testimony of gospel basics. We do this when we substitute the philosophies of men for gospel truths, engage in gospel extremism, seek heroic gestures at the expense of daily consecration, or elevate rules over doctrine. Avoiding these behaviors will help us avoid theological blindness and stumbling.[8]

When these doomsayers arise, it is alarming and indeed troubling to see Latter-day Saints pulled into these extreme philosophies.

I offer a remarkably simple antidote with an experience. Some years ago, upon receiving a new calling, I was trained by the Senior President of the Seventy. He said to me, "There are truths that are *taught* and those that are *caught* by close observation. Pay close attention to the First Presidency and Quorum of the Twelve." A clear application to today is the unrest caused in our society by the wearing of masks during the COVID-19 pandemic. Yet the Brethren were clear in their commentary. They encouraged us to wear masks and be vaccinated.[9] That was *taught*.

To those paying attention, the following was *caught*: we were the first church—before any government recommendations—to move to home worship. The Church spent considerable amounts of time and money to bring missionaries home to protect them during the pandemic, including on charter flights as necessary. Every member

---

8. Quentin L. Cook, "Looking Beyond the Mark," *Ensign*, March 2003, 40–44, abn.churchofjesuschrist.org/study/ensign/2003/03/looking-beyond-the-mark.
9. Section 38.7.13, *General Handbook*.

of the Quorum of the Twelve and First Presidency modeled mask wearing and social distancing at four separate general conferences held during the pandemic as of this writing: April and October 2020 and April and October 2021. Several General Authorities posted pictures on social media of receiving the vaccine. President Nelson encouraged us to pray for a vaccine and acknowledged divine intervention in its rapid development.[10]

Consider the professional training of the First Presidency: all three have advanced degrees from top universities in America and reached the heights of their professions in medicine, law, and business. Can you imagine a First Presidency more prepared to direct the Church through the COVID-19 crisis? Now overlay the professional qualifications with inspiration and we see the hand of the Lord in raising up this First Presidency at this time.

So, if you want clarity in times of trouble, pay attention to those we sustain as the mouthpiece of the Lord and not to the doomsayers. Do not allow your personal political views to supplant science and good counsel.

## Be Humble

I keep a copy of President Benson's classic conference talk "Beware of Pride"[11] and try to read it a few times each year. Too many people in politics become caught up in themselves. Be willing to admit mistakes, both personal and those of your party. Defend principles, not bad decisions. When your party leaders stray, be willing to admit the error. This will give you credibility.

Richard Nixon violated the trust of the American people and the law when he engaged in criminal behavior in the Watergate scandal. He defiantly resigned before impeachment proceedings commenced.

---

10. Sydney Walker, "Timeline: How the Church has responded to the global COVID-19 pandemic," *Church News*, The Church of Jesus Christ of Latter-day Saints, March 10, 2021, thechurchnews.com/history-revisited/2021-03-10/covid-19-church-response-timeline-missionaries-temples-191247.

11. Benson, "Beware of Pride."

A generation later, Bill Clinton committed perjury when he lied about inappropriate personal behavior, leading to his impeachment. The behavior of both should have been appalling to everyone regardless of party affiliation. I believe the country might have forgiven both if they had been humble and honest about their actions instead of ignoring or dismissing the significance of their poor choices. When we see the beam in the eye of the opposite party without recognizing the beam in our own, we have become tribal. It is all too prevalent these days.

Humility also means that you recognize that you should use your God-given intelligence to decide the controversies of the day, instead of expecting to find a specific scripture on every issue. Remember that Christ offers a blueprint for individual salvation, not a legislative agenda. I find it interesting that neither Christ nor the Apostles turned to government to help them establish the kingdom of heaven. Do not confuse your politics with a divine agenda. God's transcendent message is one of love, repentance, and salvation, not conservatism, liberalism, or any other secular ideology. Do not assume God is on your side.

I am reminded that Joseph Smith said, "The Lord has not given me a revelation on politics—I have not asked Him for one."[12] Never assume that the Church or, even worse, God favors one party.

### Be faithful and an example in all things

Be the most dedicated Latter-day Saint you can be. Magnify your callings. Pay your tithing. Make it difficult for the critics to dismiss you. Do not give anyone cause to question your commitment to the gospel, based on your political choices. At the same time, do not question someone else's commitment to the gospel when their political opinions differ from yours. Don't ever compromise your standards for political expediency.

You do not have a church life, a professional life, a political life, a personal life, and a family life. You have a life. Balance it. Be willing

---

12. *Documentary History of the Church*, 5:259.

to serve the Church and the public. Don't abandon your community. Involve your family in these activities. Over the years, I have given my kids plenty of lectures, few of which did any good. Sermons of example are more lasting. Let me share one such example.

On January 17, 1987, a small group of people in Forsyth County, Georgia, held a march to commemorate the birthday of Dr. Martin Luther King, Jr. They were violently attacked by several groups, including members of the Ku Klux Klan. The next morning, the attack was reported in headlines across America. My wife and I, like many Americans, were outraged as we read the story. We decided that I should go to Atlanta to participate in a second attempted march the following week.

I was not at all prepared for what I would experience. When we arrived in Forsyth County, a car pulled into a parking space next to us. We exchanged pleasant glances, and then the occupants opened the trunk of their car and began robing themselves with the white robes and tall hats of the Klan. I was shocked.

We were organized in a long procession and marched to City Hall without major incident. A few rocks and bottles were thrown by counter demonstrators. We walked silently with some occasional singing. Both sides of the procession were protected by a continuous line of the Georgia state police. I experienced some of the foulest language I had ever heard from young mothers with children in their arms, from teenagers, from older people who stood on the side-walk and expressed their anger and hatred against everything the march stood for.

On the flight home, I wondered why I went. I concluded that I went because I was afraid that I would be slipping if all I did was *talk* of brotherhood—afraid that while teaching and preaching about the kingdom of God, I might miss it all together. I was worried I might become complacent and comfortable in my own little world and not be grieved for the afflictions of others, regardless of what they might be. I remembered Dr. King's statement: "We will have to repent in this generation not merely for the hateful words and actions of the bad people but for the appalling silence of the good people."[13]

One might ask, was it worth it? Did it really accomplish anything? Did it change the attitudes of the counter protesters? Did it engender greater social harmony? The answer to the first question, was it worth it, is a resounding yes for me personally. The answer to all the rest is probably no. So what was the practical value?

The answer came several weeks later when my oldest son, who was in kindergarten, came home with a booklet that his class had put together in which each child drew a picture and described something they had learned recently. Most of the children wrote about the kinds of things you expect from kindergartners, such as play time, finger painting, toys, and so on. My son talked about learning about Dr. King and the struggle for equal rights, and added that his "daddy had gone to Georgia to fight for the rights of all people." That was my unequivocal answer for whether it was worth it. I am grateful I went for the message that it sent to my children and to my future grandchildren. I didn't go to be "seen of men" (Matthew 23:5), not even my children. I went to take a personal "stand for truth and righteousness."[14]

The Brethren constantly tell us of the "ongoing Restoration."[15] It is clear to me that their emphasis on ending racism is part of "bringing all things together in Christ" (Ephesians 1:10). We need to ask ourselves, what are the messages we unknowingly communicate to

13. Dr. Martin Luther King, Jr., "Letter from Birmingham Jail," April 16, 1963, University of Pennsylvania African Studies Center, africa.upenn.edu/Articles_Gen/Letter_Birmingham.html.

14. The former Young Women motto, abn.churchofjesuschrist.org/study/manual/young-women-personal-progress/young-women-motto-and-logo.

15. "Latter-day Saint Prophet, Wife and Apostle Share Insights of Global Ministry," *Newsroom*, The Church of Jesus Christ of Latter-day Saints, October 30, 2018, newsroom.churchofjesuschrist.org/article/latter-day-saint-prophet-wife-apostle-share-insights-global-ministry.

our families and community? May we not be guilty of "sleeping through the Restoration."[16]

## Reject Apathy

Far too many Americans and Latter-day Saints are simply apathetic about politics. They reject involvement at any level beyond voting. This attitude is simply not in keeping with gospel principles. Elder Henry D. Moyle said:

> We sometimes permit ourselves, around election time, to become concerned with politics. We should always be active. Now is the time to prepare for the next election. It is upon politics we must rely in large measure for the kind of government that we have. In turn we must rely upon that government for the protection of our rights, for the enforcement of our laws, and for the protection of our principles. . . . Our efforts should not be confined to the times of political elections. We should be on duty always.[17]

Elder Melvin J. Ballard added:

> It is indeed strange to hear, in a republic, of some who boast that they have nothing to do with politics; but it is stranger to hear of leading men who feel that this attitude is a proper one. In light of the gospel teachings, is this attitude correct? The Lord has given us positive instructions to see to it that we select wise men to make and administer the laws. . . . In the United States especially, where complete rights of suffrage have been given to the entire people, there arises a sacred responsibility, binding upon every member of the Church, to honor and magnify his political rights.[18]

---

16. Dieter F. Uchtdorf, "Are You Sleeping Through the Restoration?" April 2014 general conference, abn.churchofjesuschrist.org/study/general-conference/2014/04/are-you-sleeping-through-the-restoration.

17. Henry D. Moyle, April 1949 general conference, davidson-law.net/CR/1949%20Apr%200301%20MoyleHD%2012.pdf.

18. Melvin J. Ballard, "The Political Responsibility of Latter-day Saints," *Improvement Era,* 1954.

## Don't Let Political Differences Get in the Way of Serving in the Kingdom

A wonderful example from Church history illustrates this principle more than any other I know. Utah was the second territory in the Union to grant suffrage to women in February 1850. Wyoming was the first in December 1849, but the first women to actually cast ballots in any state or territory was in Utah, two days after suffrage was granted. Unfortunately, when Utah became a state in 1896, the women of the territory lost the right to vote because women's suffrage was allowed in the US territories but not in the states.

Two eminent men of the Utah Territory attended the state constitutional convention as delegates in 1895: B. H. Roberts, called as a General Authority in 1888 as one of the presidents of the Seventy, and Orson F. Whitney, later called to the Quorum of the Twelve in 1906. They were dear friends but vehemently disagreed on the issue of women's suffrage. Their debates were heated, yet their friendship remained intact. It is amusing to read in Whitney's and Roberts' autobiographies how they each viewed that debate. They both thought they had won the debate.

Roberts quoted the *Salt Lake Tribune*: "Roberts annihilates the suffragists . . . Whitney . . . disposed of . . . Mr. Roberts's speech the event of the day; Women suffrage means Bitterness, Strife, and unsettled conditions."[19] Whitney, describing the same event, quotes the rival newspaper, the *Salt Lake Herald*—"Seldom before, in the history of the Territory, has there been such a great debate as this. . . . Whitney, differing as much in oratory as in person from Roberts, but not less able and impressive, subjected him (Roberts) to scathing speech. Roberts' courage was turned to ridicule. . . . Whitney held

---

19. B.H. Roberts, *The Autobiography of B.H. Roberts* (edited by Gary Bergera, Salt Lake City: Signature Books, 1990), 192.

the convention. . . . Whitney was vociferously applauded, and after adjournment was overwhelmed with congratulations."[20]

Elder Whitney, a Democrat, was also the brother-in-law of Reed Smoot, a Republican, who later became a US senator from Utah. They served together in the Quorum of the Twelve. There are many examples of General Authorities who were divided by politics yet remained friends and continued to work together in the highest councils of the Church.

The gospel transcends our political views, and we must not forget that. President Hugh B. Brown said in 1968:

> Strive to develop a maturity of mind and emotion and a depth of spirit which enables you to differ with others on matters of politics without calling into question the integrity of those with whom you differ. Allow within the bounds of your definition of religious orthodoxy variations of political beliefs. Do not have the temerity to dogmatize in the issues where the Lord has seen fit to be silent.[21]

### The second great commandment does not include a political exemption

As Latter-day Saint Christians, we are commanded to love one another (Matthew 22:36–40). That is a tall order. This is not a simple suggestion. It is as strong a command as any taught by the Savior. Yet when it comes to differences in politics, many folks view vitriol as excusable, just part of the battle. We can disagree on issues, but we must never allow the language of hate to enter our conversations. Sadly, this vitriol is far too prevalent in social media, even among members of the Church who should know better.

---

20. Orson F. Whitney, *Through Memories Halls* (Independence, MO: Zions Printing and Publishing, 1930), 211.

21. Hugh B. Brown, "God is the Gardener" (commencement address, Brigham Young University, Provo, Utah, May 31, 1968), speeches.byu.edu/talks/hugh-b-brown/god-gardener/.

Even when we agree with people, we can't have our political party be just a place where we find connection in throwing "bombs" at the other side. Although it brings connection, it also generates fear and anxiety of others and exacerbates division even further. Dr. Brené Brown refers to the tendency to create a common enemy in her book *Braving the Wilderness*: "Common enemy intimacy is the opposite of true belonging. If the bond we share with others is simply that we hate the same people, the intimacy we experience is intense, immediately gratifying, and an easy way to discharge outrage and pain. It is not, however, fuel for real connection."[22]

A notable example of disagreement without vilification comes from political opposites in 2017. Hawk Newsome, president of Black Lives Matter of Greater New York, traveled to Washington DC to a rally on behalf of Donald Trump with the intention to counterprotest. Newsome knew there was potential for ugly and violent confrontations but was surprised to be invited onto the stage by event organizer Tommy Hodges. Newsome spoke about the Black Lives Matter movement and the need for justice for African Americans killed by police officers, while some of the crowd chanted in response, "White lives matter." *The Washington Post* reported that he concluded his remarks by saying, "If we really want to make America great, we do it together." Despite those chants, Newsome received a positive response from most members of the crowd, as well as supportive messages on social media after he had returned home.[23]

I remember participating in a mock election in elementary school and learning for the first time that my father was on the ballot as a candidate for local office. He obviously had not put a

---

22. Dr. Brené Brown, *Braving the Wilderness: The Quest for True Belonging and the Courage to Stand Alone* (New York: Random House, 2017), 136.

23. Kelyn Soong, "How a Black Lives Matter activist took the stage and got Trump supporters to listen at last weekend's DC rally," *Washington Post*, September 20, 2017, washingtonpost.com/news/inspired-life/wp/2017/09/20/how-a-black-lives-matter-activist-took-the-stage-and-got-trump-supporters-to-listen-at-last-weekends-dc-rally/.

tremendous amount of effort into the race since his children didn't even know that he was running. I think he was simply filling the slot at the request of the local party leadership. Nonetheless, I later learned something about that campaign that greatly impressed me. Prior to the election, my father received a phone call from a political ally with damaging information about his opponent. It would have likely guaranteed my father the election and would have been destructive not only to the political prospects of my father's opponent but also to his professional and personal reputation. I asked my father why he didn't do anything with it, and he said that there are some things more important than political office. The information would have ruined his opponent in the eyes of the community, his profession, and his family, and he did not want to be party to such destruction. It taught me a great lesson.

## The redemptive power of love

Elder George F. Richards bore witness about mercy in the October 1946 general conference, about a year after World War II ended. Many who heard him had lost sons or husbands in the war; all had suffered in various ways and had reason to be bitter. Elder Richards set aside his prepared manuscript and spoke instead about "Love for Mankind."[24]

He reviewed the teachings and example of Jesus Christ "in life and in death, a voluntary gift for us, a manifestation of love that has no comparison." He professed love for all who could hear him "in the Church or out of the Church . . . good or bad, whatever their condition of life," and reminded his listeners that in the premortal life, we lived in love together and "ought to love one another just the same here."

He said, "The Lord has revealed to me, by dreams, something more than I ever understood or felt before." He first told of a dream from forty years before, in which he stood in the presence of the Savior and felt indescribable love for Him. Then he described a more recent dream in which he and some of his associates were in a

---

24. George F. Richards, "Love for Mankind," October 1946 general conference, content. ldschurch.org/chpress/bc/media/GFR/George-F-Richards-1946-10-06.pdf.

courtyard where German soldiers led by Adolf Hitler were preparing weapons to slaughter them. A circle was formed, and Elder Richards dreamed that he faced Hitler. Then Elder Richards spoke to him:

> "I am your brother. You are my brother. In our heavenly home we lived together in love and peace. Why can we not so live here on the earth?"
>
> And it seemed to me that I felt in myself, welling up in my soul, a love for that man, and I could feel that he was having the same experience, and presently he arose, and we embraced each other and kissed each other, a kiss of affection.
>
> Then the scene changed so that our group was within the circle, and he and his group were on the outside, and when he came around to where I was standing, he stepped inside the circle and embraced me again, with a kiss of affection.
>
> I think the Lord gave me that dream. Why should I dream of this man, one of the greatest enemies of mankind, and one of the wickedest, but that the Lord should teach me that I must love my enemies, and I must love the wicked as well as the good?
>
> Now, who is there is this wide world that I could not love under those conditions, if I could only continue to feel as I felt then?[25]

## Conclusion

There is no question that political factionalism and judging among members of the Church has risen to the level of concern among the Brethren, so much so that President Oaks addressed the issue in the April 2021 general conference. I can think of no more fitting counsel to conclude this chapter than President Oaks' own words:

> There are many political issues, and no party, platform, or individual candidate can satisfy all personal preferences. Each citizen must therefore decide which issues are most important to him or her at any particular time. Then members should seek

---

25. Ibid.

inspiration on how to exercise their influence according to their individual priorities. This process will not be easy. It may require changing party support or candidate choices, even from election to election.

Such independent actions will sometimes require voters to support candidates or political parties or platforms whose other positions they cannot approve. That is one reason we encourage our members to refrain from judging one another in political matters. We should never assert that a faithful Latter-day Saint cannot belong to a particular party or vote for a particular candidate. We teach correct principles and leave our members to choose how to prioritize and apply those principles on the issues presented from time to time. We also insist, and we ask our local leaders to insist, that political choices and affiliations not be the subject of teachings or advocacy in any of our Church meetings.[26]

It is my prayer that as Latter-day Saints, we acknowledge the beam in our own eye rather than the mote in another's eye and rise to the Lord's expectation for us to love one another.

---

26. Dallin H. Oaks, "Defending Our Divinely Inspired Constitution," April 2021 general conference, churchofjesuschrist.org/study/general-conference/2021/04/51oaks.

# CHAPTER 10

# MINISTERING TO THOSE WITH QUESTIONS[1]

I love the restored doctrine revealed through the Prophet Joseph Smith and want more people to connect with this doctrine that brings hope, healing, and peace. This restored doctrine includes Heavenly Parents who love us and with whom we can have a personal relationship; the infinite Atonement of Jesus Christ to forgive sin and heal our broken hearts; the plan of salvation that gives us understanding of and perspective for our mortal life; power of covenants; the Book of Mormon's ability to bring us to Christ; and personal revelation.

Once a month, we share our hearts in sacrament meeting about these beautiful teachings and our love of the Savior. It is common for people to say "I know" at the beginning of their sentences: "I know God lives. I know the Church is true. I know Joseph Smith was a prophet." I share their sentiment and make similar declarative statements myself.

But I am aware that many people feel that because they cannot say "I know" with such confidence, they do not belong with us. They have questions about doctrines, concerns about Church policies,

---

1. For more on this topic, please read my brother David Ostler's book, *Bridges: Ministering to Those Who Question.*

and doubts about historical claims. They wonder how people will respond if they open up with their questions.

## The Restoration Began with a Question

The foundation of the Restoration of the gospel was a young man asking a sincere question in prayer. I appreciate Joseph Smith's pondering before that prayer, as explained in the Pearl of Great Price—he did not just wake up one morning and go to the woods to pray on a whim. For two years, he had read the scriptures, attended religious services, asked questions of knowledgeable people, and thought extensively about spiritual things.[2]

Many Church leaders encourage members to ask sincere questions in this same productive way. For example, President Ballard posted the following on Facebook, which was shared by *LDS Living*:

> There is absolutely nothing wrong with asking questions or investigating our history, doctrine, and practices. The Restoration began when Joseph Smith sought an answer to a sincere question.
>
> When I have a question that I cannot answer, I often turn to those who can help me—such as trained scholars and historians. Blessed by the information they provide, I am better equipped to seek the guidance of the Holy Ghost.
>
> To those of you with questions, I invite you to turn to your parents; auxiliary leaders; Church teachers, including seminary and institute; bishops; and stake presidents.
>
> And to those of you offering answers I say, please do not simply brush the question off. Do not tell him or her to not worry about the question. Please do not doubt the person's dedication to the Lord or His work. Instead, help the person find answers to their questions. We need to do better in responding to honest questions. Although we may not be able to answer every question about the cosmos or about our history, practices, or doctrine, we can provide many answers to those who are sincere. When we don't know the answer, we can search to find

---

2.  "History, circa summer 1832," 1, josephsmithpapers.org.

answers together—a shared search that may bring us closer to each other and closer to God.

Of course, we may not always find satisfying answers to our questions. At such times, it's good to remember that there is still a place in religion for faith. Sometimes we can learn and study and know; sometimes we have to believe and trust and hope.[3]

## Creating Space for Differences in Testimonies

In November 2018, I asked this poll question on Twitter, which garnered 1,169 responses: "For those of you who hold a temple recommend, please indicate your testimony of the Church: 1) know it's true OR 2) believe it's true OR 3) hope it's true OR 4) not sure if it's true."[4] The results were as follows:

- *Know*: 41%
- *Believe*: 33%
- *Hope*: 15%
- *Not sure*: 11%

A few days later, I asked this second poll question: "If you are an active Latter-day Saint and in a faith crisis, is to your hope to 1) find a way to stay OR 2) find a way to leave?"[5]

Eighty-eight percent of the 335 respondents indicated they wanted to find a way to stay within the Church. After meeting with hundreds of individuals sharing their faith crises with me, this result

---

3. "Elder Ballard: We Need to Be Better at Answering Difficult Questions and Never Brush Them Off," *LDS Living*, January 28, 2017, ldsliving.com/Elder-Ballard-There-s-Nothing-Wrong-With-Asking-Questions-About-Church-Topics/s/84321.

4. @Papa_Ostler (Richard Ostler). "For those of you who hold a temple recommend, please indicate your testimony of the Church. Thank you." *Twitter*, 15 Nov. 2018, 10:13 a.m., twitter.com/Papa_Ostler/status/1063087653669634048.

5. @Papa_Ostler (Richard Ostler). "If you are an active Latter-day Saint and in a faith crisis, is your hope to find a way to stay or find a way to leave." *Twitter*, 18 Nov. 2018, 2:45 p.m., twitter.com/Papa_Ostler/status/1064243296573128704.

did not surprise me. I repeated both Twitter polls in July 2021, with similar results.[6]

While these are hardly scientific studies, these eye-opening results are worth pondering. It is interesting to note that less than half of the temple recommend holders who responded are confident enough in their testimony to use the word *know*, yet it is the most common word we hear in our fast and testimony meetings. Even though temple recommend holders are often considered to be our strongest members, over half responded with "believe," "hope," or are "not sure."

We can take comfort in the scriptural teaching that to some it is given to "know" and to some it is given to "believe" (D&C 46:13–14). Both "knowing" and "believing" are listed in those verses, along with other gifts of the Spirit. The Savior explained, "All have not every gift given unto them; for there are many gifts, and to every man is given a gift by the Spirit of God" (D&C 46:11). We should honor that scriptural doctrine of different spiritual gifts (some believing and others knowing) and be fine with that.

I believe it strengthens our church to have people with different spiritual gifts. The Savior further explained the reason for bestowing different gifts: "To some is given one, and to some is given another, that all may be profited thereby" (D&C 46:12).

Saying "I know the Church is true" should not be a requirement imposed by others, ourselves, or our culture to be a fully participating member of our congregations, the body of Christ. Elder Uchtdorf taught, "I know of no sign on the doors of our meetinghouses that says, 'Your testimony must be this tall to enter'."[7] All different types of testimonies should be welcomed and valued in our congregations.

---

6.  @Papa_Ostler (Richard Ostler). "For those of you who hold a Temple recommend, please indicate your testimony of the Church. Thank you." *Twitter,* 11 July 2021, twitter.com/Papa_Ostler/status/1414292989619363840. "If you are an active Latter-day Saint and in a faith crisis, is your hope to:" *Twitter,* 11 July 2021, twitter.com/Papa_Ostler/status/1414292383060140033.
7.  Uchtdorf, "Receiving a Testimony of Light and Truth."

No honest testimony should ever feel like a second-class testimony. I believe that the person behind each testimony is a daughter or son of our Heavenly Parents, doing the best they can to live their covenants and come unto Christ. All testimony types need to be heard and valued.

If you have an "I know the Church is true" testimony, please continue to share it. We need to hear your testimony! If you have a "hope" or even "I *want* to believe" testimony, please share that as well. If someone sits in our congregations and all they hear is "I know the Church is true" with every testimony, they may think, "I don't belong here because I don't have that type of testimony. What am I doing here? Is there anyone else like me?" Hearing all testimony types helps everyone feel that they belong as we create Zion.

## My Own Faith Journey

I had previously assumed that a faith crisis was a result of sin or a lack of praying, reading scriptures, or attending church. I learned firsthand that this was not true, because my own mini faith crisis occurred while I was a bishop, giving everything for the cause. I felt some feelings of being "switched off" and "squeezed out."

In his book *Planted,* Patrick Mason defines being "switched off" or "squeezed out"[8] of the Church. In both cases, these may be long-time members with a deep commitment to the core teachings of the gospel of Jesus Christ.

The "switched off" group encounters troubling new information regarding our history or doctrine. This new knowledge does not align with what they were previously taught. It is unsettling and causes them to wonder what else they have not been told. They often find it hard to continue to trust the Church and its leaders.

---

8.   Patrick Q. Mason, *Planted: Belief and Belonging in an Age of Doubt* (Salt Lake City: Deseret Book, 2015), 2–3. In those pages, Mason pointed out that the words "switched off" and "squeezed out" were coined by Latter-day Saint historian Richard Bushman.

The "squeezed out" group feels they just do not fit in at church, usually because of what Mason calls "the dominant political conservatism among the members (at least in the United States)"[9] or other current issues. They often embrace the core of the gospel but ask heartfelt questions about the Church's policies for its LGBTQ members, whether girls and women have the same opportunities for spiritual growth and recognition that boys and men do, and/or other issues. Their strong feelings may be dismissed by fellow members, and they may be suspected of not being faithful to the gospel. In reality, it is often their commitment to Christ's teachings that motivates them to ask sincere questions.

Jana Riess came to similar conclusions in her book, *The Next Mormons: How Millennials Are Changing the LDS Church*. In her research, the top reasons she heard for leaving the Church are concerns such as these: an individual could not reconcile personal values with Church policies, some stopped believing some basic concepts, and others felt judged or misunderstood.[10] Young people in particular identify with feeling attacked and condemned if they express concerns or challenges. Some people feel isolated at church and conclude that there is no place for them despite their core commitments to the Savior and His gospel.

The observations of Patrick Mason and Jana Riess line up with my experiences as a bishop, both working with ward members and in my own life. In our YSA ward of three hundred members, about two hundred did not attend. I reached out to as many as I could find, connecting through text and social media. Many were willing to meet with me, and over time, about half of the non-attending YSAs told me their stories.

Since my release, I continue to visit with individuals with questions in my home. I am honored to have heard hundreds of stories from wonderful people. Listening to them has helped me better

---

9. Ibid.

10. Jana Riess, *The Next Mormons: How Millennials Are Changing the LDS Church* (New York: Oxford University Press, 2019), 225.

understand why some of our good members struggle and why some step away.

I love these words from Elder Uchtdorf, who shows empathy and kindness to those with questions, who may be unsure of their future in the Church: "One might ask, 'If the gospel is so wonderful, why would anyone leave?' Sometimes we assume it is because they have been offended or lazy or sinful. Actually, it is not that simple. . . . Some of our dear members struggle for years with the question whether they should separate themselves from the Church."[11]

Although my faith crisis has passed, I sometimes still feel "squeezed out." I encourage everyone to make space for people with all kinds of feelings about how to best follow Jesus, as I respect and make space for those who see political and social issues differently from me.

Earlier, I shared this quote by Henri Nouwen: "A minister's service will not be perceived as authentic unless it comes from a heart wounded by the suffering about which he speaks. The great illusion of leadership is to think that others can be led out of the desert by someone who has never been there."[12]

While I do not think that anyone has to have personally experienced every problem to help others, I do believe that life experiences can help build understanding and empathy.

I am now grateful for this mini faith crisis, because it gives me better tools to "lead others out of the desert" and have greater understanding for those who have stepped away from the Church. I know that desert. It was one of the most difficult things I have experienced. It affected almost everything in my life, including my emotional health. I am particularly grateful to my wife, Sheila, my family, my stake president, and others who have helped me so much along this journey. I no longer look at that experience as a step

---

11. Uchtdorf, "Come, Join with Us."

12. Nouwen, *The Wounded Healer: Ministry in Contemporary Society.*

backward. I look at it as "falling upwards" and an important part of my eternal progress.

My home stake president, David Sturt, effectively ministered to me at the beginning of my mini faith crisis by listening when I opened up about my concerns. He gave me permission to have a "fallen domino or two" as I continued to make my way forward as a faithful Latter-day Saint. Usually when one domino falls, they all fall—but President Sturt was wise enough to give me space. He did not ask me to change my feelings or give me a spiritual checklist of things to do that would somehow align my feelings with most members. I have not yet resolved some of my concerns, but I remain a deeply committed member with a firm testimony of our restored gospel. He helped me focus on dominoes that are firmly standing with deep roots that form the core of my testimony—doctrines of Heavenly Parents who love me, the plan of happiness, the restored priesthood, a modern-day prophet, the truthfulness of the Book of Mormon and its ability to help me come unto Christ, the power of temple covenants, and the Atonement of Jesus Christ.

I would not invite anybody to seek a faith crisis, but if it is part of someone's journey, it need not be a big setback. It could be part of their mortal plan that their Heavenly Parents knew they needed to help them grow in unique ways that wouldn't otherwise be possible, and develop better tools to help others.

As I "fall upwards," I do not think I can ever go back to what I used to believe. I move on with a different understanding. It is never going to be the same. For me, there is some grief for the earlier faith I used to have—yet I make my way forward as a committed Latter-day Saint because of our restored doctrine that brings hope and healing to my life.

## Holding Space for Concerns within the Ongoing Restoration

One thing that comforts me in my unresolved concerns is that President Nelson has stated clearly that the Restoration is not complete: "We're witnesses to a process of restoration. If you think the Church has been fully restored, you're just seeing the beginning.

There is much more to come. . . . Wait till next year. And then the next year. Eat your vitamin pills. Get your rest. It's going to be exciting."[13]

As a Church claiming the fulness of the gospel, we should be careful to not lock ourselves into believing that we already have all we need from God, that there is nothing more to know. The ninth article of faith states, "We believe that God will yet reveal many great and important things pertaining to the Kingdom of God." In the introduction of this book, I shared this quote from Elder Uchtdorf: "Remember, it was the questions young Joseph asked that opened the door for the restoration of all things. We can block the growth and knowledge our Heavenly Father intends for us. How often has the Holy Spirit tried to tell us something we needed to know but couldn't get past the massive iron gate of what we thought we already knew?"[14]

The Restoration is not finished. There is still so much more to learn.

As we create a safe place for people to ask questions, we also need to hold space for those who have had a difficult leader experience. In his October 2013 conference address, Elder Uchtdorf acknowledged:

> To be perfectly frank, there have been times when members or leaders in the Church have simply made mistakes. There may have been things said or done that were not in harmony with our values, principles, or doctrine. I suppose the Church would be perfect only if it were run by perfect beings. God is perfect, and His doctrine is pure. But He works through us—His imperfect children—and imperfect people make mistakes.[15]

---

13. "Latter-day Saint Prophet, Wife and Apostle Share Insights of Global Ministry," Newsroom.

14. Uchtdorf, "Acting on the Truths of the Gospel of Jesus Christ."

15. Uchtdorf, "Come, Join with Us."

In most cases, I do not believe there was any malice behind the mistakes made by members or leaders. Even though these mistakes may have caused us pain, realizing in most situations there was no intent to harm may help us move forward. Part of the progress of the Restoration is the progress of members of the Church learning to treat each other more kindly, apologizing when mistakes are made, and extending grace and forgiveness to each other.

Perhaps a person's concern will be resolved by Church leaders in a future policy adjustment. I have seen that happen many times, including in early January 2019 with wording adjustments to the temple ceremony,[16] and in May 2019 with discontinuing the one-year waiting period for temple sealings after civil marriage.[17]

The most dramatic example in my lifetime occurred in June 1978, when I was a seventeen-year-old driving to work. I still remember being in my car at the intersection of 33rd South and 27th West in Salt Lake City when I heard the joyful news on the radio that the Church was changing its policy and priesthood ordination was extended to all worthy male members of the Church. It was a day I will never forget.

In addition to holding space for members with questions about current issues, we need to hold space for different feelings about elements of Church history such as race and the priesthood. In 2013, the Church released a Gospel Topics essay which states:

> Over time, Church leaders and members advanced many theories to explain the priesthood and temple restrictions. None of these explanations is accepted today as the official doctrine of the Church. . . .

---

16. "First Presidency Statement on Temples," Newsroom, The Church of Jesus Christ of Latter-day Saints, January 2, 2019, newsroom.churchofjesuschrist.org/article/temple-worship.

17. Sarah Jane Weaver, "First Presidency Discontinues One-Year Waiting Period for Temple Sealings After Civil Marriage," *Church News*, May 7, 2019, churchofjesuschrist.org/church/news/first-presidency-discontinues-one-year-waiting-period-for-temple-sealings-after-civil-marriage.

Today, the Church disavows the theories advanced in the past that black skin is a sign of divine disfavor or curse, or that it reflects unrighteous actions in a premortal life; that mixed-race marriages are a sin; or that Blacks or people of any other race or ethnicity are inferior in any way to anyone else. Church leaders today unequivocally condemn all racism, past and present, in any form.[18]

Holding space for feelings about race and the priesthood is taught by my friend Paul Reeve, active Latter-day Saint, professor of Mormon Studies at the University of Utah, and expert on race and Latter-day Saint history. In the podcast, Paul shared that we should create space in our congregations for those who believe that withholding the priesthood and temple blessings from Blacks was not God's will:

> You can be a faithful Latter-day Saint and not believe that the racial restrictions were of God or of divine origin. In fact, as a historian, that's where the evidence is. When you respond by calling my faith into question, that is really hurtful. I've experienced it and it doesn't feel good. So you're asking me to believe that God was a racist rather than a prophet, a human, a fallible human was a racist? That's what it boils down to.
>
> The information I have about God is that He and She are not respecters of persons and that They treat all of their children the same. All are alike unto God. To me, that makes sense because I'm a parent. I love all my kids. I think Heavenly Father and Heavenly Mother love all of Their children as well. You have to tie yourself into some pretty tough knots to try to then suggest that somehow the priesthood and temple ban was of divine origin.
>
> Please don't suggest that someone's faith is somehow suspect because they don't believe that the racial restrictions were of divine origin. In fact, the evidence is in their favor, and yet we sometimes call their faith into question? In my estimation,

---

18. "Race and the Priesthood," Gospel Topics, The Church of Jesus Christ of Latter-day Saints, accessed May 7, 2021, churchofjesuschrist.org/study/manual/gospel-topics-essays/race-and-the-priesthood.

people who study the racial history of the Church and understand its complexities are exercising a great deal of faith—and charity—in their discipleship. They are willing to acknowledge weaknesses in themselves and in their leaders, and remain committed. That is a wonderful example of faith. There's more than one way to be a Latter-day Saint.

My understanding is that we're supposed to let Jesus be the judge. We're not supposed to judge each other. Because you may not like the message, that doesn't mean the messenger's faith is somehow suspect. We are all walking a stumbling path with God. I stumble all the time. As such, I try to be more accepting of my fellow Latter-day Saints who are stumbling.[19]

How we feel about this issue is not a temple recommend question, nor should it be a litmus test of our commitment to the gospel of Jesus Christ. I hope that Latter-day Saints who share Paul's feelings on this issue—as well as those who see this differently—are equally welcome and needed in our congregations. Further, before firming up our own conclusions on this topic, we should listen to Black Latter-day Saints to understand their feelings, since they are the group most impacted by past restrictions.[20]

Understanding that substantial changes have been enacted in the past can prepare us in anticipation of further developments in the future. In the meantime, we should extend support and grace to our leaders who are called of God and have priesthood keys and authority to lead the Church, as well as to individuals who are unsettled about various aspects of our doctrine and organization.

## Normalizing Questions

Jared Halverson, an institute teacher at the University of Utah, teaches a class called "Foundations of the Restoration," which

---

19. *Listen, Learn & Love* podcast episode 278.
20. See listenlearnandlove.org/black-latter-day-saints for episodes with Black Latter-day Saints.

addresses difficult issues in Church history. He shared this on the *Listen, Learn & Love* podcast:

> The class started with maybe thirty students. Once they realized, wait, we're going to really talk about this thorny stuff, the next week they brought friends and we were at sixty and the next week . . . a hundred. By the end of the semester, we had two to three hundred students meeting in the chapel to talk about these issues.
>
> One wonderful young man wanted to give the Church one more chance. He said he had asked some of his early questions at church and had been ostracized and felt, "There's no place for me in the Church if I have questions." But he decided to give Institute one shot. He happened to come into the chapel where the Institute class was taught, probably because it was easy to hide in the back and not get called out. We were talking about prophets, and he asked one of the questions that had really been weighing on him for years: "Prophets don't claim to be infallible. So how do you follow fallibility?" It was a great question.
>
> The next day he sent me an email and said, "I was scared to death." He gave me his background and told me what a leap of faith it was to come into the class at all. He felt, "Maybe I could venture my question here," and raised his hand. He said his hand was shaking when he did. He was just scared to death that a bunch of heads would turn to see who the apostate was that snuck into the back. And sure enough, when he asked his question, a bunch of heads turned and he thought, "Yep, it's going to be the same as before."
>
> I thanked him for the question and said to him, "If you weren't going to ask it, I was going to," and clicked to the next slide in the PowerPoint. And there was his question. It led to some great one-on-one conversations between this young man and me, multiplied by dozens and dozens and scores of students over the past years, as they felt comfortable. I told the class at one point, if space becomes an issue and we can't fit in this room anymore, I'll kick out the active Latter-day Saints to make room for the ones who are really struggling.
>
> It's been neat to see a generation of young people wanting to become better equipped to respond kindly and competently

to the questions that their family members, their old mission companions, their friends and roommates might have about the Church.[21] What a blessing to be able to say to the person, "That's a great question and I don't know the answer, but I'd love to spend some time studying it and hope you would join me." That happened in the mission field all the time, right?

It is about normalizing questions and "de-demonizing," if that's a word, to let them know that the questions are welcome. You can ask anything, and I'm not going to judge you or second-guess you or question your commitment, just because you happen to have a question.

You don't have to be an expert to be a conversation partner. You may need to turn to people who know specific answers to Church history issues or doctrinal concerns. But what people need first and foremost is a listening ear: "You're a human being and your story matters, and your experience is as valid as anyone else's, and I want to hear it. You deserve to be heard and to be validated, to be welcomed and loved."[22]

## Encouraging Questions

President Ballard taught the following at a Church Education System (CES) training broadcast:

> Gone are the days when a student asked an honest question and a teacher responded, "Don't worry about it!" Gone are the days when a student raised a sincere concern and a teacher bore his or her testimony as a response intended to avoid the issue.

---

21. It's worth noting that Brother Halverson points out that this generation of young adults may not have the usual level of parental support because both parents and children are confronting new information simultaneously with the dramatic expansion of access to historical documents via the internet. In the podcast, he said, "This might be an area where you can't go to your parents. They might have the same question you do. But your children will not have this problem. We have to get one generation over the hump, so to speak. We have to help one group navigate it more on their own, so there can be 'inoculation' from now on. When today's generation become parents, they can say, 'I found those same kinds of issues when I was a kid, and this is what I did'."

22. *Listen, Learn & Love* podcast episode 259.

Church leaders today are fully conscious of the unlimited access to information, and we are making extraordinary efforts to provide accurate context and understanding of the teachings of the Restoration. The Gospel Topics essays provide balanced and reliable interpretations of the facts for controversial and unfamiliar Church-related subjects. It is important that you know the content in these essays like you know the back of your hand. "Seek learning, even by study and also by faith" as you master the content of these essays. Remember that "Why?" can be a great question that leads to gospel understanding.[23]

It is my hope that our homes, congregations, and seminaries and institutes are safe places—like Brother Halverson's classroom—where we can ask questions and feel like we belong. I worry that if Latter-day Saints feel that the only safe places to ask their questions are sources outside the Church—or they are made to feel less faithful because of their questions—they may conclude that outside the Church is where they belong.

Indeed, President Ballard talked about the importance of *belonging*—and used this word over fifteen times—in his April 2021 general conference talk:

> The Mayo Clinic recently noted: "Having a sense of belonging is so important. . . . Nearly every aspect of our lives is organized around belonging to something." This report adds, "We cannot separate the importance of a sense of belonging from our physical and mental health"[24]—and, I would add, our spiritual health.[25]

---

23. M. Russell Ballard, "The Opportunities and Responsibilities of CES Teachers in the 21st Century" (Church Education System address, Salt Lake City, Feb. 26, 2016), churchofjesuschrist.org/broadcasts/article/evening-with-a-general-authority/2016/02/the-opportunities-and-responsibilities-of-ces-teachers-in-the-21st-century.

24. Jennifer Wickham, "Is Having a Sense of Belonging Important?" *Speaking of Health* (blog), Mayo Clinic Health System, March 8, 2019, mayoclinichealthsystem.org.

25. Ballard, "Hope in Christ."

I also worry that sometimes our classroom culture at church has become the "best answer club." Yes, we need the best answers, but we also need to create space where people can ask a question without feeling judged. It takes a lot of courage to say, "I feel differently" or "I don't understand." Members without the best answer but instead with an honest question also need to feel a sense of belonging. I once saw a dear sister share a concern and several class members immediately addressed it. It was almost like they were waiting for a situation to share their expertise. I watched her. She sank in her chair. Their answers were correct—but they could have first validated her concern and courage for asking her question. I hope if someone in church asks a vulnerable question or gives an honest comment, the response from class members recognizes their courage. The teacher could perhaps say, "Thank you for the courage to ask your question. Many people may have the same question." That follow-up will help them know that church is a safe place, their contributions are needed, and help them feel like they belong.

In general, I think an effective style of teaching is not to answer the question immediately, but to ask the person their thoughts on their very own question. They likely have insights, perhaps lots of research done, and might actually have a good answer already but not realize it. Perhaps all they need is a safe place to think out loud and explore their concerns in a Spirit-filled atmosphere of support among fellow seekers of truth. That creates a feeling of connection as you believe in them. If the teacher answers their question right away, it can be almost dismissive, as if to say, "That was an easy question; you should have known the answer." But if you sit with the question for a little while, inviting responses and deeper thinking, it validates both the question and the person asking it.

Brother Halverson also shared this experience on the podcast:

> A young woman was asking about plural marriage. We probably spent two hours on it, but nothing seemed to be sticking. So I backed up and said, "Tell me a little bit more about your question and why are you asking it? Where does it come from?" For her, plural marriage was becoming a personal question as she was getting older and starting to wonder about her marriage prospects. "Will I marry a widower, for example, who is already

sealed to someone?" All of a sudden, I understood that yes, this is a historical question, but really, it's also a personal one.[26]

Once Brother Halverson really listened to her question and discovered what was behind it, he could see that the answers to the historical question of plural marriage were far different than the answers to the personal question of what her future held if she married someone who was already sealed to another. Truly listening without dismissing her question was the key to helping this sister move towards finding peace.

## The Good Shepherd Knows His Flock

Jesus tells about the shepherd caring for a flock of one hundred sheep when one sheep is found to be missing (Matthew 18:11–14). He physically leaves the ninety-nine to find the lost one. The shepherd "goeth into the mountains" to seek the sheep that is lost (verse 12). The word *mountains* is interesting here. I believe it illustrates the effort required on our part to go out to minister to those with questions. As the shepherd, Christ didn't stand at the edge of the flock and call out to the one. He left and actively sought the missing sheep. He knew the one well enough to know why they left and where to find them.

How can we minister to those who have questions if we don't have some understanding of what brought them to where they are?

An elders quorum president once told me of an experience visiting a member who didn't attend church meetings. After creating a genuine friendship of trust with this good man, the president asked him why he didn't attend. The man told him, with tears in his eyes, "I've lived in this ward for over twenty years, and no one has ever asked me this question." He was touched by one Church member's desire to understand him, and a genuine friendship was established. One of the conclusions I draw from this is that we need to do a better job of creating safe places for members to share their concerns and questions. Twenty years earlier, perhaps this member

---

26. *Listen, Learn & Love* podcast episode 259.

would have stayed if he felt safe opening up, welcome, understood, and his participation needed.

I wish I had understood this principle earlier in my life. I was once a ministering brother to a member of our ward who was not active. During our visits, we would have a nice conversation and end with a prayer. Both of us seemed to be going through the motions, and neither of us brought up the elephant in the room: why he didn't attend church anymore. If I could go back in time and redo this assignment, I would try to first develop a genuine friendship with this man to earn his trust. Then I could ask about his feelings toward the Church, hoping he would feel safe responding. If I had known the reasons he didn't attend church, perhaps I would have had better insights into how to minister to him more effectively.

I hope we can follow the example of Christ—the perfect shepherd—and develop better tools to minister to those in our lives with questions and concerns.

## Being Prepared to Respond to Concerns

The story of the Good Shepherd calls us to be prepared for those honest and vulnerable conversations. In my experience, members are nervous about disclosing a faith crisis to local Church leaders, friends, or family members. Another Twitter poll I created asked, "If you are an active Latter-day Saint and in a faith crisis, have you told your current bishop?"[27] Eighty-six percent of 606 participants said no.

Think about that for a moment. Eighty-six percent said no. Now, I did not create this poll to pick on our good bishops. The bishops I know are immensely dedicated to bringing others to Christ and have blessed my life and my family for decades. But it is sometimes hard for people to talk about their questions.

---

27. @Papa_Ostler (Richard Ostler). "If you are active Latter-day Saint and in a faith crisis, have you told your current bishop?" *Twitter*, 1 Dec 2018, 11:10 p.m., twitter.com/Papa_Ostler/status/1069081357668691969.

Sadly, many Church members equate those who doubt with the elect who will be deceived in the last days (see Matthew 24:24) or the tares instead of wheat (see Matthew 13:18–30). How can people feel safe opening up to a local leader, parent, or friend if our culture has already defined them like this? I have personally felt some of this judgment and it is painful. I wondered if someone like me is welcome. I am able to navigate these experiences, but what about others? These regrettable comparisons have created fear about sharing one's heart that I believe is a stumbling block to minister to these members in an effective way.

When I meet with someone in a faith crisis, I ask, "Is your goal to stay in the Church or to step away from the Church?" By far, most say they want to find a way to stay, which is consistent with the Twitter poll mentioned earlier in this chapter—eighty-eight percent want to stay.

What I try to do for others—and the best thing people did for me when I opened up about my own faith crisis—is to listen, listen, listen. Validate how they feel with sincere phrases like, "Thank you for telling me. I can see how hard this is for you." This does not mean that we need to agree with their feelings. I do not believe that validating them deepens any wedge between them and the Church. We can heal and give hope when we listen and support their feelings and concerns. There is no need for everyone to feel the same or be the same, as we share the common goal of coming unto Christ. Each of us is a work in progress in our respective journeys.

As we seek to act like the Good Shepherd, we can walk with others as they deconstruct their faith and then help them reconstruct it in a sustainable way. We should not be afraid of walking this road with them. I believe it helps to have supportive Latter-day Saints in their lives, so they are not walking this road alone.

Brother Halverson describes deconstructing as a process to unpack what one believes in. It may include helping the person consider questions like: "Do I believe in God? Jesus Christ? What about sin? Atonement?" They can then explore those fundamental questions, hopefully resolving them, and reconstruct.

I have been involved in the lives of many who are deconstructing and reconstructing their faith. That process allowed many of them to remain members of the Church. But my goal in walking with them is not a specific outcome—but rather to love them, trust them to make the best choices for themselves, and be a safe person in their life to help them along the way.

Our love for one another shouldn't be motivated only by a desire for someone to stay in the Church. Harper Dawn Forsgren, a returned missionary, tweeted: "We as members of the Church need to stop focusing on 'We need to love people because our love will bring them back to the Church' and instead focus on 'We need to love people because people deserve to be loved.'"[28] I agree with Harper. Love with no agenda is the kind of love that keeps families and friendships together. In my experience, people on the receiving side of this kind of love feel healing and support, and are the most likely to open up if their feelings change or they need help.

Brother Halverson extends an invitation that I believe represents effective ministering: "I've often said, even if you're angry, if you want to come and ask hard questions, if you've left the Church and you want closure, if you need a good pair of shins to kick, I'm glad to have that conversation with you."[29]

## Overcoming "Us Versus Them" Culture

Some Latter-day Saints have noticed an "us versus them" element of our culture that does not resonate with their understanding of Christ's ministry and makes church feel less of a safe place to share their honest questions. For example, sometimes a discussion in a Sunday class takes a negative turn from a fact-based discussion to a fear-based and condemning narrative about other groups—which feels inconsistent with the way Christ treated others.

---

28. @harperforsgen (Harper Dawn Forsgren). "Sunday Thoughts," *Twitter*, June 24, 2018, 4:21 p.m., twitter.com/harperforsgren/status/1011011450960109568.

29. *Listen, Learn & Love* podcast episode 259.

Elder Uchtdorf invited us to live a higher law based on love and not a lower law based on fear and manipulation:

> Fear rarely has the power to change our hearts, and it will never transform us into people who love what is right and want to obey Heavenly Father. . . .
>
> One of the ways Satan wants us to manipulate others is by dwelling on and even exaggerating the evil in the world. . . .
>
> Let us serve God and love our fellowmen. Let us do this with a natural confidence, with humility, never looking down on any other religion or group of people. . . .
>
> I don't believe God wants His children to be fearful or dwell on the evils of the world. "For God hath not given us the spirit of fear; but of power, and of love, and of a sound mind" (2 Timothy 1:7). . . .
>
> I pray with all the strength of my soul that we may become liberated from this fear by the divinely appointed antidote to fear: the pure love of Christ, for "perfect love casteth out fear" (1 John 4:18).[30]

When President Ellis Ivory and Sister Katie Ivory led the England Manchester Mission in 1979, they felt that the missionaries were demonizing the Church of England rather than delivering a positive message of The Church of Jesus Christ of Latter-day Saints. To change the culture, President Ivory did something unusual. He held an all-mission conference at a prominent parish of the Church of England called St. Michael and All Angels Church.[31] Both President Ivory and the vicar Reverend Norman Scott shared remarks that day.

This event dramatically changed the direction of the mission. Our teaching became a positive message about our restored truths. Our doctrine stood on its own merits. Yes, we could have a

---

30. Dieter F. Uchtdorf, "Perfect Love Casteth Out Fear," April 2017 general conference, churchofjesuschrist.org/study/general-conference/2017/04/perfect-love-casteth-out-fear.

31. "St. Michael and All Angels, Hawkshead," The Benefice of Hawkshead with Low Wray and Sawrey and Rusland and Satterthwaite, accessed May 7, 2021, hawksheadbenefice.co.uk/hawkshead.htm.

fact-based discussion about the differences with other faiths, but we did not allow it to deteriorate into manipulative discussion based on fear and emotion. The result was that our convert baptisms soared, and we became the highest baptizing English-speaking mission in the Church, with more than 300 baptisms per month. I say this not to focus on statistics but to show that this approach was not only kinder but also highly effective.

Over thirty years later, in 2016, one of those missionaries, Brent Brown, visited the same parish church. When he learned that they were raising money to save their tower bell, Brother Brown recruited donations from our group of former missionaries. The next year, a check of £15,000 (approximately $20,000) was presented at an event with President and Sister Ulrich of the England Manchester Mission, Reverend John Dixon of St. Michael and All Angels, current Latter-day Saint missionaries, and members of the parish congregation.[32]

In my last year as a bishop of a YSA ward, I began to post kind things about our LGBTQ friends on social media (often linking to Church resources), as well as a picture of me having dinner with some LGBTQ friends. What happened stunned me. Many of the YSAs, including those who didn't attend church, concluded that if I was open about sensitive topics and said positive things about LGBTQ people, then perhaps they could talk to me about other matters without fear of being judged. No additional LGBTQ people came out to me, but many ward members felt safe for the first time sharing the issues close to their hearts.

As a parent or local leader, we can create a culture in which our children and ward members feel safe telling us about things in their lives. Some of my most meaningful moments in either parenting or Church service are when someone is candid about a difficult challenge, and we work together to resolve it. As we follow Christ's

---

32. Nicholas Read, "Mission Fundraises for St. Michaels," *United Kingdom & Ireland Newsroom*, The Church of Jesus Christ of Latter-day Saints, accessed May 7, 2021, lds.org.uk/mission-fundraises-for-st-michaels.

example to be with and say kind things about others in a nonjudgmental way, people around us know they can safely talk to us about difficult things. They will be more likely to turn to us when they need a trusted parent, Church leader, or friend. We cannot fully minister to others until they feel safe sharing how they truly feel and what they are actually experiencing.

## Don't Preach, Rather Love

At a BYU devotional, President Ballard addressed the question of fellowshipping family or friends who are not participating in the Church:

> Question: If I have family or friends who are less active, how far do I go in my attempts to bring them back?
>
> My answer is please do not preach to them! Your family members or friends already know the Church's teachings. They don't need another lecture! What they need—what we all need—is love and understanding, not judging. Share your positive experiences of living the gospel. *The most powerful thing you can do is share your spiritual experiences with family and friends.* Also, be genuinely interested in their lives, their successes, and their challenges. Always be warm, gentle, loving, and kind.[33]

This is exactly what Tom Christofferson's parents did when he was in a same-sex relationship for two decades. One of my favorite quotes from his book, *That We May Be One,* are these words from his parents to his siblings at a family reunion: "The only thing we can really be perfect at is loving each other. The most important lesson your children will learn from how our family treats their Uncle Tom is that nothing they can ever do will take them outside the circle of our family's love."[34]

---

33. Ballard, "Questions and Answers," emphasis in the original.

34. Tom Christofferson, *That We May Be One: A Gay Mormon's Perspective on Faith and Family* (Salt Lake City: Deseret Book, 2017), 19.

In another BYU devotional, professor Eric Huntsman quoted the same book. He said, "We should never fear that we are compromising when we make the choice to love. As Brother Tom Christofferson noted: 'Accepting others does not mean that we condone, agree with, or conform to their beliefs or choices, but simply that we allow the realities of their lives to be different from our own'."[35]

I mourn when someone steps away from the Church. All the good in my life comes from living the teachings of the gospel. I invite everyone to stay and live the teachings of the Savior as found in The Church of Jesus Christ of Latter-day Saints, but let's not engage in "sad heaven" thinking, as explained by my friend Jon Ogden. It is the idea that we mourn a future outcome now. It is like mourning that my favorite basketball team, the Utah Jazz, will lose the next playoffs, and feeling the pain of that loss now.

We need not mourn now a potential empty seat at the table in the next life. We cannot know the ending of anyone's eternal story now. Nor can we control the actions and choices of our family members and friends; we can only control our own response to them. Ben Schilaty, a gay Latter-day Saint and BYU Honor Code administrator, recently shared this observation in a *TedxBYU* talk: "They're going to do what they want to do, whether we like it or not. But we get to choose how much they will be in our lives. Choosing to cheer on those around me brings more joy into my life."[36]

Elder Robert C. Gay poignantly spoke in general conference about giving his sister a blessing before she died and better seeing her as God sees her:

> She had a challenging life. She struggled with the gospel and was never really active [in the Church]. . . . I gave her a blessing

---

35. Eric D. Huntsman, "Hard Sayings and Safe Spaces: Making Room for Struggle as Well as Faith" (devotional address, Brigham Young University, Provo, Utah, August 7, 2018), speeches.byu.edu/talks/eric-d-huntsman/hard-sayings-and-safe-spaces-making-room-for-both-struggle-and-faith/.

36. Ben Schilaty, "How Far Are You Willing to Love?: Including Isn't Agreeing." *TEDx BYU*, May 2021, youtube.com/watch?v=63lwcxP8ZVQ.

to peacefully return home. At that moment I realized I had too often defined my sister's life in terms of her trials and inactivity. As I placed my hands on her head that evening, I received a severe rebuke from the Spirit. I was made acutely aware of her goodness and allowed to see her as God saw her—not as someone who struggled with the gospel and life but as someone who had to deal with difficult issues I did not have. . . .

During that final evening with my sister, I believe God was asking me, "Can't you see that everyone around you is a sacred being?" . . . From the Spirit's rebuke at my sister's bedside, I learned a great lesson: that as we see as He sees, ours will be a double victory—redemption of those we touch and redemption of ourselves.[37]

I believe that the book *Bridges: Ministering to Those Who Question,* written my brother David Ostler, is the best book on this subject. I hope all Church leaders, parents, and members read this book. Regarding empty chairs, David gives this counsel: "At our house, my wife and I talk about having no empty chairs at the dinner table, around the pool, on a vacation, at their life events, and in all the chairs from our children's lives."[38] I like his vision which concentrates on things that are within our control and turning the things we can't control over to our Heavenly Parents, especially as we respect others' agency.

In an article published by *LDS Living,* David gives six tips for parents of adult children who do not believe in the Church:

1. Don't preach or lecture.
2. Listen to understand and validate.
3. Use words that affirm; don't use labels.
4. Accept and love them fully.

---

37. Robert C. Gay, "Take upon Ourselves the Name of Jesus Christ," October 2018 general conference, churchofjesuschrist.org/study/general-conference/2018/10/taking-upon-ourselves-the-name-of-jesus-christ.

38. David Ostler, "6 Tips for Parents of Adult Children Who Don't Believe in the Church," *LDS Living,* June 8, 2019, ldsliving.com/6-Tips-for-Parents-of-Adult-Children-Who-Don-t-Believe-in-the-Church/s/90940.

5. Remember agency and the love of our Heavenly Parents.
6. Take care of yourself.[39]

As a researcher, David dove into the subject, gathering both empirical data and stories to provide an important work to help Latter-day Saints minister to individuals with questions. He wrote:

> Listening and accepting the person for who they are is the first step in building loving, ministering-based relationships. When our ministering is based on compassion and acceptance, people are more likely to trust us and to open up about issues that are important to us both. [It] isn't about happily ever afters. In a way, that is beside the point. While our hearts and desires might be to help others return to being fully believing and participating Latter-day Saints, those who question or leave the Church are precious children of our Heavenly Parents. They want us to love them, comfort them, and mourn with them, and we are blessed when we do. With Christ as our example, we minister, listen to, understand, and are blessed by Savior as He ministers to us and heals each of us on our own journey.[40]

## More Resources

In addition to the books referenced in this chapter, I recommend *Listen, Learn & Love* podcast episodes this subject, including Fiona and Terryl Givens (355), Jared Halverson (259), Patrick Mason (366), Thomas McConkie (157, 356), David Ostler (17, 167), Anthony Sweat (346), and many others.[41] Further, I also encourage you to familiarize yourself with the excellent podcasts and work from Faith Matters.[42]

---

39. Ibid.

40. David Ostler, chapter 9, "Key Principles of Ministering," *Bridges: Ministering to Those Who Question*, 104.

41. See listenlearnandlove.org/lds-faith-questions for episodes focused on those who question.

42. See faithmatters.org.

I hope this chapter helps give insights to improve our culture around having doubts, asking questions, and sharing concerns within our families and church community. Building Zion means working together to come unto Christ and experience healing and hope from the Savior's gospel.

# EPiLOGUe

Imagine with me for a moment. What would our church culture look like as we *listen, learn and love* and act on the impressions we received as we read this book?

In that world, there would be far less judging others and far more loving others. Church callings would be equally valued and respected—not used as a measure of self-worth, our Heavenly Parents' love and trust, or one's ability to contribute to build the kingdom. Women's voices would truly be sought and honored. Pornography use would be met with better tools and more understanding to resolve it. Hope-filled repentance would abound. Those experiencing mental illness would be lifted with compassion and support, the same as any other kind of illness. Missionary service would be honored regardless of its length or scope. Differing political affiliations would be seen as a strength, with people bringing their varied perspectives for a common purpose to create Zion. LGBTQ members would feel needed as their unique insights and contributions would be sought after, to help us become more united as the body of Christ. Questions about the gospel would not only be tolerated, but actually encouraged, recognizing that the entire Restoration began with a question.[1] In that world, we would have unity in *diversity*—not the lower bar of unity in *sameness*—fulfilling Alma's charge to have our "hearts knit together in unity and in love one towards another" (Mosiah 18:21).

---

1. "Elder Ballard: We Need to Be Better at Answering Difficult Questions and Never Brush Them Off," *LDS Living*.

In that world, all voices are equally valued and all people are equally needed and welcomed. All are not just safe, but are contributing their unique gifts, talents, and insights. That culture matches Christ's example in His ministry: everybody is welcome. There are no classes here, no status differences here. Everyone's voice is valued. Come as you are. This is a judgment-free zone. When we do this, our Church culture mirrors the doctrine of Christ. He taught this principle clearly in Matthew 20:26–28: "Whosoever will be great among you, let him be your minister; And whosoever will be chief among you, let him be your servant: Even as the Son of man came not to be ministered unto, but to minister." Even Jesus, the greatest of all, came to serve others and to lift them up.

As we do this, we are fulfilling the words of Elder Joseph B. Wirthlin: "The Church is not a place where perfect people gather to say perfect things, or have perfect thoughts, or have perfect feelings. The Church is a place where imperfect people gather to provide encouragement, support, and service to each other as we press on in our journey to return to our Heavenly Father."[2]

Let me close with an experience that my mother shared with me that happened during her shift as a temple worker. She related that the ordinance worker prayed in that sacred setting for the senior leaders of the Church, and then prayed for all those that serve behind the scenes so faithfully, who are so needed—the librarians, the nursery leaders, and the people who lock up the building at night. Afterwards, a patron mentioned, "You don't know what that meant to me, to hear those people equally prayed for in that setting, along with the senior leaders of the Church."

Those people are the lower lights—easy to overlook, but serving so faithfully in so many ways. To leave you humming, here is the chorus to the hymn I mentioned earlier:

---

2. Joseph B. Wirthlin, "The Virtue of Kindness," April 2005 general conference, churchofjesuschrist.org/study/general-conference/2005/04/the-virtue-of-kindness.

Let the lower lights be burning;
Send a gleam across the wave.
Some poor fainting, struggling seaman
You may rescue, you may save.

Everyone is so needed, their voices are important, and everyone does belong.

# contriButor inDex

# ABOUT THE AUTHOR

Richard H. Ostler, a former YSA bishop, speaks in church settings about how to more fully embrace LGBTQ Latter-day Saints, see their gifts and contributions, and better support them on their unique road. He is the host of the *Listen, Learn & Love* podcast (listenlearnandlove.org) which provides a platform for Latter-day Saints to share their stories on a number of topics.

He is the author of the book *Listen Learn and Love: Embracing LGBTQ Latter-day Saints* available at Deseret Book. He is also the author of two *Ensign* articles: "How the Savior's Healing Power Applies to Repenting from Sexual Sin" (August 2020, YSA digital only) and "7 Tips for Overcoming Pornography Use" (October 2020, page 72).

He is deeply committed to The Church of Jesus Christ of Latter-day Saints and to improving our culture to be more understanding and supportive for everyone—a goal started during his service as a YSA bishop as he learned to set aside past assumptions to better fulfill his stewardship responsibility to meet the spiritual needs and create a feeling of belonging for of all ward members.

In addition to serving as a YSA bishop, he has served as a stake Young Men president, high councilor, and ward mission leader. He currently serves as a temple worker. He has a BS from the University of Utah and an MBA from Brigham Young University, and is a small business owner. Richard and his wife, Sheila, live in Salt Lake City, Utah, and have six wonderful children and several grandchildren.

# notes

# notes